Advance Praise for *The Conductor*

"The moral brilliance of Rev. John Rankin in his quests for racial justice comes to life in Caleb Franz's finely-written, well-documented biography *The Conductor*. Every American should know the story of Rev. Rankin, who was the mentor of the renowned abolitionist William Lloyd Garrison and whose bold anti-slavery writings and lectures were brimming with timeless wisdom. Consider that 200 years ago Rev. Rankin wrote, 'The love of gain first introduced slavery into the world and has been its constant support in every age.... It gives energy to the tyrant's sword, drenches the earth with blood, and binds whole nations in chains.'"

—Ann Hagedorn, award-winning author of *Beyond the River: The Untold Story of the Heroes of the Underground Railroad*

"You've heard of the Underground Railroad. Now meet the Conductor. Caleb Franz unearths the story of Reverend John Rankin, who fought against slavery in all its forms, from the early 19th century, when he stood nearly alone, until its destruction. In this discerning book, Rankin finally gets the treatment he deserves."

—Chris DeRose, *New York Times* bestselling author of *The Fighting Bunch* and *Congressman Lincoln*

T0179748

The CONDUCTOR

The CONDUCTOR

THE STORY OF REV. JOHN RANKIN, ABOLITIONISM'S ESSENTIAL FOUNDING FATHER

CALEB FRANZ

A POST HILL PRESS BOOK
ISBN: 978-1-63758-989-2
ISBN (eBook): 978-1-63758-990-8

The Conductor:
The Story of Rev. John Rankin, Abolitionism's Essential Founding Father
© 2024 by Caleb Franz
All Rights Reserved

Cover design by Conroy Accord

Post Hill Press
New York • Nashville
posthillpress.com

Published in the United States of America
1 2 3 4 5 6 7 8 9 10

To Randy Franz, who first introduced me to
Rev. John Rankin so many years ago.

CONTENTS

INTRODUCTION

S ome people seem predestined to lead extraordinary lives, commanding history with stories that feel almost mythical. America has a rich heritage, riddled with such extraordinary tales. Few are as legendary as that of our first president, George Washington. In the heat of battle at the onset of the French and Indian War, just to the east of what is now Pittsburgh, bullet holes ripped through his coat and hat, yet he walked away without a scratch. Horses were blown out from underneath him as fellow officers were slain left and right. Yet he left the battlefield miraculously unharmed. Stories quickly spread that Colonel Washington was bulletproof.[1] It was just the beginning of the mythologized legacy of our first president. In the years that followed, Washington led a ragtag revolutionary army out of the clutches of British victory, often seizing the upper hand in the nick of time. To be sure, it was Washington's strategy, resolve, and moral character that inspired his troops to victory during some of these pivotal moments throughout the American Revolution. Yet, at other times, it seemed only the hand of God himself controlled the outcome.

But this book does not focus on a familiar figure like Washington. Our subject reminds us that not every significant historical figure is a household name. Most, in fact, are not. Some are remembered simply because they made the right choice, in the right place, at the right time. Others are scarcely remembered at all. There were men and women from communities across America who led extraordinary lives that influenced countless individuals and helped build a freer society—often at great personal cost—whose important legacies have since been swallowed by time, and relegated to the footnote of history. I speak, of course, of folk heroes. These regional figures may not be as legendary as someone like a George Washington, but they still possessed the bravery and conviction needed to contribute to the fulfillment of the vision outlined in the founding of America. Their courage and wisdom inspired thousands in their time and often influenced the leaders of the next generation.

The Reverend John Rankin of Ripley, Ohio, was one such leader, and he is the subject of this story

Rankin's story is as unlikely as it is unknown. This Presbyterian minister came from a world where slavery was a fact of life. Born and raised in eastern Tennessee, he grew up surrounded by suffering and oppression. While the difficulties of frontier life were enough to harden the hearts of even the holiest men, Rankin's faith in God strengthened, and with it his moral clarity of right and wrong, justice and injustice, and his abiding belief in human liberty. Nothing disheartened Rankin more than seeing his neighbors exercise dominion over his fellow man. To him, slavery was the ultimate sin—an absolute disgrace to the Creator. He became disgusted by his fellow clergymen in the South, who would selectively preach scripture to sing the praises of slavery. Such an interpretation Rankin believed to be blasphemous.

Typically, we think of preachers as having a unique gift for oratory. The ability to stand in front of a room full of people and command moral authority through the Gospel is almost a prerequisite for any aspiring minister. Yet, this gift was notably absent for much of Rankin's youth. Preaching and public speaking didn't come naturally to him; they were skills he had to develop over time. Despite missing this talent at birth, the issue of slavery pulled it out of him. The more he spoke out against America's greatest sin, and the more feathers he ruffled, the more confident in his convictions he grew. Rankin's belief in the God-given right to liberty drove every action he took like a loco-motive engine. It was his guiding light, always shining, even during his darkest moments.

Those darker moments crept beside him from his early days in Tennessee, when he was driven out of his community by slave-holding congregants and forced to migrate north. They lingered even into his later days on the banks of the Ohio River, where mobs, riled by his attack of slavery, would occasionally form near his home. Eventually, he was forced to move to a hilltop on the outskirts of town that over-looked the great Ohio River. In time, fugitive slaves crossing the river began to identify Rankin's home as a beacon of liberty and a pivotal stop on the Underground Railroad.

These deeds and experiences alone make Reverend John Rankin an exciting and inspiring figure to study. However, it was his influence on a national scale that drove the eventual abolition of slavery. This outspoken minister from Tennessee came of age when the United States was facing its first identity crisis. When Rankin started his journey to Ohio, the generation of the American Revolution was dying at an alarming rate. The spirit of '76, while still present, now had to compete with the spirit of expansion. Manifest Destiny was gaining popularity across the country. The principles of liberty and republicanism became secondary to visions of national greatness. Budding leaders of this new generation envisioned a country that would stretch across the continent and compete with European powers. This vision captured the imagina-tion of both pro and anti-slavery advocates. The founding generation left the question of slavery for their heirs to address. As the sun set on the days of Washington and Thomas Jefferson, the days of Henry Clay and Andrew Jackson were just beginning. Clay, although not a fan of slavery personally, made concessions to the slave powers, ensuring it would grow as an influential institution in the emerging American political system.[2] At the same time, the Jacksonian Democratic Party soon became the home of slaveholding interests. Territorial expan-sion and the expansion of slavery became more intertwined as the years became decades. This new generation of political leadership, while often well-intended, preserved the institutionalization of slavery. Ironically, in their efforts to maintain national harmony, they sowed the seeds for civil war.

Out of this era of compromise and expansion, Rankin used his influence to shift public opinion toward a favorable view of abolition. The emerging national environment and Rankin's personal convictions on the issue of slavery finally collided upon his discovery that his brother from Virginia, Thomas Rankin, had recently purchased a slave himself. This affected Rankin so much that he wrote a series of public letters, rebuking every prominent argument in favor of slavery that he could muster. The publication of his *Letters on American Slavery* had an impact larger than Rankin could have possibly imagined. What the Federalist Papers did for the Constitution, Rankin's *Letters* did for abolitionism. In doing so, Rankin gave abolitionism an intellectual foundation. He became known as the "Father of Abolitionism." William Lloyd Garrison—today remembered as an abolitionist firebrand—credited Rankin's *Letters* as "the cause of my entering the anti-slavery conflict." Later, Garrison would even call Rankin his "anti-slavery father."

Rankin and his *Letters* set the world ablaze, directly influencing the creation of the American Anti-Slavery Society, which unified the scattered handful of anti-slavery communities across America. All under the common cause, the abolitionists started to organize. Anti-slavery societies began to pop up in states and localities across the country. Rankin met abolitionists, such as Theodore Weld, and traveled on anti-slavery speaking tours. And all the while, his involvement in the Underground Railroad increased. Stories spread of slaves crossing the Ohio River using candlelight from Rankin's hilltop house as their guide. In one account from Rankin himself, he assisted a runaway slave woman with a child on their journey to freedom. He told the story to his friend and fellow theologian Calvin Stowe, whose wife, Harriet Beecher Stowe, also sat and listened attentively. Harriet proceeded to use it as inspiration for a section of the most influential literary work of her life—*Uncle Tom's Cabin*.

Rankin led quite an impactful life, yet today his presence is largely missing in the story of slavery in America. This is unfortunate. His story is a key piece of the puzzle in understanding America's struggle to defeat the most heinous institution that we have ever faced. Rankin and the abolitionists that followed him didn't always make the right decisions. It's only natural for a movement to make a few missteps time and again. Their moral convictions sometimes got the best of them, alienating people who would otherwise be allies from their cause. Indeed, this was a major reason why the cause of abolition took several decades before it finally succeeded with the passage of the Thirteenth Amendment. Perhaps most damagingly, many abolitionists, such as Garrison, Rankin's most famous disciple, adopted a policy of disunion, refusing to participate in a system of government that permitted the institution of slavery to exist. These mistakes set the cause back more than many abolitionists realized at the time. Whatever mistakes were made, Rankin's voice of moral authority came at a critical time when the country needed it most. When the political leadership of his time danced around the issue of slavery, Rankin was one of the earliest figures in the country to take it head-on.

For whatever reason he has largely been overlooked, it is time we elevate him to his proper status in American history. Without Reverend John Rankin, the abolitionist movement as we understand it would not have existed. We cannot hope to fully understand how slavery was abolished without first understanding the role played by this rural Presbyterian minister—no Washington, but nonetheless a hero worthy of renown.

WHEN HEAVEN FELL SILENT
1783–1793
PROLOGUE

"**N**o!" exclaimed a defiant John Adams. "Rather than relinquish our claim to the western territory, I will go home and urge my countrymen to take up arms again and fight till they secure their rights, or shed the last drop of blood."[3] The American delegation of Adams, John Jay, and Benjamin Franklin was negotiating a treaty with Great Britain to finally put an end to the American Revolution. The British were insistent that the western boundary of the United States be at the Ohio River. Franklin, a diplomat, was inclined to yield. As valuable as the region north of the river was to Americans, he reasoned, it was better to give it up than to risk the fate of the treaty itself. The ever-boorish Adams refused to budge, holding that the territory north of the river was vital to the future success of the United States. If negotiations failed, it would take little for Adams to convince his fellow countrymen to take up arms against their former oppressors again. The West was a vast expanse of opportunity, economically and otherwise. Many adventure seekers looked eagerly to the frontier to establish new lives for themselves and their posterity. None were eager to have British troops traversing across the great territory above the river, depleting resources that would otherwise belong to them. Few had forgotten how the British instigated Indian tribes during the revolution in retaliation against American soldiers. Yet, as Franklin worried about securing a desirable treaty and putting the bloodshed to rest, Americans had the upper hand. Lord Shelburne had recently become Prime Minister of Great Britain, and viewed American independence as an opportunity. After establishing diplomatic ties with the United States, Great Britain could have a new trading partner, rather than spending blood and treasure on colonies that didn't want them there. With Shelburne at the helm, the British were far more willing to bend to the demands of the Americans. With Adams, John Jay concurred; the northwest territory was not something to budge on.

The British yielded. By signing the Treaty of Paris, the United States secured its independence and nearly doubled in size.[4]

News of the Treaty of Paris only magnified interest in Western lands. Squatters became a frequent problem in the early days of the republic. It quickly became clear that this land needed an established ordinance—one that offered clear definitions of property rights.

This new, northwestern territory presented a unique opportunity for the American government. The revolution wrecked the economy of this new nation. The government had little revenue, and what money it did have was losing value at an alarming rate. Thousands of veterans were now owed compensation for their service in the war, while the Articles of Confederation made it difficult to raise revenue by any means. The longer veterans waited for compensation for their service, the angrier they became. The vast amount of land secured through the Treaty of Paris allowed the government to kill two birds with one stone. Instead of raising taxes, an option few Americans desired, they could raise revenue through land sales. In lieu of revenue, the government could offer land grants as payment to Revolutionary War veterans. It wasn't the most efficient system, but it played into the frontier fever that swept the country in the wake of the revolution. Americans had won their independence, and with it came a newfound ambition to make the most of it. This aspiration, however, proved challenging to fulfill within the populated regions east of the mountains.

Eager to capitalize on Americans' itch to go west, Congress began working on an ordinance to provide a legal framework in the new territory. In Annapolis, Maryland in 1784, Thomas Jefferson took on the responsibility of primary author, as he had with many vital documents before. Jefferson's 1784 Ordinance offered five key provisions to serve as the basis for "both the temporary and permanent governments" that would be formed within the territory. Anticipating the influx of migrants from the east, the territory was to eventually be divided up into new states, admitted to the confederacy with equal standing to the original thirteen states. The new states would form republican governments, pay their apportionment of federal debts, and would "forever remain a part of this confederacy of the United States of America." These provisions were straightforward enough, but it was the last provision that sparked controversy.

Jefferson's draft included the condition that after the year 1800, "there shall be neither slavery nor involuntary servitude in any of the said states," except for "punishment of crimes whereof the party shall have been convicted to have been personally guilty."[5] This was not the first time Jefferson had sparked debates over the issue of slavery. As he drafted the Declaration of Independence in June of 1776, Jefferson had initially included a section that lambasted the King's role in the slave trade, laying the institution at his feet. He proclaimed that King George III "waged cruel war against human nature itself."[6] In fact, it was the largest grievance in Jefferson's original draft. Adams would later reflect that he was "delighted with its high tone...especially that concerning Negro Slavery."[7] Not everyone in the Second Continental Congress was as quick to praise this condemnation of slavery. Despite his personal approval, Adams confessed he suspected Jefferson's "Southern Brethren would never suffer to pass in Congress." His suspicion proved to be accurate. To succeed in resisting their mother country, the American colonies required unity, and nothing threatened unity like the question of slavery. Once Congress received Jefferson's draft, several edits were made before it adopted the final declaration that we know today. The grievance over slavery was the most significant section left behind.

In 1784, just as in that summer in Philadelphia, the special interest of southern slaveholders threatened to interfere to preserve their institution. This time around, there was a key difference in Jefferson's provision. Unlike the rhetorical condemnation proposed in 1776, the 1784 Land Ordinance had the power to save countless families from the clutches of slavery. When it came to a vote, however, the Confederation Congress decided to punt the issue. On April 25, 1784, Jefferson wrote to his friend James Madison, agonizing over the vote. "You will observe two clauses struck out of the report," with the latter concerning slavery, he reported to Madison. "The second was lost by an individual vote only." He proceeded to break down the votes. "Ten states were present," Jefferson explained. Seven states were needed, but only six states voted affirmatively. "South Carolina, Maryland, & *Virginia* voted against it. N. Carolina was divided as would have been Virginia had not one of its delegates been sick in bed" (emphasis his).[8]

The outcome of this vote seems to have significantly impacted Jefferson's attitude toward the political realities of abolishing slavery in his lifetime. Save for a few specific instances, he became silent on the issue throughout the remainder of his career. It seems he preferred to spend his political capital on matters that would achieve some degree of success. Still, his inability to quarantine slavery to the original southern colonies haunted him throughout his life. Two years later, Jefferson mournfully wrote in reflection of his clause being struck: "We see the fate of millions unborn hanging on the tongue of one man, and heaven was silent in that awful moment!"[9]

After the 1784 Land Ordinance passed without the clause prohibiting slavery, Jefferson was appointed minister to France, set to replace the aging Franklin, who was the first to fill the role. While Jefferson grew pessimistic that his visionary land of liberty would prevent the spread of slavery, others held out hope.

Back in Philadelphia, Massachusetts clergyman and Revolutionary War veteran Manasseh Cutler lobbied Congress for an ordinance closer to Jefferson's original vision. Cutler played a significant role in drafting a section of the ordinance that prohibited slavery in the territory. Massachusetts delegate Nathan Dane presented the new Northwest Ordinance to Congress with Cutler's provisions. Finally, in July 1787, just over eleven years since American Independence was declared, it happened. The Confederation Congress passed "An Ordinance for the government of the Territory of the United States northwest of the River Ohio." It included, for the first time in American history, a prohibition of slavery by the general government. While the scope of prohibition was limited, the precedent was set for what could be achieved in the future. In all territory north of the Ohio River and east of the Mississippi River, "there shall be neither slavery nor involuntary servitude in the said territory, otherwise than in the punishment of crimes...."[10]

Ten years after Jefferson failed to include his condemnation of slavery in the Declaration of Independence, and just over three years after he failed to prevent its spread into western lands, the government made its first law restricting slavery. In a single moment, the Ohio River became a physical and metaphorical divide between freedom and slavery.

* * * * *

This ordinance set the stage for the next century of debate, battles, and conflict. It was equally inspiring and nerve-wracking. With each new state added and territory acquired, the question of slavery would inevitably be addressed. The race west was driven in large part by pro and anti-slavery forces continuously offsetting one another.

Further, it was widely recognized that new states would emerge from more than just the new territory. Many existing states were far too large to be governed effectively, and were sure to split into separate states, opening new opportunities for slavery's westward expansion. Transportation and communication means were primitive for the budding nation, and states with capitals east of the mountains stretched all the way to the Mississippi. Pioneers in the bluegrass of Kentucky county couldn't rely on their government in Richmond to appropriately address the challenges they faced. Any laws passed east of the mountains were virtually unenforceable on the other side.

The idea of state cessions of land was gaining traction. It would simultaneously create states that were much more manageable while providing the general government an opportunity to again raise revenue via land sales instead of taxes. Many residents west of the Alleghenies were already petitioning separation from their home states in favor of forming their own. However, there was a much larger problem boiling throughout the country.

Under the Articles of Confederation, the government had no teeth to enforce the rule of law. This made upholding any policy relating to land claims nearly impossible. Squatters could claim land that had been given to someone else without fear of retribution. Most founders agreed that the Articles were a flawed system, but controversy accompanied proposed solutions. Those who favored decentralization leaned toward a series of reforms that would, in theory, preserve state sovereignty and individual rights while strengthening the government's authority under the Articles of Confederation. Others believed the inherent problem was with the Articles, and thus believed it was better to start from scratch with an entirely new governing system.

Within the context of these mounting pressures, it makes sense that the Constitutional Convention in Philadelphia overlapped with the passage of the Northwest Ordinance in 1787. While members of the Confederation Congress were finally able to make headway with the cause of emancipation, members of the Constitutional Convention found the issue much more difficult to resolve. Throughout the summer of 1787, debates raged over which system of government they should adopt. The once unified nation of 1776, full of romantic visions of liberty and justice, had fallen into deep-seated division. Nearly every issue that arose caused controversy. The Federalists, led by Alexander Hamilton, sought a large central government with broad, implied powers to do whatever it deemed necessary and proper to stand equally against the European nations of Great Britain, France, and Spain. In fact, much of Hamilton's vision for government had been directly inspired by the British system—an attitude Hamilton toned down to secure votes during the convention, though it remained his inspiration throughout his political career. On the other hand, the Anti-Federalists were concerned that by attempting to rival the nations of Europe, we may become like them. Anti-Federalists feared that the level of centralization Hamilton and his Federalists sought threatened the very liberties so many had fought a revolution to secure. Federalists assured citizens that the government they proposed would only have the power to do that which was specifically outlined in the Constitution. Anti-Federalists quickly pointed out that much of what was outlined in the Constitution was vague, and the nature of government was to expand its own authority. A federal government, they argued, would never stick within its confines.

The debate over the Bill of Rights became the driving controversy of the convention. But the debate over slavery revealed a much darker strain within the country, which would define the next century of American history. Southern interests refused to support anything prohibiting the institution of slavery. Northerners and certain members of the Southern delegation who valued liberalism were inclined not to give their southern neighbors the time of day. This dynamic threatened the entire American experiment. Without a union, slavery would remain, and the principles that Jefferson proclaimed in 1776 would have nowhere to spread if the country were to fracture and dissolve before it had an opportunity to take root. Thus, Madison and others made a series of compromises that neither expressly forbid nor specifically endorsed slavery. Under the new Constitution, slavery would be left to the states. As it was then written, however, the words "slave" or "slavery" could not be found. This would continue to be the case until the Thirteenth Amendment, where it was constitutionally prohibited. By doing so, Madison had found a way to ensure that southern states could find the new Constitution agreeable enough without institutionalizing slavery itself.

It was an uneasy truce, and it depended upon many variables. Yet, it was a way to preserve the Union while giving the next generation tools to fight back against slavery.

* * * * *

After vigorous debate, the Constitution was signed in Philadelphia on September 17, 1787. The misgivings of the Articles of Confederation loomed over the minds of many delegates. Angry, unpaid veterans of the Revolutionary War added pressure on the delegates, as memories of Shays' Rebellion weighed on their minds. The government's inability to raise revenue and pay off its debts, to both war veterans and foreign nations, threatened national stability. These pressures persuaded many delegates to forego their skepticism of central authority. Still, some delegates' reservations were too great to ignore. Out of the forty-one delegates present at the signing of the Constitution, three refused to put pen to parchment. Massachusetts delegate Elbridge Gerry, along with Virginia delegates Edmund Randolph and George Mason, all refused to sign. According to Madison, Mason had earlier proclaimed that he would "sooner chop off his right hand than put it to the Constitution as it now stands."[11]

Regardless, the Constitution was passed and went to the states for ratification. After New Hampshire became the ninth state to ratify, the new Constitution went into effect the following year. As the first Constitutionally elected president, George Washington was inaugurated on April 30, 1789. As with the confederation, many of the nation's first challenges revolved around land. The general government continued to propose that states cede their land west of the mountains. Slowly but surely, states agreed that this was the best course of action. As Virginia looked to cede the land west of the Allegheny Mountains, a piece of the northwest territory just above the Ohio River was to be reserved as debt repayment to Revolutionary War vets. Out of concern that in a mad rush, all the "good land" might be taken, the 1784 deed of cession read, "the deficiency should be made up to the troops in good lands to be laid off between the rivers Scioto and the Little Miami, on the northwest side of the Ohio."[12]

One benefactor of Virginia's strategic reserve included war veteran, surveyor, and pioneer Colonel James Poage. A native of Staunton, Virginia, located in Augusta County, Poage had come to Kentucky in 1778. Anyone experiencing life in the early days of Kentucky knew only strife and hardship. The frontier campaign of the American Revolution was particularly harsh in an already tiring war. Indian raids were frequent and often gruesome. Yet, out of the conflict arose heroic stories of men like George Rogers Clark, and of course, Daniel Boone. Poage, while not to the same level of notoriety as the likes of Boone, would have experienced the same threat of danger. During this time, he led surveying parties across the region. He earned a reputation as a protector of pioneer families in the rugged frontier. As fearless as he was, Poage was a man of reason and compassion. This treatment was extended to his Indian adversaries who, when met in the open, were received kindly and with fairness. It was an attribute he also extended toward African slaves, who joined him in his ventures on the frontier. Poage owned twenty slaves, to his own dismay. He viewed slavery as a curse and sought to cleanse himself of this sin.

Poage first resided near the heart of the Bluegrass region of Kentucky in Clark County, and even served as its representative in the Legislature in 1796. Soon, his brothers George and Robert came to Kentucky with their own families. They settled a tract of land in the northeastern part of the state "lying between the mouth of the Big Sandy River to the narrows" in 1799. There, the Poage brothers laid the roots for the community that would eventually become present-day Ashland, Kentucky. Poage enjoyed his time with his family here, but the presence of slavery continued to gnaw at him.

He was born into a strong Presbyterian family and the weight of his moral conviction guided him. It made his own slave-owning that much heavier of a burden to bear. At church, Poage frequently engaged in spats with slave owners, and washing his hands of slavery became his chief priority. He moved upriver on flatboats to Mason County,

Kentucky, across the river from his land claim in Ohio. He had been compensated 1,000 acres in the reserve Virginia had set aside for troops. His claim began at "two sugar trees and a mulberry running down the river, crossing the mouth of Red Oak Creek to a sugar tree and two buckeyes on the bank of the river." In 1804, Poage decided it was time to make his final trek across the river and claim his property. Ohio had become a state the year prior, and was the first to never permit slavery on its soil. As Poage crossed the river and landed on the Ohio shore with his wife and ten children, he was accompanied by his twenty slaves. As they left their boat, they walked on free soil; thus, Poage pronounced their freedom.

Poage had expected them to flee toward a better life somewhere to the north. After all, residing on the border of a slave state carried certain risks, such as being captured and sold back into slavery. Yet, to his astonishment, they remained. It was a testament to the level of respect people held for him, free or otherwise. Together, they took apart their flatboats and used the logs to build shelters, as free people. Poage named this settlement Buck's Landing. Later he renamed it Staunton, after his Virginia home.[13]

* * * * *

As Poage wandered throughout Kentucky, hoping to atone for his sin of slaveholding, Richard Rankin and his wife, Jane Rankin, traveled through the heart of slave territory. The Rankin family had a long lineage of indomitable spirits. In the late 1600s, the Rankins were Scots-Irish martyrs of the faith. Richard's great-great-grandfather, Alexander Rankin, hailed from Scotland, and suffered the loss of three out of his four sons, all killed for their faith. He and his surviving son, William, fled to Derry County, Ireland in 1688. The following year, both Alexander and William helped repel the siege of Londonderry—part of deposed King James II's attempt to regain the throne. One of William's sons, John, left Ireland and joined the wave of immigrants pursuing a new life in the new world. He arrived in Philadelphia in 1727. His son, Thomas Rankin, continued his family's tradition of resistance to tyranny as a captain in the American Revolution. Like Alexander and William in the siege of Londonderry, the four eldest sons of Thomas Rankin joined him in the revolution as privates in the Continental Army. His son William even witnessed the surrender of Cornwallis at the conclusion of the battle of Yorktown.[14]

The Rankins were by no means a wealthy family, but what they lacked monetarily they made up for spiritually. Each generation seemed to pass down the same honest character and steadfast devotion to their faith that the previous one possessed. This devotion to God and integrity made them fearless, yet humble in nature. But this humility didn't stop them from pursuing new opportunities. Thomas moved to the frontier of Tennessee after selling his land for Continental currency, which was next to worthless. In Tennessee, the land was abundant and extremely affordable. Richard, who also served with his father and brothers in the American Revolution, left his home to apprentice as a blacksmith for a man named Samuel Steele, who lived in Augusta County, Virginia. During his time in Virginia, Richard met Samuel's daughter, Jenette (Jane) Steele. They fell in love and Richard took her hand in marriage.

After they wedded, Richard and Jane had their first child. Preparing new lives for their family, Richard and a fellow pioneer, John Bradshaw, pressed deeper into the frontier. Around 1786, they found their way to what would soon be eastern Tennessee in the Dumplin Valley region. Richard and Bradshaw felled some trees, cleared a space, and began to build log homes in the heart of the virgin forest. This region was especially sparse at the time. One white man could stretch countless miles before he ran into another. Indians were another story. It was by no means a safe place to raise a family, yet opportunity and freedom awaited those who confronted and conquered the dangers of the frontier. Richard and Bradshaw prepared the necessities of their settlement and returned to fetch their families. Soon, two of Richard's brothers, Samuel and Thomas, along with their families, joined him in the wild forests of Appalachia. Their presence continued to grow, as did their families and community. By 1792, there was enough of a population surrounding the Rankin's settlement to form a county. When it came time to name their new county, it wasn't a difficult choice. They named it Jefferson County.

Richard and Jane started their new family in an often cruel and unforgiving world. Life in the wilderness could be merciless. Medicine was primitive, commerce was scarce, and the presence of warring Indian tribes was a constant threat. If something were to happen to a father in this world, the safety of the entire family would be in jeopardy. This is not to mention the political battles that raged, particularly over slavery. The Northwest Ordinance had prevented its spread north of the Ohio River, but it was alive and well in neighboring counties. The idea that slavery could be eradicated in a single lifetime would have seemed preposterous.

It is no coincidence that this is the environment in which the man who would ignite the flame to burn slavery into the ground was born. On February 4, 1793, three years before Tennessee acquired statehood, Richard and Jane welcomed their fourth boy into the world. In their secluded cabin, situated by a spring of Assumption Creek, the forceful life of John Rankin had begun.[15]

EXODUS
1793–1817
I.

The winter months in eastern Tennessee were barely more desirable than they were throughout the country's regions to the north, where most of the population resided in 1793. The vast wilderness along the edges of the Appalachian Mountains proved not to be for the faint of heart. Fortunately, Richard and Jane Rankin made anything but a timid family. So, on the winter day of February 4, 1793, when a midwife delivered Jane's fourth son, they believed themselves up to the challenge. The birth of John Rankin went about as smoothly as possible for a log cabin in the middle of unbroken wilderness. His mother held him, looking into his crying eyes, envisioning a relatively simple life ahead of him. Life on the frontier was slow at times, but it forged a strong character that, tied with biblical teachings, would give Rankin a good head on his shoulders. If she had known what was in store for him as he cried in her arms, she would view it as a blessing from God, selecting her son to achieve great things. At the time, however, she was simply thankful that her baby boy was healthy in her arms. As simple as his parents may have envisioned his life would be, Rankin was born at an extraordinary time. The United States were barely older than Rankin himself. President George Washington's first term was approaching its end, and there was much uncertainty over future. Of course, slavery stood at the center of this uncertainty.

Many delegates to the Constitutional Convention had fought to keep the slave powers at bay to prevent America from becoming totally corrupted by its influence. But the influence had already crept into the politics of the day. Coincidentally, on the same day that Rankin was born, the House of Representatives passed the Fugitive Slave Act of 1793 by a margin of 48–7.[16] Within a week, the bill passed both chambers of Congress. The act came in the wake of a crisis on the border of Pennsylvania and Virginia concerning the slave status of a man named John Davis. In 1780, Pennsylvania became the first state in the country to adopt a law abolishing slavery. The act provided gradual emancipation; a system favored by many of those opposed to slavery at the time.[17] The idea was that immediate emancipation would create too much shock in society, further dividing former slaves and their former masters. This teased the threat of a race war, with the former slaves holding a disadvantage. Gradual emancipation, legislators reasoned, would allow slave owners to get their financial house in order over time, rather than having it uprooted overnight. It also allowed emancipated black people time to acquire the skills and resources needed to live a truly free life in a post-slavery world. While imperfect, many abolition advocates believed this would be a practical solution to the slavery question.

Under the new Pennsylvania law, any child with slave parents born after March 1, 1780, would be free, following a period of indentured servitude. For a master to retain his slaves not freed on that date, he would need to register them with a court clerk before November 1, 1780, and pay a two-dollar-a-slave registration fee. Any slave not registered by that date would be immediately freed. The real controversy with this law came along the Pennsylvania-Virginia border. Boundaries between states were somewhat ill-defined in the 1780s. In 1779, commissioners from both states came to an agreement concerning the exact borderline. While Pennsylvania passed a resolution the following year accepting the border, it wouldn't be until 1784 that Virginia did. Slaveowners along the border risked losing their slaves if they were to find out that their land was, in fact, in Pennsylvania rather than Virginia. In 1782, Pennsylvania extended an olive branch to the communities in disputed territory. To provide relief amid the uncertainty, relevant counties had until January 1, 1783, to register. Still, some slave owners refused, asserting their mistaken belief that they were in Virginia.

One slave owner, a Mr. Davis of Maryland, believed he had moved to Virginia, but was, in fact, in Pennsylvania. Davis missed the deadline, and as a result, his slave John (who used Davis as his last name) was legally freed. Both seemed unaware of this. Davis subsequently rented John to a man in Virginia in 1788. A group of men believed to be members of the Pennsylvania Abolition Society then found John and brought him back to Pennsylvania. The man that Davis rented John to was outraged, and afraid that he would be held responsible for losing John. He hired three Virginians to go into Pennsylvania, kidnap John, and bring him back to his supervision. In May 1788, they did just that. As a result of John fleeing to Pennsylvania, Davis sold him to a planter along the Potomac, definitely in the slave territory of eastern Virginia. The capture of John, however, sparked fury. The three Virginians hired to capture John were indicted for the abduction. The slave catchers, while indicted, remained free to roam in Virginia. John, meanwhile, remained in slavery, despite being legally free. This sparked an interstate crisis over slavery and was a terrible precursor of what was still to come over the next several decades.

In 1791, the Pennsylvania Abolition Society petitioned the governor to extradite the three Virginians and bring them to justice. Pennsylvania Governor Thomas Mifflin consented to the petition, and sent Virginia Governor Beverley Randolph copies of the indictments and a note requesting the extradition of the Virginians. Randolph reviewed the request and brought the matter to the Virginia Attorney General, James Innes, who opposed the request. Innes made the strange argument that since the men were accused of "*violently*" kidnapping John, and not "*feloniously*," the crimes they were accused of could not be considered a felony. Furthermore, he asserted that the kidnapping of a freed black person in Virginia merely amounted to "a trespass" between parties, and thus, they could only be guilty of a minor offense in either Virginia or Pennsylvania.

Innes seemed to have recognized that his arguments were weak, so he provided another opposing the extradition: since the kidnappers had broken Pennsylvania law, rather than Virginia or federal law, he claimed he was under no obligation to make the arrest. Randolph responded to Mifflin in July with a refusal to extradite and included Innes's arguments. This, of course, only created further controversy, and Mifflin brought the matter to President Washington. It was clear to the president and his administration that this issue threatened the stability and harmony of the Union. There was also the threat of overcorrection, with the federal government exceeding its authority to intervene in a matter between states. United States Attorney General Edmund Randolph noted that only "a single letter has gone from the Governor of Pennsylvania to the Governor of Virginia." Washington sent back his recommendations for what each state should do next. His efforts were futile. The two governors continued to go back and forth over what next steps should be taken. Meanwhile, Washington took the matter to Congress. After some initial debate and discussion, the solution that Congress settled on was the Fugitive Slave Act of 1793.[18]

The issue at the heart of this came in two forms. Pennsylvanians accused Virginia of harboring fugitives of the law. Meanwhile, Virginians accused members of abolition societies in Pennsylvania of stealing slaves away from their masters and harboring them in their state. Congress tried to treat fugitives of the law and fugitive slaves in a similar manner under the 1793 law. The execution, however, greatly favored the slaveholders. To apprehend fugitives of the law, there needed to be probable cause, and any fugitive would be afforded due process. To apprehend a fugitive slave, the law merely required they be seized under the "disposition of two or more credible persons." Furthermore, fugitive slaves, or black individuals accused of being fugitives, could not accept a hearing that would verify their slave status once caught.

Perhaps most tragically, the bill did nothing to address the case that sparked its adoption in the first place. John Davis remained in slavery, and the three Virginian fugitives of the law never faced justice. Despite the obvious oversights of the bill, and the dangerous precedent it would set, Washington signed it on February 12, 1793.

* * * * *

The 1793 Act would prove to be one of the greatest influences on the life of John Rankin. It would remain law until its eventual replacement in 1850. Rankin would spend most of his life directly opposing the law, both in public rhetoric and in private actions. Throughout the 1790s, though, Rankin was preoccupied with his own upbringing. He was more privileged than most children his age in eastern Tennessee by the simple nature of his parents being highly literate. "This section of Tennessee," Rankin later explained in his autobiography, "was first settled with a very low, ignorant, and immoral class of people." The predominant attitude of the time in this section of the frontier was that education only led people astray. Secular pioneers were repulsed by how high-browed an education seemed to make people. Americans everywhere resented aristocracy, and nowhere was this truer than on the frontier. "This made it difficult to form churches and schools," Rankin later reflected. Some were even "opposed to having schools." Even frontier ministers objected to "larnin," believing that pursuing knowledge opened Pandora's box, resulting in worldliness, rebellion, and sin. Rankin recalled how "there were preachers of some orders who could not read a sentence in the book they took their texts." Supposedly, "larned" preachers were corrupt sellouts who only did ministry to enrich themselves by fooling the common man. They didn't have the calling to preach the way that more spiritual preachers did. Likewise, those preachers who did have the calling to preach the Gospel needed only to rely on this, not education.[19]

Richard and Jane Rankin weren't formally educated in any meaningful sense. They never attended college, but they understood the value of the pursuit of knowledge. They studied the Bible as well as other books of theology, philosophy, and history. Expanding their own understanding of the world was a priority. They viewed it as their Christian duty to possess a deep understanding of their own faith, to defend it and pass it on to their children. Despite the scoffing of ministers "of some orders," Rankin recalled how "they read much in the best of books, and by that means gained much knowledge, which qualified them for training their numerous family." Both Richard and Jane left an earnest desire to learn in the heart of Rankin from an early age. Jane taught him to spell using Thomas Dilworth's spelling book well before he attended any sort of formal school.[20] When he finally did attend school at a young age, he had to walk two and a half miles on a path that was "narrow and rugged and passed over a high rock." School was a log schoolhouse with earthen floors and "clapboards weighed down with heavy polls to form the roof." It was only one story with no loft, and large gaps were made between the logs to allow light in. The schoolmaster taught Rankin and his peers reading, writing, and arithmetic, although with an emphasis on the first two. Rankin later mused how sometimes "arithmetic was in the master's head and sometimes there was none there." A typical day started very early in the morning and continued until about noon when they would break for lunch and play. When in class, the schoolmaster was rigid about powering through lessons without a break. They read from Dilworth's spelling book and an assortment of history books. They also read from the New and Old Testaments—in that order. If students were lazy or misbehaving, the schoolmaster utilized the switch to command his room. Schooling took place, before the days of universal public education, for three months throughout the winter. Thus, Rankin spent only a few winters attending school. "There were no free schools," he'd later reflect. "Teachers were paid by those whose children they taught. There were no Sabbath Schools, no religious papers, no Bible and Tract Societies, no Missionary Societies, home or foreign, no steamboats, railroads nor telegraphs." These days were the days "of small things," he'd recall.[21]

With his scarce formal education, most of his schooling remained with his parents and his own ambition to learn. Like many boys and girls of his day, he spent ample time with his mother and father at home, attending to the chores that required attention around the house and farm. This allowed him to form a close bond with his parents. Rankin's father, Richard, was a calm and steady force in his early life. He provided security and stability in a world where both were frequently missing. Richard assumed the duty of spiritual guide of the house. He wasn't harsh or terribly outspoken in matters of controversy, but when he needed to take a stand, he stood for what he believed was right. Rankin was especially impressed with how morally consistent and pure his father was. He was consistent in his church attendance, prayed frequently, and valued the integrity of his word. He was honest, and if he made a promise, he intended to keep it. Despite living in the frontier, where swearing and cursing were all too common, Rankin could not recall an instance where his father used foul language. Either he was very good at hiding it from his son, or it wasn't in his vocabulary. "While he was not infallible nor sinlessly perfect," Rankin later pointed out, "he did set before his children a religious example, which was deeply impressive." He compared his father to Abraham, commanding "his children and his household after him." Much of Rankin's education also stemmed from his father's love of reading. On Sundays, he would, of course, read from the Bible, and on weekdays, he enjoyed reading books on history aloud for Rankin to hear. Rankin sat attentively as his father took him on a journey throughout history after a long workday. Much of Rankin's education came in this way.

Occasionally, Richard would go out to hunt or join a patrol to fend off roaming Indian tribes. As he was away, Jane stepped in, not only to care for their children but to serve as a moral authority for Rankin and his siblings. He had a special bond with his mother. He loved her dearly, of course, but Jane was outspoken and opinionated in a way that few women were in those days. She was steadfast in her faith and opposed the use of whiskey or tobacco. Although she enjoyed dancing in her youth, she came to believe it was a sinful practice after embracing her faith entirely. When Richard was out, she prayed with her family. Rankin would occasionally catch her praying in private just as earnestly as she would in front of her children. This example left a lasting impression on young Rankin. "The influence of a mother is more impressive than that of a father," he later wrote. Where Richard had a calm and steady presence about him, Jane possessed an indomitable spirit and an iron will that few could match. As he matured into adulthood, Rankin's actions would reveal glimpses of both of his parents throughout his life. [22]

* * * * *

Outside of the education Rankin received from his parents and from the school he attended, there was one external influence that helped define the trajectory of his life. The Second Great Awakening, kicked off with the Great Revival of 1800, swept the frontier while Rankin was still a boy. Questions on religion had filled his mind from some of his first memories. "From my earliest recollection I had serious thoughts on the subject of religion," he wrote in his autobiography. The vast and awesome nature of an almighty Creator who loved His creation so much that He joined them in human form and died for them was a concept that excited Rankin. It also, at times, confused and terrified him. He would go on to become a great preacher, using the word of God as his chief weapon to slay the behemoth of slavery. Yet, in his adolescence, he was equally amazed and confused by the nature of the Almighty. In addition to this, the debate over doctrine and theological practices were beginning to intensify up and down the spine of the Appalachian Mountains.

In June 1800, Presbyterian Minister James McGready led a Scottish sacrament service at the Red River Meeting House in Logan County, Kentucky. The seven-day "holy fair" struck a chord with the locals in the region. More multi-day tent services known as camp meetings started to appear in neighboring communities. Before long, religious fever held a grip across the entire Cumberland region of Kentucky and

Tennessee. Whereas before, the frontier people lacked any sense of moral compass to guide them through the wilderness, now, there were thousands sweeping the western states willing to put their life of abuse and immorality behind them, supposedly for good. Of course, it didn't always stick, but there were plenty of those who had a genuine change of spirit that would influence those around them.[23]

The First Great Awakening swept the colonies on the other side of the mountains in the 1730s through the '50s and was an important precursor to the American Revolution. For the first time, many colonists felt a personal connection with the Almighty. As their souls started to awaken, they began freeing their consciousnesses. Colonists began to view the Church of England as corrupt, leading souls astray. This led to dissatisfaction with the mother country itself. With this awakening came enlightenment. Likewise, the Second Great Awakening was an important precursor to the conflict over slavery that defined the 1800s.

For Rankin, the latter revival was both wonderous and concerning. He recalled how "immense camp meetings were held," attracting people from great distances to take part. They spent days praying, singing, and worshiping in a way many participants never had before. Rankin, however, was raised in a strictly Calvinist household. His family valued reason, reflection, and reservation. Those caught in a wave of emotion could hardly be considered legitimate converts, they believed. It was not doctrine new converts were caught up in, but the charisma of a frontier pastor. Rankin worried that amid these emotional explosions, people could be tricked into believing false biblical teachings. He later reflected on his experience with these revivals—"A wonderful nervous affection pervaded the meetings. Some would tremble as if terribly frightened, some would have violent twitching and jerking—others would fall down suddenly as if breathless and lie during hours."

It was a transformative time for American Christianity. Rankin noticed that in the areas where sound theology was taught, Presbyterian churches passed through "that wonderful time of excitement" with little change to their official doctrine. Some even capitalized on the excitement and grew their membership. To Rankin, this demonstrated the importance of sound theology over the emotional fever of man. Without sound doctrine, he concluded, a passionate man could bend the Word to say anything he wished. This would prove painfully true for him in the coming decades, as he confronted the arguments slaveholders made, who claimed their institution was ordained by God.

It wasn't all hysteria, however. Rankin admitted that "although Satan took advantage of the extreme excitement to mislead many souls, it is believed there were many genuine conversions." His faith was put to the test. This period of great religious excitement was followed by a period of great anxiety. He described it as a "season of coldness," and noted that he "passed into a state of darkness and doubt." Amid the camp meetings and animated revivals he attended with his father, he was forced to confront certain aspects of his faith that he found troubling. Specifically, the Calvinist teachings of predetermination—that God selected only certain individuals to carry out divine purposes. Although Rankin tried to rationalize it away, he determined that such a doctrine was, in fact, true to scripture. Confronting this brought him to an utterly defeated conclusion. "I felt as if I had been passed by and was not one of God's elect." He kept his troubled thoughts concealed as he experienced episodes of severe depression and anxiety. He continued reading the Bible and did so with pleasure, until he was reminded of his anxiety over the subject. Rankin specifically mentioned "great anguish" over the ninth chapter of Romans, which contains the apostle Paul's own anxieties.

"Therefore hath he mercy on whom he will have mercy" Paul explains in Romans 9:18 (KJV), "and whom he will he hardeneth." Rankin very much felt as if he were in the latter category. As he wrestled with this apparent certainty, he attempted what he called "mental adjustments" to carry on without becoming too overwhelmed by the moral dilemma he faced. Still, doubts would occasionally seep back into his mind as he entered young adulthood.[24]

* * * * *

As revival swept the region, there was an incident on the other side of the mountains that forced Rankin to confront another grave matter. Almost a decade earlier in 1791, Haitian slaves rose up in rebellion against their masters in Saint-Domingue. In the wake of the French and American revolutions, slaves in Haiti were inspired to also take freedom into their own hands. White slaveholders were slaughtered across the island as the Haitians in bondage ignited their own revolution. Although the sentiment may have been shared by many across the world, the imagery of planters being slaughtered in their homes was a tough pill to swallow. As some white slaveholders escaped to the United States, they recounted the horrors they experienced in Saint-Domingue as a warning to slaveholders in the American South. Word of the uprising also spread to slaves across the South, inspiring them that freedom was within their grasp if only they took it. One who took inspiration from the Haitian rebellion, as well as the American Revolution, was a slave named Gabriel Prosser. Unlike many other slaves of his day, Gabriel knew how to read and was trained as a blacksmith. When he heard of the rebellion in Saint-Domingue, he was inspired to make something similar occur in the United States—or at least in Virginia.

Gabriel was born and lived near the Richmond area of Virginia. Using the religious and social networks he had amassed over the years, he built a slave network ready to claim their liberty. Leading up to 1800, Gabriel had devised a plan that would, hypothetically, force the Virginian government to put an end to the cruel system of slavery it maintained. In the plan he devised, he and his supporters would launch a mass uprising, akin to that of the Haitian slave revolt. They had planned on marching into the capital, seizing the arsenal, taking the weaponry from there, and capturing the state government, including Governor James Monroe, until they agreed to end the system of slavery in Virginia. While they made a point to avoid needless death, it seemed as if they had little regard for whether their uprising would create casualties among white slave owners and government officials. Gabriel had even planned for his own master to be among the first victims of the rebellion. The group's primary concern was not vengeance and blood-shed, but terror and negotiation. Gabriel carved out specific groups of anti-slavery white people to leave alone in the mayhem. He mentioned Methodists, Quakers, and Frenchmen as likely allies to the cause, as well as poor white Republicans. "Death or Liberty!" became their battle cry, borrowing from the slogan used in the Haitian slave revolt—also borrowed from Patrick Henry's sensational 1775 speech, which took place not far from the rebellion they were planning.

This revolt would have realized many of the founders' greatest fears about slavery. Many prominent members of the founding gener-ation believed slavery was a ticking time bomb, especially in the wake of spreading revolutions around the world. As much as many wished for slavery to meet its end, they had prayed for peaceful revolution. The worst thing that could happen, they believed, was for the issue to result in a violent bloodbath. Although their concern about blood-shed was valid, Gabriel's Rebellion wouldn't be the cause. As it turned out, the weather foiled Gabriel's uprising. On August 30, 1800, the region suffered one of the worst thunderstorms that it had experienced to date. Gabriel was forced to postpone his scheme until the follow-ing night. By this point it was too late. Two slaves, apparently fearful of the consequences such a revolt may bring, tipped their masters off to the conspiracy. Rumors of the uprising spread like wildfire among fearful whites in the Virginia aristocracy. Governor Monroe protected the capital with state militia units. Before long, Gabriel and many of his co-conspirators were caught. The Virginia government acted swiftly and decisively to quell any lingering spirit of rebellion. Seventy con-spirators were tried and forty-four were convicted. Of those convicted, twenty-six were hanged, including Gabriel. He didn't regret his actions, though. During the trial, one of Gabriel's co-conspirators proclaimed that "I have nothing more to offer than what General Washington would have had to offer, had he been taken by the British and put to trial by them. I have adventured my life in endeavoring to obtain the liberty of my countrymen, and am a willing sacrifice in their cause." It was a sentiment that Gabriel shared.

An air of shame swept Virginia and the country in the wake of Gabriel's failed rebellion. As Monroe wrote to his mentor, then Vice President Thomas Jefferson, about the coming executions, he wrote ambivalently that it would be a "question of great importance" when he was to "arrest the hand of the Executioner." Hoping to console his friend, Jefferson replied that "There is a strong sentiment that there has been hanging enough. The other states and the world at large will forever condemn us if we indulge a principle of revenge." Evidently, there were plenty of Virginia legislators happy to indulge in such a principle. Shortly after the trial ended, many state legislators capitalized on the fear and hysteria the failed uprising caused. Rather than ending slavery in Virginia, as Gabriel had hoped, life became even harsher for the black population, both free and slave. Laws were passed to prevent another slave like Gabriel from becoming too literate or from being hired out— key elements, some legislators believed, that made the near revolt possible. To many Americans the response by the Virginia legislature was repugnant. Clearly, many believed, the cause of the rebellion was the nature of slavery itself. Making life more difficult for the poor slaves in Virginia wouldn't solve the problem, but make it worse. Abolitionists then, as few as they were, noticed another irony: for years, southerners justified slavery by suggesting that blacks were genetically inferior to whites, and not intellectually capable of existing on their own in modern society. Gabriel's would-be rebellion wouldn't have been possible if their assumptions were accurate. The legislature's response to the incident—restricting a slave's ability to learn—only gave more credit to a black person's ability to learn.[25]

Upon hearing this news, Jane Rankin was repulsed by the government's response to greater oppression. While both of Rankin's parents were against slavery, Richard let his true feelings known to few. Jane, on the other hand, was more than happy to express her true thoughts on the matter. She was a forceful opponent of slavery, believing it cruel and immoral, especially in a nation that proclaimed the blessings of liberty.

News of the incident out of Richmond gave her great sorrow, leaving a mark on Rankin. Whereas his spiritual state largely stemmed from his father, it was his mother that influenced his passion against slavery.[26]

That passion only grew as Rankin furthered his education, both formal and otherwise. His commitment to abolition progressed alongside his faith. He remained committed to the idea of pursuing ministry professionally, despite his occasional doubts and seasons "of coldness." Through discipline, meditation, and prayer, Rankin strengthened his mental health to the best of his ability until he was twenty years old. It was at this point in his adolescence that he began formally studying theology.

In his teenage years, Rankin traveled seven miles on foot from his home to Dandridge, Tennessee, which was the nearest town to his residence. The town was named in honor of First Lady Martha Dandridge Washington. Rankin's purpose was to receive education from his then-pastor, Reverend David Weir, with a focus on Latin. However, due to the unstable financial state of the Rankin household, Rankin wrote that "At the end of three months the school ended and I was left without the hope of getting an education." Rankin's father often struggled to make ends meet, but he prioritized his children's future. After some time, Richard had afforded enough for Rankin to enroll in college at Washington College in East Tennessee. Although Richard was unsure how long he could sustain his son's pursuit of education, he was nevertheless able to provide Rankin with this opportunity. It was at Washington College that Rankin made probably the most influential connection of his early life when he became acquainted with Reverend Samuel Doak. Doak established a school and Presbyterian church about eight miles from Jonesborough, Tennessee, which eventually transformed into Washington College. He served as the president of the college and taught many classes himself. It was no insignificant matter that Doak had established such an institution in East Tennessee. He himself had studied at the College of New Jersey, later renamed Princeton University, under the tutelage of Reverend John Witherspoon. Witherspoon was not only president of the college, but was also a signer of the Declaration of Independence and mentor to several Founding Fathers, including James Madison. Having a pupil of Witherspoon come to the frontier to establish an institution of high learning represented the ideas of the revolution itself spreading across the wilderness that then dominated most of the United States.[27]

Rev. Samuel Doak, President of Washington College in Eastern Tennessee, became one of John Rankin's earliest mentors

Despite owning slaves himself, Doak was a prominent voice in opposition to slavery. He knew slavery was evil and made no excuses for the institution. He confessed that there was no simple solution to ending slavery, as it was so ingrained in the fabric of the country at that time. However, when it came to the moral question of slavery, Doak made no compromise. The duality between the moral certainty of slavery's evil and the practical dilemma of how to address it would go on to influence much of Rankin's attitude and actions over the next several decades. This perspective separated him from some of his New England colleagues, who would oppose slavery to the point of threatening disunion if abolition could not be achieved.

Doak's mentorship of Rankin helped the latter grow in his intellectual and spiritual capacity. Doak armed him with a stronger understanding of scripture that Rankin later weaponized in his crusade against slavery. Just as importantly, Doak allowed him to grow confident in his own arguments. Rankin later recalled how it was required to "write a composition every week and read it to the president. When I had read my fast composition, the president commended it and said 'you are used to writing.' This was encouraging and it was true. I had been accustomed to writing articles on various subjects." Rankin's editorial skills would become a defining feature, both of his years in the ministry as well as his dedication to abolition.[28]

* * * * *

Geopolitical events in the early 1800s would prove to be one of Rankin's first major tests of faith and resolve. Since the close of the American Revolution, the Americans and British established uneasy peace. Many in Great Britain refused to respect American sovereignty, believing that the country would soon collapse under the weight of newfound independence. To make matters worse, the spark of revolution was beginning to sweep the world. Inspired by the success of the American Revolution, the French successfully orchestrated their own rebellion against the monarchy. In France, the outcome was something much darker. Bloodshed and violence gripped the country as former French monarchs and aristocrats lost their heads to the dreaded guillotine. As many Americans received news of the terror happening in France, they reacted with horror. Many of the allies who helped secure American independence were now dead at the hands of the French mob. French bloodlust proved not to be isolated, either. In 1793, the same year as Rankin's birth, the French government sought to spread its new, revolutionary principles across Europe and declared war on Great Britain. This war would continue and only intensify after a young military chieftain named Napoleon Bonaparte staged a coup and was declared First Consul of the French Republic in 1799. Napoleon's ambition for conquest would prove unrelenting.

After a temporary peace in 1802, Great Britain declared war on France again the following year. In the wake of war and anarchy, Napoleon was coronated as Napoleon I, Emperor of the French, in 1804. The conflicts between Napoleonic France and opposing European nations led to Great Britain gaining control of the seas. Often, US ships were caught in the crossfire. Toward the end of the Jefferson administration, impression of American sailors by the British was reaching a fever pitch, compelling President Jefferson to act. He signed into law the Embargo Act of 1807, which established a general trade embargo on foreign nations in response to British impressment and French conquest. It backfired, proving more economically harmful to the United States than either the French or the British.

As Madison was inaugurated president in 1809, the United States continued its embargo policy. Eventually, however, it became the conscience that a physical war would do less damage to American interests than the administration's adopted policy of continual economic warfare. Thus, on June 1, 1812, President Madison addressed Congress requesting a declaration of war against Great Britain, which Congress granted on June 18.

The Rankin boys were patriotic and eager to support their country. Four of Rankin's brothers—Thomas, Samuel, William, and David—joined the war effort as troops. David was engaged to be married to a young Virginian woman, but his sense of duty to his country became his priority. Before he was wedded, he returned home to volunteer to fight the against British as a lieutenant.

Throughout the war, tribes of American Indians fell on both sides of the conflict. The United States was aided by the Cherokee, Choctaw, Seneca, and Creek Indian tribes. The British were aided largely by Tecumseh's great confederation of Indian tribes. In the southern theater of the war, General Andrew Jackson led a coalition of American and Indian forces against the Red Stick Creek Indians at Horseshoe Bend in the Mississippi Territory. Jackson's American forces were largely composed of Tennessee militia, and David Rankin was among them. While he was initially overlooked, David insisted he be allowed to fight, even offering to go as a private if it meant he could help. This proved unnecessary, as he was allowed to join the campaign while maintaining his rank of lieutenant.

As the battle of Horseshoe Bend commenced in March 1814, Rankin attended his second year at Washington College. He continued to benefit from the experience, but it was an experience that seemed as if it would soon come to an end. His father was running out of money and struggled to pay for his education. That was when the Rankin family received a devastating blow. David had perished at the Battle of Horseshoe Bend, shot through the chest early in the fight. Mortally wounded, he died minutes following his injury. The American force's decisive victory against the Red Stick Creek Indians provided little solace to the Rankin family, grieving their treasured member. The Rankins no doubt must have recognized the cruel irony that David was never meant to go to battle in the first place. It was David's sense of duty that put him in harm's way, and ultimately forced him to pay the ultimate cost. Rankin was distraught. He had lost not just his brother, but one of his best friends. "He was two years older than myself and was my companion from childhood to manhood," he later wrote in his autobiography. "He was a kindhearted brother. The news of his death caused me inexpressible sorrow. To my father and mother it was a terrible blow." David's death was the first that Rankin's family dealt with. Yet, despite this, Rankin's faith in God's grand plan for his life seemed stronger than ever. Although he was made anxious by the Book of Romans in his youth, it gave him comfort in the wake of his brother's death. "And we know that all things work together for good to them that love God, to them who are the called according to his purpose," states Romans 8:28 (KJV). Rankin seemed to pull inspiration from this passage as he continued to write about the tragedy in his autobiography:

His purposes are never caused to fail. He orders and controls all events and uses the free agency of men to accomplish his purposes. All events are part of one great plan by which the greatest good will ultimately be accomplished, and the highest glory of God displayed. Satan prompts men to commit the most abominable crimes and the mighty God causes those very crimes to ruin Satan's kingdom. Juda's [sic] incest and David's adultery were essential to the birth of the Savior and his crucifixion was the salvation of the world. No crimes could be greater than these, yet they resulted from exercise of free agency. Thus the Lord worketh all things after the counsel of his own will.[29]

As confident as Rankin was in God's will, the grieving process is difficult for even the strongest of wills. He loved his brother, and was crushed to hear of his death. It's likely that this played a significant influence on Rankin's attitude toward war in general. In the years leading up to the Civil War, he remained committed to the notion that a peaceful resolution to the issue of slavery should be obtained if possible. Although he was no pacifist, he viewed violence as a matter of last resort. Life was a gift from God, thus it shouldn't be wasted if a peaceful alternative were available.

By 1814, popular support for the war in the United States waned. Despite Jackson's victory at Horseshoe Bend, the United States faced dark days ahead. Washington, DC was a smoldering shell of itself after the British torched the city in August—retaliation for how the Americans torched government buildings in York (now Toronto), Canada earlier during the war. In the early days of the war, Republican war hawks would beat their chest and rattle their sabers, boasting the ease at which Canada could be conquered for the United States. Speaker of the House Henry Clay even infamously boasted that "the militia of Kentucky are alone competent to place Montreal and Upper Canada" at the feet of the American government.[30] It seemed to not have dawned on the hawks that the Canadians may prefer loyalty to Great Britain. Between the failed Canadian campaign and the burning of the Capitol, Federalists were ready to act against the Republican government of the Madison administration. New England Federalists felt the sting of conflict with Great Britain early on. Highly dependent upon trade, the Embargo Act of 1807 did more economic damage to New England than anywhere else in the country. This was "Mr. Madison's war," they claimed, and his government had no right to force New Englanders to pick up the tab for Republican interests.

Since the election of 1800, when Vice President Jefferson defeated Federalist incumbent John Adams, the Federalists were a dying political faction. By 1814, they were on life support. These circumstances forced their hand into something dramatic. Starting in December 1814, New England Federalists held a secret convention in Hartford, Connecticut, to discuss what should be done about the Republican-controlled government. The convention agreed to advocate for several Constitutional amendments in response to Madison and Jefferson's policies. The proposed amendments included limiting the presidential term to one term, prohibiting embargos lasting longer than sixty days, removing the three-fifths compromise from the Constitution, and requiring new presidents to be from a different state than the predecessor, among others. Although it seemed unlikely that it was seriously considered by the convention, murmurs of secession also became more prominent. Regardless of how seriously this was discussed, it was a proposal that many New England Federalists favored. New Englanders felt they lived in a separate country from the one that the South and the West experienced. At the outset of the war on July 4, 1812, New England Federalist Daniel Webster even made a passionate anti-war speech, warning that New England may exercise their right to secede if Washington, DC continued to execute what he saw as tyrannical policies. "We are, sir, from principle and habit attached to the union of the states. But our attachment is to the substance and not to the form," he warned. "If a separation of the states ever should take place, it will be on some occasion when one portion of the country undertakes to control, to regulate and to sacrifice the interest of another." Coming shy of directly advocating for secession, he told his audience that the "present course of measures will prove most prejudicial and ruinous to this country."[31]

Just a couple of years later at the Hartford convention, it seemed that the "prejudicial and ruinous" hour was soon approaching. While mention of secession wasn't included in the final report of the Hartford convention, it was in the New England air. What the secret convention didn't know was that the American peace delegation had reached an agreement with the British in the city of Ghent, in what is now Belgium. American and British delegates signed the Treaty of Ghent on December 24, 1814. The Hartford convention held its final meeting on January 5, 1815, before news of the treaty reached North America. To make matters worse for the New England Federalists, Jackson led American troops to victory at the Battle of New Orleans three days later. News of the Hartford convention, the Treaty of Ghent, and the Battle of New Orleans engaged in a three-way race to Washington, DC. Word of the convention arrived first, infuriating Republicans. This was to be expected, but Republicans were vindicated as news of Jackson's decisive victory in New Orleans reached the government. As if that weren't enough to shame the New England Federalists, the Treaty of Ghent was finally ratified in February 1815, officially putting an end to the war. Although the Americans didn't "win" the war per se, they didn't make any prominent concessions, either. Many incorrectly believed that Jackson's victory had been the final nail in the coffin, despite a peace agreement being reached a few weeks earlier. The Hartford convention made New England Federalists look foolish at best, and treasonous at worst. This proved to be the dying Federalist Party's last breath.[32]

Although the convention killed the political viability of Federalists, its impact was felt throughout the remainder of the early nineteenth century. Speculation of New England secession had circulated since the Jefferson administration. No matter how serious the idea had been, it became a source of inspiration for future separatists in both the North and the South. Specifically, in New England, as the debate over slavery grew tense, many abolitionist associates and colleagues of Rankin would soon advocate for disunion if abolition could not be achieved. It was a precedent that damaged the credibility of the abolitionist cause in the eyes of many Americans.

* * * * *

The Rankin Family continued to grieve the loss of David, but Rankin used his grief as motivation. David's tragic death allowed him to continue his education to become a minister; because David was killed in battle, the government provided the Rankin family with compensation that helped pay for Rankin's tuition. He engulfed himself completely in his studies. "I spent no time in sporting and playing. For these I had no propensity and for other exercises I had no opportunity," he wrote. He offered to chop wood for free for President Doak, but Doak refused. It was around this time that Rankin started developing a pain in his side, which would stick with him throughout his life. "It has followed me down to the present time and whenever I confine myself to studying. A cough set in so that I feared my lungs were affected. My nerves began to give way. I feared that I would have to abandon my studies and went on from session to session expecting each one to be the last I would be able to attend. But I persevered to the end."[33]

Coping with his brother's death and deteriorating health, one would imagine that Rankin was entering another "cold season" of his life. However, this was also the time that he encountered one of the greatest lights of his life. Rankin boarded with Doak's daughter and son-in-law while attending Washington College. Doak's son-in-law, Adam Lowry, was a devoted husband, father, and committed believer in abolitionism. He refused to own any slaves. As Rankin stayed with the Lowry family, he became attached to their lovely young daughter, Jean Lowry. Rankin had "determined to pay my addresses to her," he wrote. And on the chance that there might be a connection, "I would make her the companion of my life." Rankin had developed a crush that was budding into something much more. He was compelled by her beauty as well as her "high reputation for industry and good nature." Consumed with thoughts of religion and philosophy as a boy, Rankin was never much of a lady's man. He gained a reputation for being studious, but that wasn't much of an attractive trait for teenage girls in his region. In contrast, Jean was strong and intelligent, came from a well-respected family, and was committed to the Presbyterian faith, like Rankin. He quickly understood that she was a strong match for him. Still, it came as a shock to those who knew him that he had found his partner for life. "It was a matter of surprise to my friends and acquaintances," he mused, "because I was unaccustomed to associating with young ladies." Rankin and Jean joined in holy matrimony on January 2, 1816, only a few weeks before his graduation from Washington College. Jean even made Rankin's wedding coat for him, and he made his own shoes. He wrote that his marriage "was a matter of duty and interest as well as of affection." Concern for his parents constantly consumed his thoughts, and his marriage to Jean allowed him to remove the financial burden of his education from them. "My parents were at once relieved from all further expense."

Some believed Rankin made a mistake in getting married before his studies were complete, but he later observed that "time fully justified my professional wisdom." With his marriage behind him, Rankin was able to fully devote himself to his studies with his wife's help, and was better equipped to pursue ministry once he graduated. His marriage to Jean was something Rankin never regretted. Neither was what came from their marriage, the birth of a baby boy that November. On November 4, 1816, Rankin and Jean welcomed Adam Lowry Rankin into the world. Named after his grandfather, Lowry would prove to be not just a respectable son, but a key ally in Rankin's fight against slavery.

Things seemed to be looking up for Rankin, and it was finally time to become a minister of the gospel. Six months before he graduated from Washington College, he joined the Abingdon Presbytery. His now grandfather-in-law, President Doak, privately tutored Rankin and guided him through the ministry for eighteen months. Doak also "prescribed and furnished the books" Rankin needed to study to be licensed by the Presbytery. Preaching came with much practice for Rankin, and he did not become comfortable with it for many years. Public speaking was an obstacle in his youth as well as adulthood, and it didn't come intuitively to him as it did for other ministers. Before he went to college, Rankin attempted preaching in Dandridge. Once, in the middle of his sermon, he completely blanked. "My sermon was well memorized and I was speaking with ease," he recalled, "when suddenly I had a slip of memory and my mind seemed as blank as if there was not an idea in creation. My eyes grew dim. I could scarcely see the people, but I kept the sound going until I recovered and went well through. I suppose that not one in the audience discovered my embarrassment. Reverend Jesse Lockhart was present but did not notice anything out of the way." Nonetheless, he developed his speaking skills enough to obtain his license from the Presbytery. Many were skeptical of Rankin as a minister. Upon his approval, the Abingdon Presbytery noted in his file that he would be accepted with "suspicion and distrust because of his frequent expression of opposition to slavery."[34]

Indeed, if they wished for Rankin to remain quiet over the issue of slavery, they had good reason to be. It was a matter on which Rankin refused to be silenced. His first sermon was committed to memory and was preached with ease. His second sermon was recited nearly from memory. His third sermon was challenging, as he felt unwell and was unaquanited with the audience. Rankin also preached without notes this time, adding a new layer of pressure. As he started speaking, he became excited by the content of his sermon and delivered it with ease. As he developed his speaking skills, Rankin grew in confidence, and it wasn't long before he started to bring matters of injustice in front of his congregation from the pulpit. In the summer of 1817, he launched into a sermon where he felt compelled to mention the Bible's opposition to "all forms of oppression" and that it was the Christian duty to drive such oppression from the face of the earth. Without mentioning slavery, the congregation knew what he was referring to. The church elders were outraged. They believed that Rankin's sermons might inspire an uprising, not unlike that of Gabriel's Rebellion in 1800. The church enjoyed the membership of several slaveowners, and inciting such an incident threatened their lives, they believed. They instructed Rankin to never again preach on the subject of slavery or oppression.

It wasn't the first time Rankin put his anti-slavery beliefs to practice. He was already engaged in the Tennessee Manumissions Society, which advocated for slave owners to willfully emancipate their slaves rather than wait for abolition from the government. This society was organized in Rankin's home region of Jefferson County in February 1815 and was the first formally organized anti-slavery society of its kind. Members of the society were required to boldly advertise in their homes that "[f]reedom is the natural right of all men. I therefore acknowledge myself a member of the Tennessee Society for promoting the manumission of slaves." Rankin helped the society's leader, Quaker abolitionist Charles Osborn, by working to expand its membership in East Tennessee. But even that was different from blatantly promoting abolition from the pulpit. If the elders hoped their frustration would convince Rankin to tone it down, they were sorely mistaken. [35]

A few weeks after his sermon against oppression, a new opportunity arose. Rankin was invited by a church in the Union Presbytery, which had few slaveowners and was sympathetic to the anti-slavery cause. Perhaps it was despite the rejection he received from the Abingdon Presbytery. Maybe he was emboldened by preaching to a sympathetic audience. Whatever the reason, Rankin was gripped by righteous indignation to unleash a furious sermon against the evils of slavery and all forms of oppression. He didn't mince words, even openly using the term "slavery" in front of his congregation so that there was no confusion over what kind of oppression he was referring to. The spirit of his sermon overcame him, completely and uniformly renouncing every aspect of slavery in America.

Rankin had bitten off more than he could chew. Still young and largely inexperienced, he failed to read the room as he was caught up in his own sermon. Even a sympathetic southern congregation believed it to be a radical thing to openly speak out against slavery from the pulpit in the way that Rankin had. Afterward, the elders pulled him aside. To his shock, they suggested that if he couldn't stop preaching against slavery, it might behoove him to leave Tennessee.

This notion depressed Rankin, but he knew they were right. Even in a sympathetic region, he couldn't carry out his ministry where slavery still existed. If he wanted the freedom to speak and preach freely, he would have to do so from a free state. Word had gotten out that over the Ohio River, there was a growing frontier town settled by Virginian abolitionists. Rankin set his sights on the community after discussing the matter with his wife, and started packing his bags. Rankin and Jean's friends and family were largely upset by the notion of them leaving for Ohio. In 1817, once you left a region, it was permanent. They believed they would never see them again. For the most part, they were right. The only one who didn't seem to object was Jean's father, Adam. Despite the danger in the journey and the risk of never seeing his daughter, son-in-law, and grandson again, he understood why Rankin was making the decision. Richard, however, was another matter. He begged Rankin to stay, offering him a farm to stay on if it meant he would remain. Rankin's calling for ministry was too strong, and he believed he could only fulfill this calling by speaking out against slavery. As much as it pained him, Rankin knew he had to leave his father and mother in Tennessee. Adam was as supportive as he could be, offering the young family a horse, a two-wheeled topless carriage, and seventy dollars' worth of silver. A friend provided an umbrella in case of rain on their journey. They said goodbye to Jean's family and made one final stop to see Richard and Jane before departing north.

Rankin was surprised by how hard it was for him and his family. They loved him, and with David's death still fresh in their mind, the thought of losing another treasured son wrecked them. "My parents felt more deeply than I had anticipated," he later recalled. They provided them with a quilt and some clothes, which proved to be more than their carriage could hold. The morning came for their departure. Jane provided their breakfast, but Richard was nowhere to be found. He couldn't bear the thought of sending his son off for the final time. With his father absent, Rankin and Jean loaded their carriage and headed off. As they departed, Richard rushed on his horse to his son's side. He guided them out of the neighborhood he had raised his son in. At the neighborhood's border, rather than say goodbye and return home, Richard continued to ride with them. Concerned by his father's journey home, Rankin turned to him, asking if he needed to head back. Richard was unconcerned about how far he needed to go if it meant a few moments longer with his son. "The feelings of that parting moment I never can describe. At this late hour of life, tears start whenever I reflect upon the separation," Rankin later wrote. "I felt we were to meet no more on this Earth." Together, they rode for miles in silence, looking straight ahead, holding back their tears as they delayed the inevitable.[36]

BLUEGRASS SOJOURNER
1817–1822
II.

I n the fall of 1817, John Rankin, Jean Rankin, and baby Adam Lowry Rankin made their way north from Tennessee into the commonwealth of Kentucky. It was a challenging journey for any early nineteenth-century traveler. Roads were primitive even in America's wealthiest regions, but in the frontier country of Tennessee and Kentucky, they were virtually non-existent. Rankin walked alongside the horse-drawn carriage as his wife and infant son rode for miles in the foothills of the Appalachian Mountains. Being carriage-bound did not make the journey any easier for them. Every rock and divot made the mother and son brace for impact, making it difficult to rest in any meaningful sense. Adam still had newborn needs and Jean tried her best to accommodate. Meanwhile, Rankin was on constant alert. Traveling such a great distance in 1817 wasn't just uncomfortable, it was dangerous. Still an untouched wilderness, though not as severely as it was when Richard and Jane Rankin settled in Jefferson County, there were several animals to be wary of. Black bears, mountain lions, and poisonous snakes were abundant across the region. Of course, other travelers were the real danger. If someone were found in a compromising position, they would be easy picking for roadside robbery. For the Rankin family, that could mean life or death. Nonetheless, Rankin led his family out from his metaphoric Egypt through the wilderness toward his promised land. They traveled up from Jefferson County, Tennessee, and entered Kentucky through the Cumberland Gap.

The late Kentucky historian Thomas D. Clark called the commonwealth a "land of contrast."[37] It was full of danger and opportunity. Few regions in the country represented all of America's exciting promise and glaring contradiction as much as Kentucky. Whereas the Northwest Territory became synonymous with liberty because of its prohibition of slavery, Kentucky was a battleground state. The religious influence of many protestant denominations in the commonwealth drove this early debate. Many Presbyterians were inclined to support abolitionist sentiment, and the same could be said of Methodists. Baptist congregations were more deeply divided.

From the beginning, Baptists have been engrained in Kentucky's history. Prior to and throughout the American Revolution, many Baptists faced persecution as a religious minority in the Anglican-dominated commonwealth. They scoffed at the notion of paying taxes to support the Church of England, despite the doctrine of the church counter to their own conscience. Many in the 1770s were even imprisoned or beaten as tensions rose. One individual who ran contrary to authorities on multiple occasions was Lewis Craig. A self-taught Baptist minister, Craig devoted himself to the faith after a conversion around the age of thirty. He had no license, as was required for ministers in a dissenting minority, but he nonetheless preached in defiance of the law. In 1768, Craig and other ministers, including one of his brothers, Joseph, were arrested for being "disruptors of the peace" and preaching without a license. As they sat in a courtroom in Virginia awaiting their trial, a plain-looking man dressed in unremarkable attire entered the courtroom after riding over fifty miles to the defense of the ministers. Most in attendance had no idea who this common-looking man was, but the magistrates and prosecutors knew well who they were looking at. It was Patrick Henry.

After listening to the indictment, Henry rose in a state of disbelief. He specifically honed in on the charge of "preaching the gospel contrary to the law" and pounced on it. "May it please your worship, what did I hear read?" Henry asked. "Did I hear it distinctly or was it a mistake of my own? Did I hear an expression, as if a crime that these men…are charged with what?" He asked as the weight of the charge was beginning to settle on the crowd. "For preaching the gospel of the Son of God?" Henry had become famous for his oratory skills. Before he got another word out, the audience was aware of the gravity of Herny's rhetorical questions. He then erupted into a burst of energy and exclaimed "Great God!" before the court. After Henry made his case, they agreed to release the ministers, on the conduction that they wouldn't preach for one year. The ministers declined, and preached from their prison cell in Fredericksburg, Virginia for a month.

Craig continued to preach even after his release, not to be deterred by the threat of imprisonment. He was ordained in 1770 and became the pastor of the Upper Spotsylvania Baptist Church. Craig was also captivated by the idea of Kentucky after stories from the west started making their way back to Virginia. For religious dissenters, Kentucky seemed like the Promised Land. In Kentucky, they could enjoy fertile farming, abundant hunting, cheap land, and practice their faith without fear of persecution. Lewis had made the decision to journey over the mountains to Kentucky. When he announced his plans to his church in the fall of 1781, over half of his congregation agreed to move with him. Lewis's brother and fellow Baptist minister, Elijah Craig, was among them, and became very industrious in Kentucky. Among his pursuits, Elijah distilled whiskey, which he is most associated with today. As Craig brought his congregation across the mountains into their land of freedom, many church members also brought with them their slaves. With the spread of the Baptist denomination across Kentucky, division grew within many churches. Pastors would often preach about the immorality of slavery, but many slaveholders made up their congregations.[38]

While it existed, anti-slavery sentiment spread like wildfire, and some of the earliest abolitionist groups formed as the bluegrass was tamed. This conflict of consciousness is strongly reflected in Kentucky's first constitution, accepted on June 1, 1792, less than a year before Rankin's birth. Article IX of the Kentucky Constitution dealt with the question of slavery. In no uncertain terms, it declared that "the Legislature shall have no power to pass laws for the emancipation of slaves without the consent of their owners, or without paying their owners, previous to such emancipation, a full equivalent in money for the slaves so emancipated...."[39] From the outset, the slave-holding class ensured it would take nothing short of a constitutional convention for the Kentucky constitution or an amendment to the US Constitution to force slavery's elimination. However, in the very same article, the Constitution affirms the humanity of the slave, stating that the legislature "shall have full power to pass such laws as may be necessary, to oblige the owners of slaves to treat them with humanity, to provide for them necessary clothing and provisions, to abstain from all injuries to them extending to life or limb; and in case of their neglect or refusal to comply with the directions of such laws, to have such slave or slaves sold for the benefit of their owner or owners."

The conflict that many Kentuckians felt over slavery continued to hang over the commonwealth, but the influence of the slave-holding class proved very powerful. As another constitutional convention was held in 1799, many of the original provisions from 1792 were refined and modified. The provision concerning slavery was upheld word for word, and free blacks, Indians, and people of mixed race were further disenfranchised. "Every free male citizen (negroes, mulattoes, and Indians excepted)...shall enjoy the right of an elector." The 1799 Constitution also ensured that freemen "shall be armed and disciplined" for the defense of the commonwealth. The exception, of course, was "negroes, mulattoes, and Indians."[40]

While parts of this constitution disenfranchised free minorities in addition to slaves, it again upheld their humanity in unsuspecting ways. Article X of the Constitution stated that "all freemen, when they form a social compact, are equal, and that no man or set of men, are entitled to exclusive, separate, public emoluments or privileges from the community, but in consideration of public services." This was updated from 1792, which stated more generally that "all *men*, when they form a social compact, are equal…" (emphasis added). Yet, a few lines below, as it dealt with religious liberty, such a change was not made. "All men have a natural and indefeasible right to worship Almighty God according to the dictates of their own consciences; that no man shall be compelled to attend, erect, or support any place of worship, or to maintain any ministry against his consent; that no human authority ought, in any case, whatever, to control or interfere with the rights of conscience; and that no preference shall ever be given by law, to any religious societies or modes of worship."[41]

Kentucky became the land of opportunity after the revolution. Indian tribes were mostly pushed back, unlike in the Northwest Territory. Just as pro-slavery forces began to populate the region, anti-slavery families also came, escaping Virginia's slavery influence. The convergence of wealthy planters, religious dissenters, and anti-slavery Virginians set the stage for the constitutional battles that would occur in 1792 and 1799. Although anti-slavery proponents would ultimately lose the battle against the slaveholding class in 1799, they would continue to be a major cultural influence throughout Kentucky. By the time Rankin and his small family started to travel through the bluegrass state, the anti-slavery presence was already engrained.

* * * * *

It wasn't long into their journey that the Rankin family ran into trouble. Because of the load that they carried, as well as the state of Rankin's wife and infant child, an entire day's travel brought them only a short distance. Kentucky was still referred to as "the wilderness" at the time of their journey, "and I suppose is wilderness still," Rankin wrote years later in his autobiography. Shortly into their travel, they faced rather significant setbacks. "The axle tree [sic] of our carriage broke into two pieces," Rankin recalled. Since the axle was made of iron, he needed a blacksmith to fix the wheel. Unfortunately, this meant leaving his wife and son alone on the road with all their belongings. Rankin was hyper-aware of the risk, but he was left with little choice. If he expected to make it to Ohio, he was going to need a blacksmith sooner rather than later. As Rankin left, Jean watched over their belongings with their son by her side. Fortunately, the only traveler of note who passed by was with a large drove of pigs. The pigs, Rankin mentioned, "behaved civilly."

Eventually, Rankin found a blacksmith to fix his wheel and he returned to his wife and son. After repairing their carriage, they continued on the road until Saturday afternoon. Despite the daunting journey they faced, or maybe because of it, Rankin insisted they still observe the Sabbath. He began looking for homes the family may reside in until Monday, after the Sabbath had passed. He wished to provide his family with some rest. In addition, he also sought out an opportunity to preach. As he stopped at one home asking where he might lodge his family, they were invited to stay there. Rankin accepted the invitation and noted that the family they stayed with was very kind and their lodging arrangements were quite comfortable. As Sunday morning came around, he was met without an audience to hear him preach, save for the family they lodged with. "No notice of preaching was given out to the wilderness neighborhood," Rankin recalled. "Therefore no one came to hear." He made another discovery on Sunday morning, that the "landlord was an infidel." After talking with Rankin about religion and faith, their landlord confessed that matters of the spiritual realm perplexed him, and he found it difficult to wrap his head around such things that he could not comprehend. The landlord pulled from the story of Jesus feeding the thousands miraculously with only a few loaves of bread and fish. Such a story seemed unbelievable to him, and thus he found it difficult to have faith in such things. "He professed not to believe in the inspiration of the scriptures and to believe nothing but what he could understand," wrote Rankin about their temporary stay. He told the landlord that miracles, by definition, defy earthly explanation, and thus can only be explained through the power of God. If there was a reasonable explanation, it wouldn't be miraculous and would thus undermine the authority of Christ and the purpose of his mission on Earth. They went on with their day, and the family remained very cordial, but Rankin couldn't help but return to their discussion about miracles. Later that night, Rankin recalled the landlord telling him about a time when he had a splitting toothache and "a Dutchman took him out to a tree, performed some ceremony and cured his tooth." Rankin turned to him and asked if he truly believed that his tooth was cured. The landlord looked back at him and confirmed that he did believe it. Rankin then asked, "Why not believe the miracle of the loaves and fishes?" The landlord had "no reply to make. His inconsistency was so palpable he could not help seeing it."[42]

Monday morning came and it was time for the Rankin family to hit the road again. He paid the landlord what they agreed to be a reasonable amount for their stay. While Rankin was grateful to the landlord, he mentioned in a somewhat annoyed remark that his reason for asking them to stay was "to get pay for keeping us over the Sabbath." As they continued, their journey remained relatively unhampered by unforeseen events until they finally arrived in Lexington, Kentucky. Lexington was gaining a regard as the "Athens of the West." In the heart of the bluegrass region of Kentucky, many of its earliest settlers wished for the city to become the center of culture and agriculture in the United States. In some ways, it was accomplishing that. The aristocratic class in Kentucky flocked to the bluegrass region, predominantly in Lexington. Even today, many of the original homes of the Kentucky planters still stand. Of course, this was also the region of the commonwealth where slavery was most present. But, perhaps somewhat to Rankin's surprise, this was also where Kentucky's anti-slavery activity took place most resolutely. Rankin and his small family arrived in Lexington fifteen days after leaving his father's home in East Tennessee. Upon arrival, they called on Reverend Dr. James Blythe with the First Presbyterian Church, formerly Mount Zion Church, for lodging and an opportunity to preach. They stayed with him during "a communion season at the Presbyterian church," Rankin recalled. He was paid twenty dollars for his preaching services.

They weren't long for Lexington, however. They soon continued to Paris, Kentucky in Bourbon County, a little to the north of Lexington. There, they called on Reverend John Lyle, who came to Kentucky around 1800, near the outbreak of the Second Great Awakening. Like Rankin as a boy, Lyle was skeptical of certain religious factions spreading in the wake of the excitement that swept the region. One idea in particular that was spreading rapidly at the time was Hopkinsonianism. Named after the New England theologian Samuel Hopkins, Hopkinsonianism adopted a modified Calvinism that emphasized accepting God's will, even if it meant one's personal damnation, and proposed that moral ethics are nothing more than "disinterested benevolence." Lyle defiantly rejected Hopkinsonianism and believed it had no place in Calvinist theology. He allowed Rankin to preach and lodged him and his family. Shortly afterward, before Rankin continued his journey to Ohio, Lyle invited him into his garden for a chat. They dove into a theological discussion, specifically on whether Rankin himself believed in Hopkinsonianism. Rankin reassured Lyle that he was not a Hopkinsonian. Lyle breathed a sigh of relief, then urged him to settle in Carlisle, Kentucky, about fifteen miles from Paris. There, the Concord Presbyterian Church was trying to fill a vacant pulpit. Lyle believed Rankin could be the perfect man for the job. He had preached there several times in the past, he told Rankin, attempting to reassure him. But Rankin was somewhat taken aback by the proposal, and somewhat taken aback. "I was opposed to slavery," he told Lyle, reminding him that Kentucky was not meant to be his final destination. "I designed to go to Ohio as it was a free state." The two discussed it further, and Rankin finally relented. It was on his way to Ohio, so he agreed only to call upon the church to preach a few sermons. He made no promises that he would remain any longer than that.[43]

After Lyle paid Rankin, the family went on their way. As promised, he arrived in Carlisle and called upon the Concord Church to deliver some sermons. He had every intention to continue on to Ohio once his side mission was complete, but he again faced a hurdle. His horse collapsed from exhaustion and a sore back. He needed to give it time to recover before moving on toward the river. Rankin was keen to take a hint when he believed it came from the Almighty. His horse collapsing so near winter would mean that he would need to remain in Carlisle until spring. So, after he arrived and preached at the Concord Presbyterian Church, he agreed to serve as their temporary pastor for six months. At the end of his six months in Carlisle, he would finally finish his journey to Ohio. He was soon gripped by some of the same insecurities that taunted him as a child and during his first few sermons. He found himself giving the same sermon "every Sabbath to the same people twice a day." He was running out of steam. He wondered how he could keep it up for six months. If he couldn't keep it up for six months, how could he be expected to be minister at all? Surely it was a sign that he made a mistake getting into the ministry? He brought the matter to his wife for counsel. He confessed to her that he believed he should quit preaching. Jean Rankin refused to entertain such a notion. He wasn't lacking capacity, she told him, but needed to expand his horizon. Rankin snapped out of his state of despair and came to terms that his wife was likely right. He used the time he had during the winter of 1817–18 to acquire enough texts that would give him enough material to develop new sermons. "I selected a sufficient number of texts to give me enough to speak," he later wrote. "For I never had a talent for speaking on nothing, as some seem to have." Eventually, it started working, and his congregation took notice. "I began to preach and in this way the people began to speak of my improvement in preaching."

Rankin remained with the congregation for all six months, as he promised. Spring of 1818 came around and it was nearing time for his departure. He was initially prepared to continue his journey, but the congregation came to him and asked if he would consider staying as their permanent pastor. During his unexpected stay in Kentucky, Rankin developed a certain appreciation for the bluegrass state and the people who inhabited it. Yes, it was a slave state, but there also existed a counter-culture so strong that one couldn't help but think that if slavery could be conquered in any southern state, it would be in Kentucky. The congregation of the Concord Presbyterian Church was a significant reason for this sensation. The members of this church were strongly antislavery, so much so that many of them were instrumental in establishing the Kentucky Abolition Society. The society was one of the first of its kind and a harbinger of things to come. Over the next several decades, many anti-slavery societies would pop up across the country, largely thanks to the help of Rankin and his colleagues. Members of the Concord Church and twelve other churches across Kentucky established the abolition society as far back as 1807, well ahead of most organized abolitionist activities. In 1808, they formed a constitution advocating for the abolition of slavery, black education in Kentucky, and justice for the "negroes and mulatoes [sic] as are held in bondage." They also sought to promote the circulation of anti-slavery speeches and sermons. What really made the Kentucky Abolition Society stand out in this era was their advocacy for what would later be known as "immediate emancipation." Rankin later recalled that the society advanced the notion that "if the slave has the right to freedom at all, he has it now." This was especially unique in the early 1800s when they formed. At this time, many of the individuals or groups who supported ending slavery believed in gradual emancipation. To so openly call for an immediate end to slavery was considered radical by many.

David Rice, the late Presbyterian minister and abolitionist, was active in the Kentucky Abolition Society until his death in 1816. Sometimes referred to as the "Apostle to Kentucky," Rice was a very influential political and spiritual figure in the early days of statehood. He was a member of the 1792 convention and a powerful advocate for the freedom and humane treatment of those in bondage. While he failed to prevent the continuation of slavery as an established institution in Kentucky, the Constitution largely left the matter in the hands of individual slaveholders. In other states, like Virginia, the manumission of slaves was heavily regulated to prevent slaveholders from freeing their slaves. Ensuring that Kentuckians had the option to free their slaves was no small accomplishment in those days.

While Rankin never had the opportunity to meet Rice, his influence was certainly felt. While Kentucky remained a slave state, Rankin discovered that he wouldn't be ostracized by his congregation for supporting or promoting abolition in the way that he was in Tennessee. He decided that he would accept their offer for him to remain. "A call was presented to West Lexington Presbytery," he recalled. He was "accepted and was ordained and installed pastor of Concord church."[44]

* * * * *

Rankin's Kentucky years were crucial to his development, not just as a minister, but as a leader in abolition. Each week as he preached from the pulpit, he grew in confidence and oratory skill. His congregation made him feel appreciated, especially when it came to his conviction against slavery. He later reflected that his time preaching in Kentucky enabled him to "preach forty-four years in one place," after he completed his journey to Ohio. He even admitted that he was tempted to "preach there much longer had I chosen to do so." Although he was bound for the free soil of Ohio, he was likely not expecting how positive of an impact Kentucky would have on him. He would develop a soft spot and appreciation for the bluegrass state that stretched well into his later years. In addition to his ministry and anti-slavery activism, Kentucky is also where his family started to really expand. When Rankin decided that he would remain with the Concord Church, his love for the congregation wasn't the only motivating factor. Jean was once again pregnant, due to give birth within a few months. After accepting the church's offer to remain in Kentucky, Jean gave birth to their first daughter, Isabella Jane Rankin, on June 16, 1818. She was born in a log cabin that the Rankins rented and shared with another family. Jean's brother, Samuel Lowry, soon arrived at Carlisle and boarded with them during this time. He was taught theology by Rankin and licensed to preach by the West Lexington Presbytery. A little over a year later, Jean gave birth to yet another child, David Rankin, on September 18, 1819. Everything was going unexpectedly well, given the circumstances. It's little wonder why the Rankins included these days among "the happiest times of our lives." For some time, it even seemed the family would abandon their journey to Ohio entirely. Rankin purchased property in Carlisle and prepared to build a permanent residence there. However, several events soon took place that derailed these plans and forced him to look back to Ohio.

As Rankin settled into his preaching role at Concord and started to expand his anti-slavery activism with the Kentucky Abolition Society, he had a thought that startled him. The slaves in Kentucky had little or no way to receive the gospel. Kentucky was one of the few slave states that did not pass the anti-literacy laws, which would prevent the state's enslaved population from learning how to read and write. Individual slaveholders still usually prevented their own slaves from becoming literate, however. It was the education of a slave, after all, that led to the outbreak of Gabriel's Rebellion in Virginia when Rankin was younger. Ignorance was key in maintaining slaveholding power. But Kentucky slaveholders, many of whom were religious or heavily influenced by their religious neighbors, dealt with a dilemma. How can they permit slaves to be exposed to the gospel without allowing them to read the Bible? Rankin knew something had to budge, and he would force it to budge if he needed to. "My father became interested in the spiritual welfare of the slaves," Adam Lowry Rankin later wrote. "They were denied a knowledge of the Word of Life." He added that Rankin believed "it was an imperative duty to do something for their moral welfare."

Speaking against slavery was one thing, but educating slaves, even if it was about the gospel, posed a direct threat to the power of the slaveholding class. Rankin would need to be tactical about how he approached this controversial subject. After much thought, he came up with a proposal. He would approach the slaveholders in his region and have their permission to "gather the colored people in a neighborhood schoolhouse that was not occupied on the Sabbath afternoon." He assured them that he would not teach slaves how to read the Bible, but only provide "an oral instruction" on the teachings of scripture. Additionally, he would ensure to receive written permission from the slaveholders that the slaves were allowed to attend. He was playing with fire in a way that he hadn't done before. But Rankin was not to be deterred. They had a right, he thought, to their conscience. Without that right, nobody could truly claim to be free. Additionally, as a minister, he believed he was duty-bound to spread the gospel to all corners of the earth, including to the slave.

At first, his slave gatherings transpired without much incident. After Jean's brother, Samuel, arrived in Carlisle, he assisted Rankin in his schoolhouse instructions and was a valuable ally. His program went on for more than a year uninterrupted, but suspicion soon started to boil in the region. Word of anger in the community made its way back to him, but he brushed off the complaints and continued to instruct the slave population as he had before. It wasn't long before the quiet discontent transformed into vocal indignation. Threats were made against Rankin and Samuel, as well as their black pupils. They wanted the school shut down and the education of slaves to cease immediately. Rankin was unwilling to back down, but he also didn't intend to get anyone hurt. After receiving permission from their masters, he made the decision to move from the schoolhouse to an unoccupied private home. For several months, he was able to continue teaching in peace. This peace soon ended, when an alcohol-fueled mob formed, broke into the house, and drove off the slaves with clubs. Finally, Rankin again moved his operation to the kitchen of a friend nearby. Their hope was that because the home was an occupied residence, rather than an abandoned house, the mob might back off. Indeed, they refused to sack the house in the way they had before. Instead, they intercepted the slaves as they returned home and proceeded to give them "a light thrashing." The intimidation worked, and they stopped coming to Rankin's school. In the aftermath, Rankin approached the slaveholders, asking for their help in putting an end to the beatings. They only offered their firm disapproval of the incidents. The slaveholders weren't part of the intimidation plot, but wouldn't do anything to prevent it either. With his students scared away, Rankin had to shut his school operation down. As if this wasn't discouraging enough, it coincided with the Panic of 1819.

The inauguration of James Monroe into the presidency in 1816 unleashed what is commonly referred to as the "Era of Good Feeling." With the war of 1812 behind the United States and Napoleon's defeat and exile in Europe, the world was in a relative state of peace. Economic commerce exploded in the United States, with new industries sprouting constantly. Steamboats were beginning to open the west to commerce and travel in a way that was unheard of up to that point. The *New Orleans* made history by becoming the first steamboat to successfully traverse western waters between 1811 and 1812. It traveled from Pittsburgh all the way to New Orleans. In 1817, the *Ontario* became the first steamboat to actively operate on the Great Lakes. Each year, they populated the Great Lakes and the Ohio and Mississippi rivers, making the frontier more accessible than ever before. Gone were the days of isolated frontiersmen traversing the virgin forests west of the Allegheny Mountains, constantly surrounded by the threat of roaming Indian tribes. Life in Kentucky or within the former Northwest Territory was still hard, but it was becoming civilized. The opportunities seemed endless. This unleashed a land rush in the west, even greater than what was seen in the aftermath of the Revolution. State banks were quick to capitalize on this, incentivized with a liberal credit policy from the Second Bank of the United States (SBUS). They dished out banknotes to practically any borrower who asked. Both banks and borrowers believed that the money they would make on land out west would quickly pay off the loan. This, of course, all occurred without actually seeing the land they were purchasing. This land interest also welcomed a flood of speculators, eager to make a quick buck, even if it wasn't honest. It wasn't uncommon for speculators to sell land that they didn't actually own or to sell the same land to multiple parties. Most settlers didn't know any better and were easily swindled.

All these factors created a massive bubble that quickly became too large to contain itself. Attempting to slow down inflation, the SBUS demanded that state banks pay back their loans in 1818. Unable to do so, many banks started shutting down, kicking off a cascading effect that led to a run on the banks. The Panic of 1819 became the first major economic downturn in the history of the early republic. Rather than swift action from the federal government to achieve some kind of relief, as we are accustomed to today, President Monroe took a hands-off approach. In 1819, there was little that the president or Congress had the authority to do in the realm of the economy. Additionally, President Monroe was a Jeffersonian Republican. He believed that the federal government should have little involvement in economic affairs in the first place. He trusted the market to work itself out. In many respects, it did. Those most harmed by the panic were mostly those responsible for it in the first place—reckless bankers and dishonest speculators. There were those, however, who suffered temporary setbacks. Rankin was one of them. "When I made my contract, the country was flooded with money of independent banks," as he recalled preparing to build his home. But as soon as he was ready to construct his house, "these banks all failed and their bills were worthless, and large numbers of the people became bankrupt." The church couldn't maintain his salary during the downturn, "hence I became deeply involved in debt," he wrote.

In wake of the Panic of 1819 and the controversy surrounding his school, Rankin returned to the idea of completing his journey to Ohio. The carpenter he hired to build his house completed his job, but Rankin had no money to pay him. He borrowed from the bank to pay off some of his debts, but it was hardly enough. His home was valued at $2,000, but he could only get $400 from the bank. He used this money to pay off his debts as much as he could, but a year later he still had $1,000 of debt, $743 of which was due to the carpenter for building his home. Knowing that he was soon to leave Kentucky, Rankin gave the carpenter his property to pay off his debt. In return, the carpenter agreed to pay off the rest of the value of the home through his building services as far away as Ripley, Ohio. Rankin agreed to his terms.[45]

* * * * *

The debate surrounding slavery exploded with great intensity as Rankin prepared his final journey to Ohio. In addition to the Panic of 1819, that year was met with the crisis of Missouri's application for statehood. In February 1819, New York congressman James Tallmadge offered an amendment to the bill, which permitted statehood in Missouri. He proposed that Missouri would have no more slaves brought into it. Additionally, a system of gradual emancipation would be established for the offspring of slaves already living there. That lit the fuse. "A motion for excluding slavery from it has set the two sides of the House, slaveholders and non-slaveholders, into a violent flame against each other…," wrote Secretary of State John Quincy Adams. He continued to detail his thoughts on that matter, stating, "The President thinks this question will be winked away by a compromise. But so do not I." With great foresight, Adams believed the fight over slavery was to be "destined to survive his political and individual life and mine."[46] The Missouri debate in Congress was America's most significant debate over the issue of slavery since the Constitutional Convention. Southerners argued that the federal government could not prevent Missouri's statehood based on slavery. The Constitution, they claimed, permitted the institution of slavery. Demanding that Missouri be a free state was an overreach of federal authority and violated state sovereignty. Not so fast, said the anti-slavery proponents. They insisted that the federal government was under no obligation to permit slavery to expand into the western territories acquired by the Louisiana Purchase. Additionally, many of the most prominent framers disagreed with the notion that the federal government was bound to permit slavery. Thomas Jefferson, after all, drafted the proposal to prevent slavery in the Northwest Territory in 1784. While the Constitution gave the federal government no authority to prohibit slavery in the slave states that already existed, anti-slavery proponents insisted that it had the authority to prevent its spread west of the Mississippi River. Both sides were entrenched in their position, and for good reason. The answer to the Missouri question would determine the fate of the United States and whether slavery was a beast that could be vanquished or not.

Enter Henry Clay.

Although the Kentucky congressman was himself a slaveholder, he was no advocate for the system. He did, however, believe that a gradual system of emancipation would be best, and opposed abolitionists who demanded immediate emancipation. Clay, above all else, believed that the Union's preservation was his top priority. As the abolitionists grew in numbers and influence, he would view them as a great danger to the stability of the Union. This commitment to stability sometimes blinded him to the dangers of the compromises he would propose. Clay was Speaker of the House at this time, and as the debate over the Missouri question intensified, he started to panic. Representative Thomas W. Cobb of Georgia was openly warning of violent disunion if slavery was not permitted to expand into Missouri. Cobb said that Tallmadge was igniting a "fire that all the waters of the ocean cannot put out, which seas of blood can only extinguish."[47] Not inspiring confidence, Tallmadge gave into Cobb's rhetoric, responding that if a civil war is inevitable, then "let it come!"

Despite his concern over disunion, Clay followed the Senate's lead in composing a compromise. In February 1820, the Senate approved a compromise. In the heat of debate over the Missouri question, Maine formally requested admittance to the Union as a new state, separate from Massachusetts. Southerners bemoaned the admittance of a new state where slavery was prohibited. Without Missouri, Maine's admittance into the Union would tip the balance of power in Congress toward the anti-slavery cause. Illinois Senator Jesse Thomas proposed an amendment that Maine and Missouri's admittance into the Union would be tied together. Maine would be permitted to join as a free state, and Missouri as a slave state—no special conditions required. Additionally, any future state formed out of territory north of the 36°30′ and west of Missouri would be free. Meanwhile, states formed to the south of it would have the option of permitting slavery. In the House, Clay was relieved by the Thomas proposal, believing it to be the most practical solution to the Missouri question. With Clay pushing it through the House, the compromise passed and received President Monroe's signature in March.[48]

Henry Clay would be dubbed the "Great Compromiser" throughout his life. Many of Clay's compromises would come at the expense of men like John Rankin.

On the surface, it seemed like it was a modest proposal that would keep the balance of power in congress between pro and anti-slavery interests neutral. In truth, the South could claim much more of a victory than the North could. Missouri's admittance as a slave state meant that slavery could expand in the West. It also set a tradition that for Southerners to get what they want, they merely needed to threaten disunion. The implications of the Missouri crisis loomed ominously over the heads of the remaining Founding Fathers still alive. "I have never known a question so menacing to the tranquility and even continuance of our Union," President Monroe wrote to Jefferson, his friend and mentor.[49] "All other subjects have given way to it." Jefferson, by this point, was the "sage of Monticello," retired from public life and happy to leave political matters to men of the next generation, like Clay. The Missouri question frightened him. In a letter to John Holmes, Jefferson admitted that "I had for a long time ceased to read newspapers or pay any attention to public affairs, confident they were in good hands...." However, news of the compromise, "like a fire bell in the night, awakened and filled me with terror." Jefferson believed that the key feature of the compromise, the 36°30′, was a dangerous precedent. "A geographical line," he said, "coinciding with a marked principle, moral and political, once conceived and held up to the angry passions of men, will never be obliterated; and every new irritation will mark it deeper and deeper." As he continued to write, he reflected more broadly on slavery and how it poisoned the American experiment. "I can say with conscious truth that there is not a man on earth who would sacrifice more than I would, to relieve us from this heavy reproach, in any practicable way. the cession of that kind of property, for so it is misnamed, is a bagatelle which would not cost me a second thought, if, in that way, a general emancipation and expatriation could be effected: and, gradually, and with due sacrifices, I think it might be." As he continued in his letter, he seemed to become more depressed by the conclusion he reached. "As it is," he wrote, "we have the wolf by the ear, and we can neither hold him, nor safely let him go."[50]

* * * * *

As the implications of the Missouri Compromise started to loom over the country, many opponents of slavery started to flee slave states for free states. This was the case for many in Kentucky, including several members of Rankin's Concord Church congregation. "My people began to leave and go to free states," he later recalled. "I could not be supported, and therefore resigned my charge...." The whirlwind of events that transpired in 1819 and 1820 forced Rankin to finally leave Kentucky for what would be his permanent home in Ohio. Looking back, however, he would remember his time in Kentucky fondly as a period of great growth and personal development. Before leaving, he had yet another familial milestone—the birth of his third son, Richard Calvin Rankin, on July 24, 1821. As summer turned to fall in 1821, and as their newborn son was healthy enough to travel, the Rankin family prepared for their journey into Ohio. They gave their final goodbyes to Concord Church and, in December, finally completed the journey to Ohio that they started back in 1817. On New Year's Eve, 1821, Rankin, Jean, and their four children reached the icy banks of the Ohio River. Future fugitives fleeing slavery, who Rankin would soon help, would come to know this view well. Unsure of what the future had in store for them, but confident in their resolve, the six members of the Rankin family crossed the great divide between freedom and slavery and, for the first time, touched the free soil of Ohio.[51]

RIPLEY
1822–1824
III.

I t's hard to say exactly what John Rankin believed he was getting himself into when he crossed the river on New Year's Day in 1822, but his first impression of Ripley was anything but encouraging. He discovered a surprising contrast to the life he had become accustomed to in Kentucky before leaving. "Ripley was a very small village and badly infected with infidelity, Universalism and whiskey retailers," Rankin wrote as he recalled first arriving in the town. "It was exceedingly immoral. Drinking, profane swearing, frolicking and dancing were commonalities." While in the bluegrass region of Kentucky, there was a certain decorum one could expect from many of the residents there. The presence of slavery weighed down the region's potential, but Rankin came to appreciate the influence that faith and religion played on people's lives, both publicly and privately. Ripley, in contrast, was almost like a prototype for an old saloon town on the outskirts of the wild west. The people were rough with little regard for any kind of moral code to govern their lives.[52]

Kentucky joined the Union in 1792, with droves of people immigrating to the state for the entirety of Rankin's life. It had time to build up civilization amid the wilderness. Ohio, in contrast, was over a decade behind. There were a few cities of note rapidly expanding. Marietta, for instance, was the first legal settlement in the Northwest Territory. It had experienced a healthy level of growth since Rufus Putnam and his band of pioneers first settled in the area along the Ohio River in 1788.[53] Less than two years later, a little further down the river, Northwest Territory governor Arthur St. Clair renamed the small town of Losantiville to Cincinnati after the Society of Cincinnatus, which he was the president of. Cincinnati had been experiencing rich growth and became known as the "Queen of the West." Most of the Northwest Territory was still viewed as inhospitable due to the looming threat of Indian raids. This was the case until Major General "Mad Anthony" Wayne led American forces to victory against the Indian forces during the Battle of Fallen Timbers in 1794. People began immigrating in droves to the territory after Wayne's victory. Included in the wave of new settlers were many anti-slavery activists from Kentucky, discouraged by their inability to prevent slavery in the Constitution. With slavery outlawed in the territory and preserved in Kentucky, migration was the natural course.

Over the next decade, anti-slavery Virginians and Kentuckians left the system of slavery behind as they moved to Ohio. Their migration proliferated after Ohio acquired statehood and was admitted into the Union as a free state in 1803. Among the anti-slavery migrants to the state was Colonel James Poage, who settled the region that would one day become Ripley, Ohio in 1804. Poage had brought his family and his slaves to the Ohio shore to atone for his sin of owning slaves. After they were freed, they remained in the area and helped Poage build the first temporary structures. Not long after Poage established this area as the town of Staunton in 1812, word got out that some anti-slavery Virginians had established a settlement on the shores of Ohio. Anti-slavery activists started to populate the area in the years to come. One of the most notable individuals attracted to the region early on was Dr. Alexander Campbell. Born in 1779, Campbell could count himself part of a very distinct generation of Americans that would succeed the Founders. Like other notable figures such as Henry Clay or Andrew

Jackson, Campbell grew up amid the American Revolution. He spent the first few years of his life in Frederick County, Virginia, until his family moved to eastern Tennessee and eventually Kentucky. While he was in Kentucky, Campbell studied medicine at Transylvania University in Lexington before getting bitten by the political bug. He practiced medicine for a brief period in Cynthiana, Kentucky before serving as a representative in the Kentucky House of Representatives in 1803. Like several before him, he became disenfranchised by the state of slavery in Kentucky and moved to Adams County in Ohio in 1804, where Poage was also settling. [54]

Campbell rose quickly through the ranks of Ohio politics after getting himself established. He joined the Ohio House of Representatives in 1807 and served as Speaker of the House in Ohio in 1808 and 1809. In his final year as Speaker, he was appointed to the United States Senate, where he remained until 1813. After he retired from the Senate, he moved to Staunton in 1815, where he lived for the rest of his life. The following year, Staunton was renamed Ripley in honor of General Eleazar Wheelock Ripley, a war hero who served in the War of 1812. In Ripley, Campbell continued to be involved in both medicine and politics, but the cause that would come to define him was abolition. Sometimes referred to as "Ohio's first abolitionist," Campbell supported the anti-slavery movement both in his public and private life consistently for approximately the next forty years.

The Collins family was another antislavery family that moved to Ripley early on. Nathaniel Collins was a carpenter from Delaware. He and his sons became known as skilled carpenters in the area. He was also Ripley's first mayor. As far back as 1815, Collins and his family would help slaves escape to freedom by hiding them in the corn shocks behind their houses.[55] The wealthy banker and businessman Thomas McCague moved to Ripley in 1820, just a few years before Rankin, to start his pork-packing enterprise that would provide him with much success. McCague would put his wealth to use by also helping runaway slaves on their journey to freedom. While many abolitionists populated Ripley in these early days, the opening of the Ohio frontier brought out a wave of people migrating out west in hopes of striking it rich. When it became clear that wealth was out of their reach, they settled for whiskey. The residents of Ripley were not interested in adopting the cause of abolition and certainly weren't interested in being told that they needed to change their ways and get right with the Lord. Regardless, Rankin wasn't going to let it be from a lack of effort.

* * * * *

By the time Rankin had arrived in Ripley, it was undergoing a period of transition. A new county had recently formed around it, for instance. Brown County, named after General and War of 1812 veteran Jacob Brown, broke off from Adams County in 1818.[56] A year before Rankin's arrival, the community of Ripley was also dealt a heavy blow. Its founder, James Poage, passed away in 1820.[57] He had built himself a home on Front Street, along the riverfront, which went to his son Robert after his passing. Robert invited Rankin and his family to stay with him as they recovered from their trek. It was an invitation the Rankins happily accepted. Their journey across the river was a perilous one. Ice was quickly forming along the river on New Year's Day 1822. The night before, they lodged with an anti-slavery man named John Courtney in Kentucky. As the Rankins prepared to cross the river the next day, they saw that the river was too icy to use a large boat, they would instead need to cross with a smaller vessel. Waiting another day could make the river too impenetrable to cross. They left their horse and possessions with Courtney until the ice thawed. Adam Lowry Rankin later wrote how frightening the experience was "when we were struck by a large field of ice which nearly upset our boats. It was a slow, tedious passage and extremely dangerous…," Having made it to Ohio safely under Poage's roof, Lowry recalled how the first day of 1822 "was spent in a free state with no definite plan as to what the future would be."[58]

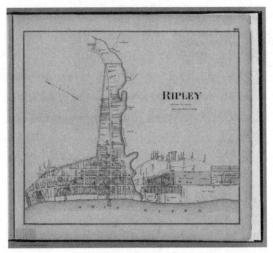

Ripley, Ohio. (Ohio History Connection)

Poage and the other abolitionists in Ripley were happy to welcome the Rankins to their community. The same could not be said for many of the townsfolks. "The majority of the inhabitants were openly immoral," Lowry wrote. "Infidelity, atheism, and drunkenness had the ascendance. Presbyterianism, Christianity, and the new pastor were openly cursed in the streets." In this instance, the new pastor was his father. Rankin was asked to preach at both the First Presbyterian Church as well as the Straight Creek church about seven miles away. He agreed to split his time between both. Any time Rankin would be out walking in the streets, usually heading to one of these churches, he would attract hecklers and protesters. This didn't bother him nearly as much as how small his new congregations were. In Kentucky, he enjoyed a large congregation that gave him both moral and monetary support. The First Presbyterian Church in Ripley only had thirty-six members when he started, "and that of Straight Creek had forty." He knew it was going to be a challenge, but confessed that "I was much discouraged." As Rankin moved his family out of Poage's home into a log home on Second Street, the protests only got worse. When Rankin would lead his family in prayer or worship, hecklers would gather to curse them and beat pots and pans, hoping to interrupt their concentration. "It seemed to be a question of endurance as to who should hold out the longest, father or the rabble," wrote Lowry. "These night scenes were indelibly impressed upon my memory."

Although slavery was largely prohibited above the Ohio River by this point, anti-black sentiment infected the country well to the North. Even individuals who were against slavery sometimes bought into the notion of black inferiority. They believed that no man should be held in bondage, or deprived of basic humanity, but that whites were clearly the superior race. Integration or equal political rights were concepts accepted by only a few across the country, no matter if they were in the North or the South. Ohio wasn't immune to this. There were many supporters of slavery in the state, and even those who were free had no intention of allowing black people to enjoy total equality. Some who supported making Ohio a free state did so not because they believed in abolition, but because they wished Ohio to be completely devoid of black people, as to prevent them from being able to compete in a free and open market. Within the first few years of Ohio statehood, this resulted in the passage of several "Black Laws." In 1804, laws were passed to prevent any "black or mulatto person" from moving to the state without court-certified proof that he or she wasn't a runaway slave. Without such evidence, a black or mixed person couldn't be hired under Ohio law. In 1807, blacks were prohibited from testifying in cases that involved whites. Blacks were prohibited from marrying whites, owning firearms, and attending most public schools. While they were technically free, true equality would take several decades to achieve.[59]

Many of those who supported and advocated for such restrictive Black Laws in Ohio lived along the Ohio River, migrating from slave states for one reason or another, but having no intention of leaving their racial prejudices behind them. Many resided in Ripley. When these sentiments were mixed with alcohol and the arrival of an abolitionist preacher like Rankin, sparks were bound to fly. Like before in Tennessee and Kentucky, Rankin's intrusive thoughts began to seep in. Rankin was again full of doubt, believing that he may have made a mistake coming to preach in Ripley. The voice of his father likely penetrated his thoughts, reflecting on how he begged him to stay with his family in Tennessee. How often he must have recalled riding along the road with his father in silence, leaving Tennessee, unsure if they would ever meet again in this life. Should he have remained in Kentucky, where he led a congregation that supported him and his anti-slavery convictions? In Ripley, he was doing more work for even less pay. "My salary was five hundred dollars," Rankin recalled as he started preaching in Ripley. It was "fifty dollars less than I had at Concord." Nonetheless, he persisted in his ministry in Ripley, speaking out against vice and immorality that seemed to only grow with his presence.

The Rankins spent almost two years in Ripley before they could move into their real home. The carpenter who agreed to pay off the remainder of the debt he owed Rankin in building services finally arrived in Ripley a week before his services were due in the fall of 1823. Rankin was underprepared for his arrival. With no money for the material or the lot to build his home on, he again borrowed from the bank. Debt was a persistent presence throughout Rankin's life. After he acquired the appropriate funds, the carpenter and his crew were finally able to finish the job. Like the Poages and Campbell, Rankin bought a lot on Front Street to build his family home. Rather than a single-family home, he wanted to try to make some money off his home to help alleviate his burden of debt. The carpentry crew was to build an apartment complex with three units. Rankin and his family would reside in one unit and he would lease out the other two. The building would have three front doors and would measure twenty-five by sixty feet. As they went to break ground on the lot, trouble started to arise. Hecklers and protesters rushed to confront Rankin and the crewmen working on his home, almost in a state of hysteria and disbelief that Rankin had the fortitude to remain in Ripley permanently. The building of his home was as symbolic as it was practical—it would take more than the insults of drunken ramblers to drive him out of town. The building of the new apartment complex commenced, but every time Rankin would go out to get new materials, saloon patrons would rush into the streets to greet him with colorful new slurs and curses. As they completed the structure, Rankin immediately moved his family into the first unit. He leased out the middle unit to a local doctor. The unit on the other end of the complex finally went to a man named David Ammen. Ammen was the editor of the local paper, *The Castigator*, and would soon play a key role in changing the trajectory of Rankin's life. At that time, however, Rankin was just happy to provide his family with some kind of stability for the first time in his life.[60]

* * * * *

As the carpentry crew returned to Kentucky, word of Rankin's journey started spreading throughout the region. The man who spent so much time educating slaves in Kentucky now lived on free soil next to the shores of the Ohio River. Rankin was not yet the famed conductor of the Underground Railroad, but the idea of having a key ally on the other side of the divide seemed promising to many slaves. Before he could lead runaway slaves to the promised land of freedom, he must surmount the adversity of Ripley locals.

"Nearly two years had passed away without any marked improvement," Rankin later recalled. Lowry's recollection was similar, stating, "For three years there was no apparent goal accomplished, only going from bad to worse...." Rankin's first mission was to improve church attendance. In the early days, he went house to house to introduce himself and spread his message in person, but this was not well-received. "The church at Ripley was at first cold and feeble. The audience was small with no hope of increase," wrote Rankin. Lowry was even more detailed about the state of the community: "The young people grew more and more immoral; no advance was made in the church in spirituality while the village was steadily increasing in vice and immorality." He recalled how fighting and even "shooting in the streets was not an unusual occurrence." For the first few years in Ripley, it was the same song and dance. Rankin would preach against these vices, pleading with them to get right with God. It might reach one or two people, but most of them only dug their heels in deeper. Their vices would take control of them even further, and the townspeople continued spiraling out of control. Rankin was totally opposed to drinking. His crusade against it in Ripley, however, didn't come about because the locals enjoyed taking the edge off after a long day's work. Rampant alcoholism infested the community, and it often led to far more nefarious activities. Rankin recalled how in some cases, "men thus engaged were starving their wives and children, and that some of them had even sold wives' clothes for intoxicating drink." Young women in the community often felt unsafe around men, enduring public harassment in the streets.

Such was the state of affairs for so long that it nearly broke Rankin's will. With no sign of improvement in the community, he felt as if he was failing as a minister. Not unlike his low point in Kentucky, he prepared to walk away from preaching in Ripley. He even drafted a letter of resignation. Again, as in Kentucky, his wife intervened. Jean encouraged him to put the letter down and wait a few more months before officially offering it. If nothing changed, Rankin could revisit his plans to step down. But, she believed, they didn't travel as far as they had just to give up now. Around this time, changes started happening in the community, some to a rather dramatic effect. There had been about four or five individuals who were leading the charge against Rankin's presence in the community, bringing out the worst of the residents of Ripley. Unexpectedly, each of them started dying, and in some instances, violently. Lowry recalled how one of them "had purchased some oil of vitriol (sulfuric acid) and put the vial containing it in his vest pocket and forgot to take it out when he went home. An hour or two after, desiring to take a horseback ride, he mounted a young horse which was not well broken and was thrown by it to the street. The vial was broken, and there was added to the pain resulting from the internal injury that caused his death, the burning of the vitriol. He had forgotten the vitriol, and, supposing it to be a special judgment from God, he began to pray most earnestly for Divine mercy. When he discovered the cause of the burning, he commenced to curse God in the most profane manner and in a few hours he died." Reasonably, his friends and many members of the community were filled "with horror and alarm."

Almost as if a spell holding the community had been broken, the churches that Rankin pastored began experiencing growth. The antagonistic nature of "the rabble," as Lowry called them, was going out of control, and many community members were fed up with their activities. After the death of the "leading infidels," Rankin lead a sermon on Revelation 3:20 (KJV)—"Behold, I stand at the door and knock." He explained how God had been knocking on the hearts of the people of Ripley "by his word, his ordinances, his spirit and finally by his judgments." Indeed, he preached that God knocked on the door of these men specifically, and they rejected him. Rankin had invited a Presbyterian minister from Kentucky, Reverend W. L. McCall, to assist him in this service, but McCall fell ill and was unable to help. It was just Rankin and the people of Ripley. At first, this prospect frightened him, but soon more and more people welcomed his message. Rankin continued to preach this sermon without assistance for weeks. Each time, several more people "publicly professed conviction." Some believed this to be a revival, but Rankin was insistent on not calling it that. "It was a conversion, not a revival. The church was not revived, it seemed as it was dead up to the close of the meetings. I have witnessed many revivals in church since that time. For many years after that time Ripley was famous for good morals."[61]

Rankin remembered how "frolicking and dancing were terminated with the very beginning of the religious excitement...." Of course, there were those who never bought into Rankin's message. Drinking wasn't entirely eliminated from the community, even among church members. Likewise, there were still residents with prejudice that persisted throughout Ripley, none too eager to rush to the aid of a runaway slave. But the "conversion" that Rankin helped usher in marked the beginning of a new era in the history of the community. Rather than being consumed by their own indulgences and vices, they were consumed by what they considered to be a higher calling. The church at Straight Creek had grown so rapidly that before long, he was able to resign as its minister, not because he felt defeated, but because they could sustain a full-time pastor, leaving Rankin to attend to the church in Ripley entirely. As the church community gained a reputation as "an active moral force" in Ripley, Rankin again returned to activism—not yet anti-slavery activism, but, rather, temperance activism. He continued to preach against the perils of the "common use of ardent spirits," both from the pulpit and in the community. Rankin asked two church elders to reach out to a few influential Methodists nearby and "solicit them to unite in forming a temperance society." They succeeded, and together they formed the first temperance society west of the Allegheny Mountains.[62]

After the initial period of conflict, Rankin succeeded in getting the people of Ripley to prioritize their relationship with God over their earthly pleasures. He spent time building up the First Presbyterian Church in town. He also started going to neighboring communities, preaching and founding new churches for their residents. Amid his battle for the soul of Ripley, Rankin and his wife Jean welcomed yet another member of the family. Samuel Gardner Wilson Rankin was born in 1822. It seemed as if Rankin had finally triumphed over his adversaries and prepared to begin a prosperous new life ministering on the banks of the Ohio River. As he returned home one day early in 1824, he discovered that his brother, Thomas Rankin, had sent him a letter from Augusta County, Virginia. He was living there as a merchant at the time. Rankin always had an attachment to his family, especially after the loss of his brother, David, during the War of 1812. A message from Thomas brought him great excitement. As he opened his letter, however, that excitement rapidly settled into dread and betrayal. His brother Thomas had purchased slaves.

LETTERS ON AMERICAN SLAVERY
1824–1829
IV.

T homas Rankin's letter hit John Rankin like a ton of bricks. How could his brother purchase slaves? All the Rankin kids had been raised to learn of the evils of slavery. They were taught it was an offense to the Almighty. Rankin didn't believe Thomas had merely made a mistake—he felt as if he had betrayed the Rankin family. For several months in 1824, Rankin pondered how he would respond to his brother. He still loved him, and didn't want this to stand between them, but how could it not? Thomas had willfully betrayed everything they were raised to believe. As he considered his response, Rankin had an idea. He approached his neighbor and tenant, David Ammen. Ammen resided on the lower level of the three-door apartment that Rankin had built, and he operated the printing services for his newspaper, *The Castigator*, on the upper level. Postage wasn't cheap, and he knew that his response to Thomas wouldn't be limited to one letter. Why not, Rankin thought, make his argument publicly? Surely whatever caused his own flesh and blood to betray the foundational principles of liberty and humanity was an illness that infected hundreds upon thousands of slave owners in the south. They were misguided into believing that blacks were inferior to whites, that slavery was good for the slave, or even that it was ordained by God and sanctioned in the Bible. Whatever response he made to Thomas would need to be heard repeatedly by slaveholders across the country. Besides, it would be cheaper for Rankin to publish his letters via a newspaper than it would be to send individual letter responses by mail. As Rankin discussed his idea with Ammen, the editor loved it. Not only was Ammen an anti-slavery man himself, but Rankin also presented an opportunity to provide a steady stream of content for his paper. Rankin was gaining a reputation as a formidable foe of slavery after his time in Kentucky. Giving people the opportunity to read the words of the abolitionist preacher of Ripley was an opportunity Ammen couldn't pass up.

After several months of contemplating exactly how he would respond, *The Castigator* finally published Rankin's first letter to Thomas on August 17, 1824. "My dear Brother," the letter opened. "I received yours of the 2d December with mingled sensations of pleasure and pain."[63] Rankin was delighted to discover that his brother wrote to him, and even more relieved to hear that Thomas was in good health and spirits. He was pained, however, "to hear of your purchasing slaves." With formalities quickly out of the way, he dove straight into the heart of the matter. "I consider involuntary slavery a never-failing fountain of the grossest immorality, and one of the deepest sources of human misery," Rankin wrote, definitely and passionately. "It hangs like the mantle of night over our republic, and shrouds its rising glories. I sincerely pity the man who tinges his hand in the unhallowed thing that is fraught with the tears, and sweat, and groans, and blood of hapless millions of innocent, unoffending people." Before writing any further, Rankin felt the need to clarify that he did not write Thomas out of anger or malice, but a duty. "A mistaken brother, who has manifested to me a kind and generous heart, claims my strongest sympathies. When I see him involved in what is both sinful and dangerous, shall I not strive to liberate him?" Rankin was concerned for his brother. It wasn't a lecture, as he feared Thomas might interpret it, but an intervention. "Shall I suffer sin upon my brother," Rankin asked rhetorically. He answered resolutely: "No—his kindness to me forbids it, fraternal love forbids it, and what is still more to be regarded, the law of God forbids it. Though he has wandered for the moment, may I not hope to show him his error, and restrain his wanderings?" Because he harbored such conviction, Rankin explained that he had "resolved to address you, in a series of letters, on the injustice of enslaving the Africans. This I hope you will receive as an expression of fraternal affection, as well as of gratitude to you for former favors. I entreat you to give me that candid attention which the fondness of a brother solicits, and the importance of the subject demands."

Following this brief introduction, Rankin proceeded to take the most common arguments of his day in favor of slavery and systematically dismantle them piece by piece, leaving no stone unturned. "I think it proper to apprise you that several things connected with the present condition of the Africans, tend to bias the mind against them, and consequently incapacitate it for an impartial decision with respect to their rights." The first bias he felt compelled to address was the common belief that the black skin of slaves was a sort of curse, damning them to subjugation. "This leads many to conclude that Heaven has expressly marked them out for servitude," he wrote. Rankin described racial prejudice as a type of prison that fortifies the mind from being exposed to "the strongest arguments that reason can suggest..." He suggested that black skin color was not "the horrible mark of Cain, nor the direful effects of Noah's curse, but the mark of a scorching sun." He proceeded to go into detail about how climate plays a role in skin color. The closer to the equator, the darker a person tends to be. Likewise, people closer to the poles tend to be white. Logically, he concluded, this would mean that all mankind are brethren, and blacks are no less human than whites. He admitted that he didn't fully understand the science behind it, or how much genetics play a role as opposed to radiation from the sun. He was confident that this demonstrated that black skin is "no peculiar mark of Heaven's displeasure," and there certainly isn't "evidence that he who wears it is doomed by the Creator to endless servitude."

Continuing to argue against the belief of black inferiority, Rankin examined their condition under slavery. "The Africans," he wrote, "are deeply degraded." During the eighteenth and nineteenth centuries, a common argument made in favor of the inferiority of slaves was the observation that they behaved like animals. Surely if they were equal to whites, many argued, they would behave more civilized. According to their observations, blacks were unintelligent and beast-like in behavior. Rankin utterly rejected this conclusion, claiming that any observation of beast-like qualities says more about their state of subjugation than it does their racial inferiority. "They are bought and sold, and driven from place to place like mere animal herds; this fetters the mind, and prevents that expansion of soul which dignifies man and ornaments civilized life." Under these conditions, he wrote, it is little wonder why any man, black or white, would have such a lack of motivation for self-improvement. "They seldom have any opportunities of improvement, any encouragement for the efforts of genius, or any inducements to enter the field of science." His frustration began to bleed through further on in the letter. "How false, how ungenerous, how unreasonable is such a conclusion!" Slavery itself, and slavery alone, is to blame for any lack of intellectual curiosity or ambition. "Under such oppression," he wrote, "powers of mind, merely ordinary, cannot unfold; the gloomy prospect of perpetual bondage hovers continually around, and cuts off every enterprise which might elicit the native energies of the soul, or give occasion for the vigorous efforts of genius. Hence talents that, under other circumstances, would appear to very good advantage, are totally obscured." Rankin predicted that the state of their subjugation is so severe that even well after their emancipation, they will be required "to pass through several generations in order to regain their original strength of mind, and give the world a fair exhibition of the powers they really possess."

In the third and final point that he made in this letter, Rankin suggested that white slaveholders delude themselves into thinking that they are physically and mentally superior to blacks due to their "love of gain." When weighed next to the love of gain, Rankin claimed that the most rational arguments made against racial inferiority "are lighter than feathers." It "first introduced slavery into the world, and has been its constant support in every age. It was the love of gain that first enslaved the African race, and it now invents every possible argument against their emancipation. This is equally manifested in the social circle, and on the legislative floor; individuals and States will argue in favor of slavery in proportion as they view their interest at stake." Rankin suspected that it is this love of gain that compelled his brother to stumble. He admitted that if Thomas were to divorce himself from the institution of slavery, it would not be an easy separation. "You, my dear brother, have considerable at stake; you must wade through much loss, if you would come to a right conclusion, and obey the imperious voice of justice; but remember that loss will be temporal, and from it may spring eternal gain." He concluded with a final plea. "Let not their color, their degradation, nor the predominating principle of self-interest, bias your mind against them," he begged of Thomas. "Let their miseries excite your pity, and incline you to justice."

* * * * *

Once his first letter was published, Rankin ensured Thomas received a copy in Virginia. Like clockwork, every successive week throughout the remainder of 1824 and into early 1825, he had Ammen publish a new letter to Thomas in *The Castigator*. He opened his second letter by restating his hope that his first letter had dispelled the influence of prejudice that might exist in his brother's mind and heart. "Inspired by this hope," he wrote, "I now proceed…to prove from the nature of the Africans that they were not created for slavery." Rankin expanded on his arguments from his prior letter. If, as he wrote, blacks aren't subhuman "beasts," then it stands to reason that they were created with the same capacity for liberty as whites. "It is most absurd to imagine that beings created with capacity for liberty were designed for bondage." Rankin believed there was no distinction of human capacity between black and white, and thus had a right to pursue their own happiness the way any white man might be inclined to. "Every man, who possesses all the original properties of humanity, desires to obtain knowledge, wealth, reputation, liberty, and a vast variety of other objects which are necessary to complete his happiness." As Rankin continued to write his second letter, he revealed his conclusion to these observations. If blacks are every bit as human as whites, and they possess the same capacity for liberty, then denying them such liberty based on skin color alone is barbaric. "How then," he asked, "can you withhold from others what is so dear to yourself? The Africans possess all the original properties of humanity, and were, as we have fairly proven from their nature, created for freedom; and, therefore, to enslave them is both unjust and cruel."

In his third letter to Thomas, Rankin shifted away from rhetorical arguments to his personal experiences with slavery. "I am now to point out more fully than the limits of the preceding letter would permit me to do." Reflecting on his journey from Tennessee to Ripley, he realized that slavery didn't exist in a vacuum. It was a threat to everyone's liberty. Slaveholders required total submission, not just bondage. This couldn't be accomplished unless the slave was kept in total ignorance. Rankin quickly discovered that even learning about "the words of eternal life" threatened to compromise their authority. The slave's soul was threatened by the slave power. Rankin also realized something less obvious, yet equally true. The right of ministers to preach the gospel was under attack. "I know from experience that this is the case," he wrote, "even where slavery exists under its best and mildest form." This form, he believed, existed in Kentucky. "If there be any place in the United States where it wears a tolerable aspect, I am persuaded it is in that State." While Rankin was careful to emphasize that he was not endorsing Kentucky's form of slavery, he felt compelled to admit that "if any slaveholding people can be generous, the Kentuckians are such." Admitting this, he made a crucial point. "The mildest form of slavery is like 'the tender mercies of the wicked.'" In other words, slavery in Kentucky was still "very cruel."

Rankin pulled from his memories of trying to educate local slaves in Kentucky. He wrote that it "often happens that the benevolent teachers

of Sabbath schools find themselves, and their poor, unoffending schol-
ars, on a sacred morning, surrounded by men armed with whips, clubs
and guns, for the violent dispersion of the unhappy and innocent victims of their rage!" It wasn't a phenomenon that was limited "to the
more ignorant parts of the State," he wrote. It "is equally manifested
in the most enlightened places." This, of course, was a reference to the
slaveholders of the bluegrass region surrounding Lexington. While they
prided themselves on being much more benevolent than the planters
of the Deep South, Rankin refused to allow their sins to go unnoticed.
On one "sacred morning," he recalled, "the poor slaves assembled at
the school-room with the pleasing expectation of learning to read the
word of eternal life: but to their sad surprise, about sixty men soon
appeared for their dispersion, armed with clubs and guns, and thus the
school was dispersed never to meet again!" It brought him no pleasure
to reveal the true nature of slavery in Kentucky, he wrote. However, he
thought it "necessary to show the real state of things even where slavery
assumes her mildest aspect; for I still believe that slaves fare upon the
whole better in Kentucky than they do in other slaveholding States."

In another letter, Rankin disputed the notion that the slaves
brought to America were in a better condition than what they would
be otherwise in their home continent. "You tell me that many of the
poor Africans will be thankful that they were brought from the dark
regions of Africa, and made slaves in a land of gospel-light, where they
have become the subjects of salvation!" Rankin had written extensively
about how many slaveowners deprived their slaves of an understanding of scripture. "I have seen the preacher and elder bow their knees
around the family altar," he wrote in a prior letter, "while their poor
slaves remained without, as if, like mere animal herds, they had no
interest in the morning and evening sacrifices!" Rankin wrote that even
if the slave or their descendants were to experience a higher quality of
life in America than they would in Africa, it is not an endorsement of
slavery itself. Using this logic, he wrote that "the Jews might have justified themselves in crucifying the Saviour." This, Rankin believed, was
a perversion of the meaning of scripture. He encouraged Thomas "to

remember that it is the province of the Almighty to bring good out of evil, and that it is not the province of man to 'Do evil that good may come.'" The Almighty's ability to turn a dire situation into a blessing, he explained, should not be confused with his permission to "promote the curse of slavery."

A few letters later, Rankin began examining the political hypocrisy of "the boasted land of freedom" infested with the backdrop of the "clanking chains of the most horrible oppression!" Slavery, Rankin believed, was the greatest insult to the American idea. "Yes, in America, the far-famed America, you may hear the clankings of the chains that bind innocent husbands and wives, and parents and children, in order that they may be forever separated from the objects of their affections and all that is dear to them in life!" Alluding to Exodus, he questioned whether or not "the tyrannical Pharaoh (could) be more cruel than" the slave states in America. The more he wrote about the perceived promise of American liberty, the more ashamed he was that so many states refused to fulfill that promise. He commented that "the eyes of the sublimely soaring eagle of American liberty are highly insulted while she is made to hover over the detestable chains of cruel bondage!" In his observation, it was no wonder that those who honored such noble values came to disdain the government that refused to uphold them. Who, he asked, "can help feeling indignant at seeing the American flag becoming the derision of tyrants!" Frustration over the American government's relationship with slavery had spread since the Missouri Compromise. This frustration would boil into raging indignation toward the Union and the Constitution by many abolitionists in the first half of the nineteenth century. In the coming decades, several notable abolitionists would openly call for disunion with a government subservient to the interests of slavers. It is one of several reasons that the abolitionists became a rather unpopular minority in American politics and culture. Rankin didn't approve of the radical notions that some abolitionists held of disunion. It would still be a few decades before anti-slavery forces popularized the concept of weaponizing the Constitution rather than rejecting it.

In a later letter, Rankin made the case that slavery wasn't just cruel and irrational, it was also "opposed to domestic peace." It was likely that, when making this argument, Rankin recalled his mother's reaction to Gabriel's Rebellion, or at least subconsciously. Slaveholders frequently accused abolitionists of inciting the threat of a slave rebellion or race war in the south. If slaves were to hear the song of freedom, they might become inspired to slaughter their masters and take it for themselves. To Rankin, this stemmed not from the abolitionists, but from the intrinsic nature of slavery itself. As he reasoned in his prior letters, the slave was every bit as human as the free white man, with the same passions and desires. Mankind was created with a yearning for freedom. But American slavery, he argued, forced the slave to indulge his or her more sinful nature. "Slaves, as we have before shown, are generally raised without moral instruction," he wrote to Thomas. They "consequently possess a low degree of moral feeling, and therefore they are not very conscientious in regard to the preservation of domestic peace." This, Rankin believed, exposed the hypocrisy of the slave system in America. Slaveholders feared that ministers like Rankin would inspire the slave to rise and claim their freedom for themselves if they were to be taught how to read or understand scripture. Yet, without the moral foundation that scripture provides, the slave would be lacking a moral compass that would restrain them from acting on their instincts for revenge against their master. It produces "fierce contention" to force a "variety of families and individuals of different habits and feelings" to live together under the whip of the overseer. "This disturbs the peace of the master's own family, and so becomes a source of perpetual vexation." Because the slave is forced into a state of low "moral feeling," their vices "are frequently made to bear upon the master's family in such a manner as entirely banishes domestic peace."

Rankin made a long list of all the dangers resulting from the existence of slavery. "Idleness is generally one result of slavery," he wrote. "Necessity is the parent of industry—few are willing to labor when necessity does not impel them; and slaveholding families seldom feel the influence of this impelling principle." He wrote that "Slavery promotes vice among the free inhabitants of slaveholding States." Not only does it lead to laziness, ignorance, and immorality, but also "Slavery must eventually tend to poverty." While many slaveholders experience short-term gain, slavery as a whole was economically damaging in the states where it existed. States that relied on free labor were beginning to experience tremendous growth, whereas slave states seemed to exist in perpetual and expanding poverty. When people were free to pursue their own happiness, they were far more industrious than those laboring for their master. When Rankin wrote his letters in the fall and winter of 1824, the states that made up the former Northwest Territory were still very rural, but the rise in their industry was rapid. In contrast, progress seemed to be all but nonexistent in the southern frontier states where slavery existed. This economic divide between free and slave states would only expand as time went on. Most dangerously, Rankin wrote, "Slavery tends to tyranny." As states permit masters to become tyrants, he argued that the founding principles of the United States are disgraced. "It is directly opposed to those fundamental principles of republicanism maintained in that part of the Declaration of Independence, which declares, 'That all men are created equal; that they are endowed by their Creator with certain inalienable rights; that among these are life, liberty and the pursuit of happiness.' These principles are absolutely denied by the slaveholding States." Not only do those states deny that all men were created equally, but they also suggest that "liberty is not an inalienable right, and that a certain class of people have not a right to pursue their own happiness." Rankin took aim at the constitutions of the slaveholding states, which largely seek to affirm the principles of liberty while maintaining a system of slavery. "The constitution of Kentucky tells us," for instance, "'That all freemen when they form a social compact are equal....' Kentucky cannot admit 'That all are created equal,' nor that even freemen are equal until they become so by social compact. Thus, she plainly denies a fundamental principle of the Declaration of Independence." On one hand, Rankin admitted, there isn't a "State in the Union that makes stronger pretensions to republicanism than does Kentucky," but despite this, the commonwealth "both theoretically and practically denies the fundamental principle upon which the whole republican system rests." He wrote that the truth is that "all the slaveholding States do practically maintain the fundamental principles of, absolute monarchy—which are, that all men are not equal, and that all men are not born equally free and independent. Every slaveholder is an absolute monarch to his slaves, and they are bound to approach him with all the sensibilities of inferiority which absolute monarchy can require."

In another letter, Rankin devoted his time to confronting the belief that slavery is sanctioned by the Almighty. As "many of the abettors of this system pretend to support it by the sacred scriptures, I deem it necessary to examine the principal arguments which they have drawn from this source." This argument Rankin took a particular offense to, as he saw it twisted the words of scripture to advance a truly wicked cause. Instances of slavery in the Bible are incomparable to the modern example of American slavery, he argued, for some significant reasons. Slavery in the Bible was limited in duration and often used as a means to pay off debt or punishment for crimes. This is in stark contrast to American slaves, who were kidnapped from Africa and sold into bondage. Additionally, "according to this law, none could be enslaved longer than from the time they were purchased to the year of jubilee." As stated in Leviticus, the Israelites were to "hallow the fiftieth year, and proclaim liberty throughout all the land, unto all the inhabitants thereof." If American slavery and the system of bondage in ancient Israel were supposed to be the same, Rankin observed, when will liberty be proclaimed to American slaves? "No joyful year of jubilee is now expected by the miserable slave!" The ancient Israelites, Rankin wrote, were given special permission directly from the Creator to hold "the heathen" in bondage. This form of slavery came with very specific guardrails ("ye shall not rule one over another with rigor") and was meant to expire during the year of jubilee. "This special grant implies that the children of Israel without it had no right to enslave even the heathen," Rankin wrote. America was not Ancient Israel, and was not given any such grant to enslave any man. "No such grant has ever been made to any people," Rankin pointed out, thus "the very text on which slaveholders rely for support, amounts to a real prohibition of slavery in all cases except the one which it specifies." In his final few letters, Rankin continued to demonstrate the concept that the "whole Bible is opposed to slavery." It is in fact "one grand scheme of benevolence. Beams of love and mercy emanate from every page, while the voice of justice denounces the oppressor, and speaks his awful doom."

As he closed, Rankin informed his brother that he was finally ending his series of letters. "I hope you will receive them as so many tokens of sincere affection for you. My heart fills as I approach the closing moment. It seems as if I am about to bid you a long and uncertain farewell!" Rankin was consumed with images of his childhood with Thomas as he closed his letters. News of Thomas becoming a slave owner was the last thing he ever hoped for. He reminded his brother that he was addressing him from a position of love and affection, wanting him to experience nothing but a life full of happiness. He understood that Thomas would be tempted to ignore Rankin's pleas and proceed in life as a slaveholder. He hoped, however, that Thomas had been persuaded to abandon his involvement in the slave system. "A brother pleads with you; nature by all her tenderest sensibilities, and the God of nature, by all those heavenly sympathies that issued from a Savior's bleeding heart, plead with you to 'do justly, to love mercy,' 'and to let the oppressed go free!' And can you refuse?" As Thomas reflected on this final question, Rankin left him with this final assurance. "If you do, I am your brother—I will not speak your doom! Farewell."[64]

* * * * *

Rankin's last letter to Thomas ran in *The Castigator* on Tuesday, February 22, 1825. He was consumed with anxiety as it went out. Could his pleading have fallen on deaf ears? Would his relationship with Thomas forever be tarnished? He didn't regret publishing the letters, but he stressed about what the future held for them. *The Castigator*'s editor, Ammen, on the other hand, was proud of the editorial accomplishments of Rankin's letters on slavery. Ammen made a note in that Tuesday's edition of his paper. "This day's paper contains the last of a series of letters, on slavery, published in this paper," he wrote. "Such are the ways of the world, that we have been censured by some, and applauded by others, for publishing them." Rankin later wrote in his autobiography that "the series of letters was well received" in Ohio, but they weren't without [65]

The "era of good feeling" had come to an end. The country seemed united four years earlier, but in 1825, it couldn't have been more divided. In the same edition, *The Castigator* reported the results of the 1824 election, which had to be sent to the House of Representatives after there was no clear winner in the Electoral College. Andrew Jackson, John Quincy Adams, William Crawford, and Henry Clay all stood in line for the presidency, each believing themselves heir apparent to the James Monroe administration. Clay came in fourth place, thus being eliminated from consideration by the House. Clay and Adams both feared the possibility of a Jackson administration, believing the hot-tempered hero of New Orleans to have all the qualities of a military chieftain in the White House. On January 9, 1825, before the House voted, Clay went to Adams's home. The two former rivals spoke for hours. The contents of their meeting are to this day unknown, but rumors began to swirl that they came to an agreement to defeat Jackson. Following this meeting, Clay extended his public support for Adams. Not only was Clay a former rival of Adams, but he was also Speaker of the House at the time. His support carried significant influence, enough to ensure that Adams would triumph over Jackson as the votes were tallied.

There was an uneasy atmosphere across the country. Many could feel the transition that the nation was experiencing. The Jeffersonian age was dead, and despite his defeat in the election, the age of Jackson had arrived. Although Jefferson and Jackson shared certain qualities, constitutional republicanism was always at the heart of Jeffersonian ideology. Jackson, in contrast, had formed a cult of personality around him. Unabashed populism drove Jacksonianism, especially in the west.

When news broke that Clay had been selected by Adams to serve as Secretary of State, Jackson supporters bemoaned that a "corrupt bargain" had taken place. Accurate or not, they were convinced that when Clay and Adams met on January 9, they had arranged a quid pro quo in which Clay would offer Adams support on the condition of being appointed Secretary of State, then considered a steppingstone to the presidency. After Clay accepted the appointment, Jackson threw up his hands in outrage, stating that "the *Judas* of the West had closed the contract and will receive the thirty pieces of silver."[66] Jackson's support would only continue to rise in the coming years, and the country would spiral into divisive populism. It was in this new age of popular politics that the slave-holding powers thrived. Supporters of slavery weaponized mob tactics to intimidate abolitionists and black community members alike. Rankin would be a primary target of this coming wave of mob violence.[67]

One such incident occurred only a few months after Rankin published his final letter in *The Castigator*. After he completed his series, Ammen had them organized and published in book form, believing they could still be further distributed. Entitled *Rankin's Letters on Slavery*, Ammen printed one thousand copies for eighty dollars. Rankin, still facing financial hardship, suspended Ammen's rent until the debt was paid off. Rankin had many anti-slavery friends in Maysville, Kentucky, just nine miles from Ripley on the other side of the river. One of these friends, Edward Cox, bound roughly five hundred copies and sold many in his bookstore. As copies were sold in Cox's bookstore, the second half of the copies remained unbound in a Maysville warehouse until Rankin could save up enough to have the rest bound and sold. The reaction to Rankin's letters in Kentucky was mostly tame at first, but clearly, there were those who felt threatened by their existence. The mixture of Rankin's letters and the aftermath of the 1824 election slowly elevated tensions in the Ohio River Valley until they finally broke in the summer of 1825. One morning, the residents of Maysville woke to a smoke-filled sky and the smell of fire in the valley. It wasn't long before they discovered the source—the private warehouse where

Rankin's unbound letters were stored had burned to the ground. The unbound copies of Rankin's letters that he intended to sell were turned to ash. To make matters worse, this was no accident; it was arson.[68]

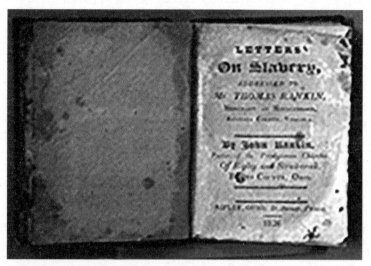

John Rankin had his letters to his brother Thomas published as a book. These letters would become a sensation as some of the earliest arguments in favor of immediate emancipation.

This was a grim development, and the world around Rankin only seemed to grow darker. There were only about six hundred copies of his letters in circulation, along with however many individual newspapers people kept. The arsonist was never found and had succeeded in preventing the spread of Rankin's letters. "I was too poor to reprint another edition," he later wrote, "and supposed it would never appear again...." Meanwhile, slave revolts, mutinies, and escapes were becoming more common. Slave states were starting to crack down hard against blacks, free or otherwise. In the north, abolitionists came to be viewed by many as troublemakers, practically inviting an invasion of slave hunters into free soil by aiding runaways. This threatened the peace and stability of residents of these states. In this atmosphere of animosity against abolitionists and blacks, and in the wake of rising populism, many residents of the Ohio Valley region turned spiteful. In 1826, *The Castigator* reported on the heightened animosity toward slaves in Kentucky. In one specific instance, a slave was "murdered in Henry County, Kentucky, in the following barbarous manner: The murderer had hired the slave, and treated him with intolerable cruelty." After the slave attempted to escape his despotic master, he was caught and tied to his master's horse "and when extremely heated, drew him through a creek of cold running water." The slave fell to the ground, unable to stand, upon which his master proceeded to dismount and "beat him to death!" Although the master was arrested, he was only charged with manslaughter. *The Castigator* reported in disbelief that "the most malicious, deliberate and barbarous murder of a slave is but man-slaughter!"[69]

With the approach of the election of 1828, America was descending into hysteria, and men like Rankin only grew in their unpopularity. In the fall of 1828, Jackson faced a rematch with Adams, this time securing decisive victory. Adams himself was a strong opponent of slavery, fueling the Jacksonian animosity toward the abolitionists. With Jackson's inauguration in 1829, a new era of conflict and controversy arrived.

It was through these tribulations that Rankin and his fellow abolitionists sparked a movement that they hoped would one day defeat slavery. At this time, Rankin again considered moving his family. Despite living on free soil and his sprouting ministry, life on Front Street in Ripley remained dangerous. The drunken mobs that first confronted Rankin upon his arrival to Ripley had been successfully tamed. Now, however, a far more serious danger threatened him and his family. As slaves continued to escape north, slave hunters pursued. Given Rankin's notoriety, he was an easy target for investigation. In the spring of 1829, Rankin looked to the hilltop behind Ripley as a prime location to resettle his family. The hilltop was removed from the dangers of living on Front Street, but provided quick access to town if needed. It also boasted a wonderful view of the river valley—one could see for almost five miles on a clear day. As he planned to make his move, Rankin took comfort that his letters had accomplished at least one intended goal. In 1827, Thomas agreed with his brother that slavery was evil and sought to divorce himself from slavery entirely as he traveled to Ohio, emancipated his slaves, and "provided them with homes a few years later in Louisville, Kentucky, where they became quite well off financially[70] Thomas' acquiescence was a ray of light in an era of growing darkness.

LIBERTY HILL
1829–1834
V.

John Rankin could rest with satisfaction that his letters had their intended consequence. Thomas had freed his slaves, and if nothing else came from the letters, their publication was worth it for that reason alone. This joyful news was soon offset by the discovery that their father, Richard Rankin, had passed away in May. This was the moment that Rankin had feared since he rode away from Tennessee in the autumn of 1817. Richard was seventy-two, leaving Jane "an aged widow." Without Richard by her side, Rankin worried excessively about his mother's wellbeing. Adding to his troubles, pro-slavery sentiment in Ripley remained strong. Despite their small victories, anti-slavery activists needed to be careful. As Rankin had discovered from the arson of his unbound letters, the slave-holding class wasn't going to roll over and allow the abolitionists to dominate conversation. Rankin had only begun to discover the lengths that they would go to preserve their power. In the wake of these concerning developments, he concluded that "town was not the best place to bring up" his family.[71] Rankin made the decision to relocate his family to the hilltop behind town, which offered sixty-five and a half acres for $700. Not only would the acreage provide safety for his family, but Rankin also believed it would present an opportunity to make some money. "The land was thickly set with the best of timber and the soil was excellent." He planned to turn the property into farmland, providing his family with a stable source of income. But even if farming proved fruitless, Rankin could still sell parts of the land to provide. This, he viewed as a worthwhile investment.

He purchased the property in its entirety in 1829, putting down one hundred dollars and paying off the rest over the next five years. Rankin was eager to remove his family from town life in Ripley, especially his son, Adam Lowry Rankin, who was about to enter his teenage years. After the purchase, he "at once put up a log house that would do for a stable and moved into it." Shortly after, Rankin sold a third of the apartment he had built in town and erected a brick house at the top of the hill. "I bought a yoke of oxen and a cart," he later wrote about his new hilltop home. He paid men to cut down many of the abundant trees around him and had Lowry take the wood into town to sell "for one dollar a cord." Soon, he wrote, he "had the ground all fenced and most of it cleared, ready for farming." The farming potential of his property was great, but only Lowry was of contributing age. Thus, Rankin would have to hire men to do much of the needed work. This he used as an opportunity to advance both his ministry and his belief in the superiority of free labor. He had his laborers pledge not to curse or drink liquor while they worked for him. They were to attend church and worship with his family. All but one agreed to his terms, Rankin wrote, and he only had to turn "one away for violating them." Rankin insisted on treating his laborers with the utmost dignity, "without regards to color." He had them eat with his family at the table and "treated them as to make them feel there is no degradation attached to labor." This was vital to his abolition work. Many people at the time believed that certain labor was reserved for slaves, or black people generally. Rankin wanted all his laborers to understand that free labor was not degrading, but empowering. Whites and blacks, he believed, could work together on a common job as equals, and put their earnings toward their personal pursuits. Only if all people were equal in honest labor could they be truly free.

One night, Rankin came home from a prayer meeting only to find a deranged drunkard at his door, terrified the townspeople would tar him. Recognizing the man was genuinely seeking help, Rankin brought him in and sheltered the man until he was sober. As he came to his senses, the man immediately felt shame, explaining to Rankin that he had "pledged his clothes for whiskey." Believing in his sincerity, Rankin offered the man employment if he agreed to his terms. Like all Rankin's other laborers, the man agreed to no cursing, no drinking, and regular church attendance. "He kept the terms faithfully and labored for me six months; then returned to his friends. He went away a grateful and well doing man."[72]

Ripley, Ohio, as viewed from Kentucky. The home that John Rankin built for his family can be seen at the top of the hill behind the town. (Ohio History Connection)

* * * * *

As Rankin and his family settled into their new hilltop home, he received surprising news. After the first edition of his *Letters on Slavery* fell victim to arson, Rankin hadn't the means to reproduce a second edition. Besides, the letters had accomplished their primary purpose in managing to convince Thomas to free his slaves, so building his new home was Rankin's priority. A mere six hundred copies existed at the time, but somehow, one of those original copies made its way to a Quaker in New Jersey, who became extremely interested in republishing them. He wrote to Rankin in 1830, hoping to receive permission to reprint the letters to a wider audience. As Rankin wrote back, he told the Quaker that he had but one purpose in publishing the letters to begin with, and that was "the destruction of American slavery."[73] If the Quaker, or anyone for that matter, believed that reprinting the letters would help accomplish this goal, then Rankin would happily permit the printing of as many editions as they believed to be necessary. With Rankin's blessing, the Society of Friends in New Jersey (a.k.a., the Quakers) reprinted Rankin's letters as a book entitled *Rankin on Slavery*. After the second edition was finally published, it received much popularity in the far friendlier region of New England. As it spread, it found its way into the hands of a young William Lloyd Garrison.[74]

At that time, Garrison was morally against slavery but supported the concept of colonization. Founded in 1816, the American Colonization Society was the most popular institution for those opposed to slavery. Proponents of colonization believed immediate abolition would create too much of a shock to the system, threatening societal unrest and even possibly a race war. Colonization, in contrast, would gradually abolish slavery and have former slaves transported to Africa, the West Indies, or somewhere in the western territories of the United States, separating white societies from black. There were several reasons people supported colonization. Since the day of the founders, many of the most vocal opponents to slavery admitted they had no idea how abolition could be accomplished without plunging society into chaos. They pointed to instances of the Haitian slave rebellion as evidence that former slaves might opt for vengeance. Occurrences like Gabriel's Rebellion only reinforced this theory. For some, supporting colonization was a matter of self-preservation. Others feared for the wellbeing of slaves if they were left to fend for themselves with few skills, education, or allies. The prejudices of angry white mobs seemed as great a threat to societal peace as slave rebellion. Others, still, preferred colonization because they simply didn't want to coexist in a world with freed blacks. Whatever the reason, many of those who opposed slavery came to believe that colonization was the most practical solution, including Garrison.[75]

When he received his copy of Rankin's letters, Garrison's entire worldview was flipped upside down. A Christian man, Rankin's moral arguments against slavery weighed heavily on him. He quickly realized that anything less than immediate abolition only preserved the slaveholding powers. Garrison not only came to endorse Rankin's belief in immediate abolition but also supported his commitment to a multi-racial society. Consumed by Rankin's arguments against slavery, Garrison abandoned his support for the American Colonization Society. By this time, he had experience as a newspaper editor, having worked for anti-slavery papers, such as the *National Philanthropist* and *The Genius of Universal Emancipation*. On January 1, 1831, Garrison combined his editorial skills with his newfound passion for Rankin's vision of abolition and launched *The Liberator* in Boston, Massachusetts. This was a weekly newspaper co-founded with Isaac Knapp that would report the news from a strictly abolitionist view. On the first page of its first issue, Garrison utterly renounced colonization and begged God to forgive his former support. "In Park-Street Church, on the Fourth of July, 1829, I unreflectingly assented to the popular but pernicious doctrine of gradual abolition. I seize this moment to make a full and unequivocal recantation, and thus publicly to ask pardon of my God, of my country, and of my brethren the poor slaves, for having uttered a sentiment so full of timidity, injustice, and absurdity." Echoing Rankin's argument that all races belonged to the same human family, *The Liberator* boasted in their motto that "Our country is the world—our countrymen are mankind."[76]

After Garrison started publishing *The Liberator*, he sought to popularize the same arguments that awakened his own anti-slavery conviction. The unfolding movement against slavery resulted in talk of the formation of a society to advance the cause. Garrison and eleven other anti-slavery men met in the basement of the Belknap Street Church, a black church and schoolhouse on Beacon Hill. There, Garrison and his associates formed the New England Anti-Slavery Society. "We have met tonight in this obscure schoolhouse," Garrison told his colleagues. "Our numbers are few, and our influence limited, but mark my prediction. Faneuil Hall shall ere long echo to the principles we have set forth."[77] Following the establishment of the New England Anti-Slavery Society, *The Liberator* became its official publication. Garrison started republishing Rankin's *Letters* each week in *The Liberator* beginning in August 1832.[78] Now, a new and much more receptive New England audience would be receiving them. Rankin's *Letters* became a craze for New England abolitionists. He later wrote how his *Letters on Slavery* "was extensively published in New England, and the Society made it a textbook for their lectures." His letters became so popular that they even made their way to England. In the coming decades, Garrison would become one of the most polarizing figures in the abolitionist movement as he advanced the principles of perfectionism and disunion. Garrison and Rankin wouldn't always see eye to eye. Like many of Garrison's colleagues, Rankin sometimes opposed his positions, both in substance and tactic. Despite this, Rankin would long consider Garrison a friend and vital ally, even if he was too abrasive at times. In reflection, Garrison would later call himself "a disciple" of Rankin. This was a claim that Rankin himself would long take pride in.

William Lloyd Garrison fully embraced the idea of immediate emancipation after he obtained a copy of Rankin's Letters on Slavery. Garrison would often tell people that Rankin was his "anti-slavery father."

* * * * *

Rankin's *Letters* took off at the perfect time. Garrison's conversion to immediatism coincided with one of the most consequential slave rebellions in American history. Eight months after *The Liberator* was published, a Virginian slave called Nat Turner launched a slave uprising with limited success. He and six others rose up and killed the family that he had been hired out to. Turner and his co-conspirators then took up arms and enlisted over sixty other slaves to aid in their rebellion. The result was a disorganized but somewhat successful rebellion that slaughtered more than fifty white people. Turner's rebellion did not discriminate on age or gender as they murdered white men, women, and children alike. It wasn't long before the rebellion was suppressed, and after six weeks of hiding, Turner was caught in October. Before the end of November, he was tried and hanged for his actions. It was a dark moment in history for everyone involved. Like Gabriel's Rebellion at the dawn of the nineteenth century, southerners used the opportunity to double down on their conviction that blacks were inferior and talks of abolition incited violence. In the immediate aftermath of the rebellion, white mobs and militia retaliated against blacks in their communities, whether they had anything to do with the revolt or not. Droves of black people were beaten or slaughtered as white mobs hoped to send a message: submit or [79]

Unlike Gabriel's Rebellion, abolitionism was beginning to attract a small but vocal minority in 1831, and with Rankin's *Letters*, they were armed with counterarguments. This was exactly the kind of threat to domestic peace that Rankin had warned about. Slavery, not talks of abolition, inspired Turner and his co-conspirators to rebel. Both sides became more entrenched in their convictions. The difference was that the slave-holding class still held all the political power in the southern states. Even in the North, like Rankin's Ohio, black codes had been established to ensure that even free blacks were treated as second-class citizens. Slave laws in the South were given even more teeth, and those on the frontlines of the divide between North and South were in more danger than ever.

Nowhere truer would this be than in Ripley. Rumors had started to spread in Kentucky that Ripley was the place where fugitive slaves went to disappear, never to be found by their masters again. There was a developing suspicion that someone, or perhaps a group of people, was helping fugitives escape into Canada. While it wasn't entirely clear when this work had begun, Rankin became a prime suspect. Some nights, the residents of Ripley noticed a lantern in the window of Rankin's hilltop home. His new house was so visible that anyone on the Kentucky side of the river could see it from miles on a clear night. It also wasn't uncommon for residents of Ripley to notice shadows passing in the alleyways, apparently headed in the direction of the lantern-lit home behind town.

The townspeople were correct in their assumptions, and Rankin's activities aiding fugitive slaves would come to define his life in more ways than one. In 1831, however, he and all the other "conductors" of the so-called "Underground Railroad" required total secrecy. Fortunately, Rankin had several key allies to trust and rely on. Many of Ripley's residents on Front Street, where Rankin had built his first home, harbored slaves after they first crossed the river until it was safe to venture up to Rankin's hilltop home. Dr. Alexander Campbell was a key ally in these efforts. The Collins boys—Thomas, Theodore, and Eli—also become vital in aiding fugitive slaves. There were also key conductors further north that Rankin could trust as he sent fugitives on their way to Canada. One of them was Reverend James Gilliland of the Red Oak Presbyterian Church, slightly north of Ripley. Further still, there was the Quaker conductor Levi Coffin in Wayne County, Indiana. Coffin's legacy on the Underground Railroad would go on to rival that of Rankin's. Before they could reach Gilliland or Coffin, fugitive slaves must cross the river, following the lantern in the window of the home set on what would become known as "Liberty Hill."[80]

* * * * *

Rankin's secret work as a conductor on the Underground Railroad was well-kept in 1831, but Rankin had no issue taking public action against racial prejudice. An opportunity arose when the Brown County seat was removed from Ripley, leaving an unfinished courthouse behind with no further plans for it. Rankin believed it to be a prime location for a new college founded on the principles of Presbyterian morality and equality. "At father's suggestion," Lowry later recalled, "the legislature of Ohio was asked to authorize Brown County officials to sell that building and also to grant a charter for Ripley College." With both requests approved by the legislature, Rankin was named president of the board of trustees of Ripley College. Other abolitionists in Ripley also sat on the board with him, including Campbell. After the remaining construction of the building was completed, the college opened. Nathan Brockway of New York was named president of the college, and the school grew substantially under his leadership. Lowry recalled how attendance "reached 250" with students coming from nearby Kentucky and as far away as Tennessee, Mississippi, and Louisiana. One individual that the college attracted was a freed slave by the name of Benjamin Franklin Templeton. Originally from South Carolina, Templeton became free upon the death of his master, Thomas Williamson, in 1813. Thomas's wife, Ann, proceeded to take the emancipated slaves to Adams County Ohio, where her abolitionist son, Reverend William Williamson, lived nearby.

Templeton's brother, John, attended Ohio University and became the school's first black graduate. After graduation, John Templeton mentored his younger brother Benjamin and, ordained as a Presbyterian minister, worked at the Chillicothe Presbytery. After some discussion, the Presbytery agreed to pay a portion of Benjamin's tuition if he attended Ripley College. As Benjamin arrived in Ripley, things proceeded without incident. Lowry later wrote that the students from the Deep South didn't seem to mind that a black man was being taught in their classroom as an equal. One day, however, tensions rose when a Ripley citizen named Frank Shaw sent a note to Brockway demanding that Templeton be removed from the college. Shaw was a notorious drunkard and was upset that a black student was permitted to attend the school even though his own brother was too poor to attend. In his mind, a black man took an opportunity that would otherwise be afforded to a white man. Shaw was so upset that he threatened to "cowhide" Templeton if his request was not agreed to. Concerned for Templeton's safety, Brockway escorted Templeton to and from the college with another professor. When they believed that the threat of violence had passed, Templeton was permitted to walk to and from college by himself again. Not even two days had passed before Shaw ambushed Templeton in the middle of the afternoon, pulled him into an alley, and mercilessly beat him until he was nearly unconscious. Shaw was arrested and forced to pay a ten-dollar fine. He fled to Mason County in Kentucky after he was freed, leaving Ripley for good.

Templeton elicited sympathy from the community in Ripley as he recovered. The debate that dominated the talk of the town, however, was whether Templeton should be permitted to continue his education at Ripley College. Many were concerned that this kind of violence was only the beginning for their small community. Allowing him to continue at Ripley College might open their community to an onslaught of mob violence from southern sympathizers and slavery supporters. To Rankin and many at the college, this was an unfortunate incident of whiskey-fueled racism, not a harbinger of widespread social unrest. They thought it absurd to ruin Templeton's future over one unruly community member taking offense. Still, there was also the concern that students from the South would walk out if Templeton wasn't removed. In the wake of growing concerns, Rankin offered a solution. If the board allowed Templeton to remain enrolled in Ripley College, he would privately tutor the young man in his home until he graduated. While he'd prefer Templeton to remain in the classroom, this was a better option than complete removal. It would also decrease the likelihood that he would be the target of such a violent assault again. The board agreed, and Templeton continued his education under the tutelage of Rankin himself until after the spring semester of 1832. After moving away from Ripley for a while, Templeton completed his education and became ordained as a Presbyterian minister.[81]

* * * * *

By the end of 1832, Rankin had risen from a local anti-slavery crusader to a national leader in abolitionist thought. His profile had risen to such a degree that he received an invitation to join fellow abolitionists in Philadelphia on December 4, 1833 "to form a NATIONAL ANTI-SLAVERY SOCIETY" (emphasis theirs).[82] Rankin agreed to attend the convention. Philadelphia was strategically selected as the location. Geographically, it was a central location when transportation was still primitive. More importantly, it held significant historical weight. It wasn't lost upon the abolitionists that this was where the United States was born almost sixty years earlier. It was also where the Constitution was debated and approved. This, many abolitionists like Garrison believed, was a great national tragedy. Garrison viewed the Constitution as a pro-slavery document, but not everyone subscribed to his view of the Constitution. It would be one of the greatest driving wedges among the abolitionists in the coming decades.

During their convention in Philadelphia, the abolitionists united in their uncompromising opposition to slavery. Drawing from the revolutionary spirit of the city's heritage, they adopted a declaration of their own. "More than fifty-seven years have elapsed since a band of patriots convened in this place," read the opening of their Declaration of Sentiments. "The corner-stone upon which they founded the Temple of Freedom was broadly this—'that all men are created equal; that they are endowed by their Creator with certain inalienable rights; that among these are life, LIBERTY, and the pursuit of happiness'" (emphasis theirs). These abolitionists found great inspiration in the actions of the fifty-six men who risked everything for the freedom of their countrymen. "They were few in number—poor in resources; but the honest conviction that Truth, Justice, and Right were on their side, made them invincible." Now, they believed, it was time to make a similar stand in favor of liberty for the enslaved. "Their grievances, great as they were, were trifling in comparison with the wrongs and sufferings of those for whom we plead. Our fathers were never slaves—never bought and sold like cattle—never shut out from the light of knowledge and religion— never subjected to the lash of brutal task-masters." As they proceeded to list their grievances against the institution of slavery, they acknowledged their own limitations under the current Constitution, conceding "that Congress, under the present national compact, has no right to interfere with any of the slave States, in relation to this momentous subject." This didn't mean Congress was helpless, though. The abolitionists affirmed their belief that the federal government should divorce itself from slavery where it had the power to do so. "Congress has a right, and is solemnly bound to suppress the domestic slave trade between the several States, and to abolish slavery in those portions of our territory which the Constitution has placed under its exclusive jurisdiction." To achieve this divorce from slavery, and abolish slavery within the states that it exists, they vowed to "organize Anti-Slavery Societies, if possible, in every city, town, and village in our land." In closing, they vowed not to rest until they have overthrown slavery entirely from the United States, "whether we live to witness the triumph of LIBERTY, JUSTICE, and HUMANITY, or perish ultimately as martyrs in this great, benevolent, and holy cause" (emphasis theirs).[83]

The Declaration was adopted on December 6, and the contents of it were published in *The Liberator* on the fourteenth. They also proceeded to adopt a constitution to govern their national anti-slavery society. "This Society shall be called the American Anti-Slavery Society," read the first Article. Most of the content of the governing document dealt with procedure and process. Still, it was also prudent to identify who was and was not eligible to be among their ranks. These abolitionists were strategic to ensure those in favor of colonization or gradualism could not be a member. Slaveholding, it read, "is a heinous crime in the sight of God, and that the duty, safety, and best interests of all concerned, require its *immediate abandonment*, without expatriation" (emphasis theirs). Simply believing slavery to be wrong wasn't enough. Members must also be committed to the equality and advancement of the black race. "This Society shall aim to elevate the character and condition of the people of color, by encouraging their intellectual, moral, and religious improvement, and by removing public prejudice, that thus they may, according to their intellectual and moral worth, share an equality with the whites, of civil and religious privileges…." As much as they were committed to abolition, they were equally committed to nonviolence. The end of the third Article affirmed that "this Society will never, in any way, countenance the oppressed in vindicating their rights by resorting to physical force." This commitment to pacifism would prove to drive yet another wedge in a movement already loosely held together over the coming decades.[84]

* * * * *

Through his involvement with the American Anti-Slavery Society, Rankin came to know many of the most influential people of the nineteenth century on the issue of slavery. Of course, he met his "disciple" Garrison. He also had the opportunity to meet and get to know the Tappan brothers of New York, Arthur and Lewis. The Tappans were wealthy philanthropists who would often fund anti-slavery causes. One individual that Rankin met during this time who had a particular impact on his life was Theodore Dwight Weld. Entering his thirties at the dawn of the anti-slavery movement, Weld was a gruff, slightly unkempt man who found his way to immediate abolitionism through his faith, his travels, and the influence of Garrison's paper. In the early 1830s, as Rankin was establishing Ripley College, Weld was scouting on behalf of the Tappans to find a location where theological training could be provided for "poor but earnest" young men going into "the western ministry" in the "vast valley of the Mississippi."[85] Weld had traveled to Cincinnati a few times in 1832, where he discovered a seminary that would serve the mission he and the Tappan brothers had envisioned for the west. A few miles north of Cincinnati, the Lane Seminary was founded in 1829 with the contribution of local merchants, Ebenezer and William Lane. It had one main structure and a few smaller, unfinished buildings. Despite its small size, Weld believed it could be the exact location he and the Tappan brothers were seeking. Weld enlisted Lyman Beecher to relocate to Cincinnati and serve as the institution's president in 1832. Originally from Connecticut, like Weld himself, Beecher moved from Boston to Ohio with his family, which included his daughter, Harriet. Lyman's son, Henry Ward Beecher, would follow the rest of his family to Cincinnati two years later, following his graduation from Amherst College in 1834.[86]

Weld enrolled in Lane and became the student-body president. Many of the students who first enrolled at Lane weren't abolition absolutists. There were some from the South enrolled, and even those from the North weren't in favor of abolition as much as they were of colonization. Even Beecher himself favored colonization.[87] Weld believed this was the great question of the age—whether abolition was feasible and whether colonization was actually a practical solution to slavery. Weld believed that getting to the bottom of it required robust debate over the subject, not silence. [88] Weld and some like-minded abolitionist students decided to host public "debates" over slavery and abolition. Ironically, there was nobody to defend colonization during these discussions. Weld hardly went out of his way to find them. The country was all too aware of the arguments in favor of colonization in 1834. What they needed, he believed, was a fair argument in favor of immediate abolition. Under the misleading pretext that both sides would have an opportunity to speak, Weld organized the discussions around two questions. "Ought the people of the slaveholding states abolish slavery immediately?" and "Are the doctrines, tendencies, and measures of the American Colonization Society, and the influence of its principal supporters, such as render it worthy of the patronage of the Christian public?" Although there wasn't much of a debate that transpired, largely by design, it did manage to bring together the abolitionists of the west to organize behind the same cause. Hearing that these discussions were happening at Lane Seminary, Rankin traveled from Ripley to witness the exciting spread of abolitionism. He sat in wonderment as he witnessed Weld and his contemporaries make many of the same arguments he had made to his brother less than a decade earlier. It must have left Rankin with a great feeling of satisfaction to hear his arguments become so popularized in the valley. But popularity didn't come without controversy. It wasn't long before Weld had taken to writing public defenses of his debates at Lane. In May 1834, he wrote a public letter to James Hall, editor of *The Western Monthly Magazine*, in the *Cincinnati Journal*, asking him, "why should not theological students investigate and discuss the sin of slavery?"[89] Many Cincinnati residents were pro-slavery or anti-black, and became irritated by Weld and his student cohort.

Lane Theological Seminary. The colonization debates at Lane Seminary ignited a firestorm of controversy. Many abolitionists, including John Rankin, were outraged that the faculty would turn their back on their students and censor them.

The Lane debates over slavery took place not long after Ripley's own school controversy. Indeed, Rankin was still educating black students in his own home after the Templeton controversy at Ripley College. Like in Ripley, many citizens in Cincinnati didn't take kindly to the fact that the Lane Seminary was educating black students along with whites. By July 1834, churchgoers were writing in the *Cincinnati Journal* that the racial mixing of black and white students in the seminary had desecrated "our Temple of God."[90] As tensions rose, the threat of mob violence targeting Lane Seminary rose too. The trustees and President Beecher began to panic. Not unlike the Templeton controversy in Ripley, the faculty and trustees feared the outbreak of violence was on the horizon. As classes ended for the summer, Beecher took to the east to raise funds for the school.

In the meantime, the trustees voted on a series of resolutions that would crack down on student activities on campus. They essentially gagged the students' ability to speak on matters they deemed too controversial, namely slavery. Any student could be dismissed or censored if they discussed prohibited subjects. The anti-slavery society that Weld and his fellow students had organized was banned. It wasn't lost upon Weld and his abolitionist contemporaries that their speech and academic freedom had to be sacrificed to appease the slave power. This was yet another regretful incident of slavery eroding away at every aspect of American life. For slavery to be preserved, freedom everywhere had to yield. Weld was not going to be stopped from speaking out, and neither were many of his peers. So, after they returned to school in the fall, seeing few options left, Weld and his anti-slavery peers at Lane Seminary simply left the school. The protest had a serious impact on the school, with a sizable portion of their student body now gone. The students that walked out quickly earned a reputation as the "Lane Rebels." *The Liberator* published a statement from the students detailing their lengthy reasoning for leaving. "Inhibition of free discussion is ruin, not remedy," they wrote. "We leave Lane Seminary with sentiments of grateful affection for the advantages which, during our membership, it so largely afforded us, and, apart from the grief we feel in being obliged to withdraw from these advantages, our heartfelt sorrow is, that in crushing the high and sacred principle of free inquiry, its ruling authorities have given a death blow to the spirit of its glory, and have dragged it down to a dishonored level with those institutions where mind becomes the crouching slave of prescription...."[91]

* * * * *

Rankin knew many of the trustees at Lane Seminary and considered several of them friends, but hearing about the incident with the Lane Rebels infuriated him. Rankin was furious that the faculty and trustees would sacrifice academic freedom to yield to the slave powers. He was embarrassed for them that the mere threat of violence would cause them to fold at the expense of their students. The draconian policies they adopted infuriated him. Rankin defiantly declared in an editorial published in the *Cincinnati Journal* that this was "a bad beginning in Lane Seminary—If it IS to be governed by the excitements of Cincinnati, and especially, excitements so unreasonable; and if the students are to be placed under laws made to appease the mob, the church will have little to hope either from its purity or its influence. When it is found that it can be governed by city excitements it may expect to be favored with enough of them." If a mob truly was going to destroy the small institution, as they feared, it would have been far better "for the Seminary and the religion" if they had succeeded. "It could have been reared again as a standing monument to integrity." After the *Cincinnati Journal* ran Rankin's scolding editorial of the Lane faculty, he had it printed in pamphlet form. Much of the content included an examination of the American Colonization Society in contrast to the anti-slavery society. He knew the arguments deserved a wider audience.[92]

The Lane Rebels scattered across the country following their departure from the seminary, each one advancing abolition to new audiences. It wasn't just students affected by the mass exodus. Asa Mahan was a trustee at Lane who resigned out of disgust for the school's treatment of the students. He was the only trustee to vote in favor of the students' ability to discuss matters of slavery. After he resigned, Oberlin College in northern Ohio asked if he would serve as their first president. Mahan agreed under the condition that the school would allow for the admission of black students. Once the school agreed to his terms, he traveled north to run the school, and many of the Lane Rebels in Cincinnati traveled with him. For his part, Weld decided to visit the Rankins in Ripley following the controversy. It was during this time that Weld had decided to dedicate the entirety of his efforts toward building up the anti-slavery movement in Ohio. Unlike in the east, where societies and social movements were a dime a dozen, it became very difficult for anything of the kind to take root in the west. People were largely more independent and worried too much about the rough aspects of life on the frontier to give any concern to community engagement in the same way that one might find in Philadelphia or Boston. Building an anti-slavery movement in Ohio would take time. It would need to be nurtured by the steady and reliable hands of leaders willing to build a movement from the ground up. Weld had already committed in his heart to achieving this end. Before the close of 1834, so would Rankin. As Weld lectured in Ripley against the evils of slavery, Rankin and the other local abolitionists activated to take a much more public stand against slavery. Indeed, Rankin had been preaching against it from the pulpit for years, but that only went so far. Weld helped him realize how much work was needed to truly evangelize the people of Ohio against the slave powers. Rankin's *Letters* were key in exciting Weld to the abolitionist cause. Now, in Ripley, Weld was able to return the favor to Rankin.[93]

Rankin wasn't the only one in his family to be influenced by Weld's presence in Ripley. Young Lowry had just turned eighteen in November 1834. With his entire adult life in front of him, Rankin was eager for his firstborn son to follow him in ministry. Lowry, as his friends called him, had not felt a calling at this point, instead wishing to learn a trade. A carpentry apprenticeship with his uncle, William McNish, had recently become available in Ripley. He desired to take it, against his father's wishes. Lowry was against slavery like the rest of his family, but their opposition was based mainly on spiritual grounds. Lowry believed in God and even passed an examination for membership into the Presbyterian Church in Ripley when he was fourteen. Yet without a calling to the ministry, Rankin understood that he shouldn't pressure Lowry into something that his heart wasn't in. He consented, reluctantly, to Lowry's apprenticeship. Still, Rankin held out hope that one day, a spark would ignite, not unlike how it did for himself when he was younger. That day would come sooner than later.

Lowry worked through his apprenticeship as a carpenter and architect for steamships. One day in December 1834, he was working on the molding of the steamer *Fair Play*. His uncle had informed him and the rest of the workers that a steamer named *Uncle Sam* was going to dock at Ripley to load five hundred barrels of pork and ship it on to New Orleans. *Uncle Sam* was said to be the largest steamer in the country in 1834, so there was great excitement from everyone in town to see the ship, especially with Lowry and the carpentry crew who would walk on its deck. As the steamer docked, Lowry boarded the ship. What he witnessed "revolutionized the whole purpose" of his life. Exploring the ship, making his way through the cabin and then to the engine room, he came across a scene that would forever be burned into his mind and animate his passions throughout the rest of his life. "Two groups of slaves, about twenty-five in each, were chained to the sides of the deck, the men on my left and the women on my right. Two long chains extended from the forward to the rear of each side of the steerage deck. The ends were bolted to the sides of the boat about four feet above the deck floor. To these chains, at about equal distances apart, were attached twenty-five shorter chains with a handcuff attached to the loose end. The handcuff was locked on the wrist of the right arm of each slave. The short chain was just long enough to enable the slave to sit or lie down on the deck, and in weight and size was that of the ordinary chain used in plowing with horses."

His mind reeled to Weld's lectures on the brutality of slavery a few weeks earlier. Weld had animated Rankin against slavery, but what Lowry saw caused an unnerving chill to shoot up his spine in a way that no lecture, sermon, or story could possibly induce. But as bad as it was, the real images of human bondage weren't even the worst of it on that day. As he scanned the room, he noticed a young, beautiful woman bound like the men. Lowry couldn't wrap his mind around why such a beautiful woman would be held in chains. "Can it be possible that she is a slave, bound for a Southern slave mart to stand on the auction block and be knocked down by some brutal auctioneer to the highest bidder?" His initial reaction was that of horror, but as he overheard the conversations of two men passing by on the ship, his horror transformed into a fit of righteous anger. "Ain't she a beauty!" he heard them say, barely noticing him standing there. The man Lowry overheard was a slave trader, who "had the usual characteristics" of one. The course-looking slaveholder spoke to a younger, well-dressed man hoping to make a sale. "The trader used the vilest language, proposing the woman as a mistress for the young man and insisting she was worth more than he asked, $2500, and swearing he could get $3000 for her in New Orleans. He knew young men, he said, who would jump to get such a well-made and good looking woman as she was." Their conversation hit Lowry like a ton of bricks. He remained frozen, observing the scene as if he were a ghost, not noticed by any of them. He turned to look at the woman, horrified at the prospect that she was about to be sold as a sex slave. She covered her face and began to sob as she overheard their conversation. The slaveholder became rage-filled, worried she was about to ruin his trade. "No more of that, you black sons of —," Lowry recalled him saying. He explained how the man "struck the woman on the shoulder and ordered her to take her hands from her face and stop her crying or he would half kill her. She obeyed, and after a little more talk the young man offered $2000." All his sympathies, Lowry noted, were "expended upon that one woman." After he left the boat, he was indignant as he prayed aloud, saying. "My God helping me there shall be a perpetual war between me and human slavery in this nation of which I am a member and I pray God I may never be persuaded to give up the fight until slavery is dead or the Lord calls me home."[94]

**Adam Lowry Rankin as a young man. Following an
unexpected encounter with slavery in Ripley in 1834,
Adam Lowry vowed to God that he would be in "perpetual
war" against slavery until he died, or it was defeated.**

* * * * *

After reflecting on the scene, Lowry decided that upon the comple-
tion of his apprenticeship, he would in fact join the ministry and fight
against slavery, as his father had desired. Ironically, if he hadn't rejected
his father's pleas and started his apprenticeship, it's hard to say if he
would have been so animated as to shift the entire trajectory of his life.
Rankin was pleased, but his life was also about to change forever. As
Weld had spoken against slavery in Ripley, he had animated Rankin
to put his entire life on hold for the cause of abolition. Rankin would
travel with Weld and other abolitionists across Ohio for a year, lecturing
against the evils of slavery in churches and at town meetings, organizing
new anti-slavery societies in the process. Weld and Rankin would force
the country to take a good look at the ugly realities of slavery. Their
activities throughout the remainder of the 1830s would attract much
attention. Everyone, from anti-abolitionist mobs and slave hunters, all
the way to the halls of Congress, would start to take notice.

ANTI-SLAVERY
1835–1838
VI.

R ipley had changed dramatically since the arrival of the Rankin family in January 1822. John Rankin had successfully exercised the soul of the community. Although it wasn't completely devoid of "intemperance," as many in his day called it, the community now had character to it that was missing before. Certainly, the town's escalating abolitionist activities helped establish that character as much as the uptick in church attendance did. Rankin's involvement with Ripley College also helped elevate it from a frontier saloon town to a respectable community with several budding leaders. The college's president, Nathan Brockway, died of cholera in 1832. After the professor who succeeded him resigned, Rankin rose to fill the office. By 1835, he was known as a respectable educator, minister, family man, and farmer. But now, all those roles would have to be put aside as he fully embraced his most important role yet—anti-slavery advocate. He realized through his interaction with Theodore Weld and the larger anti-slavery community that there were towns all across Ohio that needed help building a network of abolitionists in the way that Ripley had. He would return to his family and the community that he came to adore, but he felt a higher calling to expand the cause of abolition across the state.

* * * * *

In the early months of 1835, Rankin traveled extensively, speaking to anyone who would have him across Ohio. It must have felt like familiar territory to some extent. Travel was a staple of much of his early preaching in Tennessee and Kentucky. Sharing the same message to a new audience every few miles kept things fresh for Rankin, who came to enjoy that aspect of his early ministry. Now, as he spoke from the pulpits and meeting houses in communities across Ohio, he preached a message of liberation. He denounced the concept that slavery was sanctioned by God, and refuted many of the common beliefs associated with race in America. As popular as his *Letters on Slavery* had become, some in the communities he visited were hearing his arguments for the first time. Both Rankin and Weld understood the value of audibly spreading a message that has been written down. One can choose not to read a message, but once something is heard, it can't be unheard. After a few months of travel and stump speeches, Rankin found himself in Putnam, Ohio, in April 1835. This was the location in which over a hundred representatives from all over the state and even a handful from outside the state would meet to officially form the Ohio Anti-Slavery Society. Forming a state anti-slavery society was crucial to fulfilling the mission of the American Anti-Slavery Society, which vowed to "organize Anti-Slavery Societies, if possible, in every city, town, and village in our land." Weld was the first to arrive in the area. In March, he arrived in neighboring Zanesville, Ohio, across from Putnam on the other side of the Muskingum River. In 1872, Putnam was annexed into Zanesville as the city expanded. In 1835, the two communities were very different despite their proximity. Much like Ohio itself, Putnam was founded by anti-slavery settlers from New England. In contrast, most of the citizens of Zanesville were from southern states and had little to no issue with slavery. With these two communities of stark contrast so close together, conflict was sure to arise when the abolitionists descended upon the area. Weld had intended to give a speech for the anti-slavery society when he arrived in Zanesville, but the pro-slavery residents of the community chased him out of town. As he crossed the river into Putnam, he settled at the Stone Academy, where he was given room to deliver his lecture. This was soon disrupted by pro-slavery mobs who had caught wind that Weld hadn't left the region and was lecturing in Putnam. They crossed the river from Zanesville and forced him to take refuge in the private residence of a church elder. Weld was not deterred, but he realized he would need protection. Once he secured protection from the county sheriff, the Muskingum County Emancipation Society approached Weld, offering to host the convention for the anti-slavery society in Putnam in late April.[95]

Theodore D. Weld was an inspiration to John Rankin. Following Weld's visit to Ripley, Rankin fully devoted his life to the abolitionist crusade, both publicly and privately.

Nearly every notable Ohio abolitionist traveled to central Ohio that spring to gather in Putnam. Asa Mahan traveled from Oberlin College, as did many of the Lane Rebels. William T. Allen, James A. Thome, Henry B. Stanton, Augustus Wattles, and Horace Bushnell all left Lane in protest with Weld just the prior fall. Now they were in Putnam ready to turn their protest into action. There was Joshua Giddings, former Ohio State Representative and soon-to-be congressman from Ashtabula County, Ohio. Giddings was a driving advocate for abolition from the Western Reserve and was active as a conductor on the Underground Railroad. From Kentucky, there was James G. Birney, the former slave owner and politico who converted to immediate abolitionism after joining the Presbyterian Church. Birney, similarly to William Lloyd Garrison, had advocated for colonization for most of his life up to this point. He worked on Henry Clay's Congressional campaign in Kentucky and later was an elector for John Quincy Adams in the 1828 election. By the early 1830s, Birney had completely abandoned colonization right when abolitionism was sweeping the country like wildfire. In 1834, he freed all his slaves and compensated them for their labor. The following year, he announced his plans to open an abolitionist newspaper in his hometown of Danville, Kentucky. When mobs threatened him, he made arrangements to move to Cincinnati later that year. Birney was a rising star in the abolitionist movement, but also a controversial figure at times. With such a history in politics, Birney believed in political abolitionism—the idea that abolitionism could be achieved through the political process. This was a point of sharp division with the Garrisonians, who believed it immoral to negotiate with slaveholders. Regardless of future division, Birney was in Putnam with his fellow abolitionists in April 1835 to help form a larger movement against slavery.[96]

Then there was the delegation from Brown County. As a hotbed for abolitionist activity, it only made sense that Ripley would have strong representation at the convention. Dr. Alexander Campbell made his way up from Ripley that April. Reverend James Gilliland of the Red Oak Presbyterian Church was also in attendance. John B. Mahan was a young, but convicted abolitionist who also made his way to Putnam that spring. Mahan was a Methodist minister from a newer village in Brown County called Sardinia. He owned and operated what was known as a "temperance tavern," or a tavern which didn't serve liquor. Mahan was fully committed to abolition due to the influence of his father, Jacob Mahan. He was an Irish immigrant and a minister who preached, among other things, against the sins of slavery. In 1828, Jacob died unexpectedly after a horse-riding accident. His death had a powerful effect on his children, who fully committed themselves to the abolition cause moving forward. Mahan's tavern came to be an important stop for runaway slaves after they left Ripley on their way north. He would often send them on their way to the safehouse of Levi Coffin in Indiana. Among all of those arriving in Putnam in April 1835, none were more well-known or well-respected than John Rankin.

Of the roughly twenty-five counties represented in Putnam that April, all had come to know of the man whose *Letters on Slavery* had sparked a movement. Many of those in attendance were new to the abolitionist movement, having been personally recruited by Weld over the past few months. As they sought to expand their understanding of abolitionist thought, Rankin's *Letters* were their first stop. As Rankin arrived in Putnam, this was likely the first time he could appreciate his personal impact over the anti-slavery movement. Eventually, James Birney's son, William Birney, would recount the impact Rankin had on the first Ohio Convention in *James G. Birney and His Times: The Genesis of the Republican Party*. "The most noted abolitionist in the convention was doubtless John Rankin," Birney wrote. "Many Western men have called him 'the father of abolitionism.'" It also wasn't "an uncommon thing in (the 1830s) to hear him called 'the Martin Luther'" of abolitionism. By the time Rankin's *Letters* began to circulate in 1827, Birney noted that "John Rankin was one of the five most prominent advocates in this country of *immediate abolition*," as well as one of the earliest (emphasis his).[97]

* * * * *

The convention began on April 22, 1835. The first order of business involved the creation of several committees to nominate officers. According to the convention minutes, "the following committee was appointed by the chair to nominate officers for the convention: A. A. Guthrie, Wm Dickey, James Loughead, Theodore D. Weld, John B. Mahan, Wm. Poe, and W. W. Bancroft." Following the selection of officers, a committee was formed to bring forward new business to the convention. "On motion of Mr. Gushing...a committee of arrangements of seven members, to prepare and bring forward business for the convention, was appointed by the chair... James G. Birney, James Stewart, Theodore D. Weld, and Harmon Kingsbury," as well as the Reverends "Henry Cowles, R. V. Rogers and John Rankin." The matters that Rankin and the rest of his committee chose to bring forward to the convention included resolutions to open sessions with prayer, form a committee to draft a constitution for the Ohio Anti-Slavery Society, form one to "prepare an address to the churches," and to "draft a petition to Congress, for the abolition of slavery, and the slave trade, in the District of Columbia," as well as one "to consider and report, on the laws of the state of Ohio, with reference to the colored population within its limits," among other things. Rankin was selected to sit on the committee to form a report on the laws of Ohio. Although Rankin himself didn't write the Declaration of Sentiments for the anti-slavery society, his influence was felt. Many of the arguments made in his *Letters* were adapted to the Declaration. "We believe Slavery to be a sin—always, everywhere, and only sin. Sin in itself, apart from the occasional rigors incidental to its administration and from all those perils, liabilities, and positive inflictions to which its victims are continually exposed, sin in the nature of the act which creates it, and in the elements which constitute it. Sin, because it converts persons into things; makes men property, God's image, merchandise." As the Declaration of Sentiments came to a close, they "solemnly consecrated" themselves "to the cause of EMANCIPATION, IMMEDIATE, TOTAL, AND UNIVERSAL, we subscribe our names to this Declaration; The principles which it embodies we will, by the grace of God, forever cherish and fearlessly avow, come life or death" (emphasis theirs). Rankin was proud to sign his name to it. The constitution that the convention approved was much shorter than its declaration but no less bold in language. After it affirmed that it would be named the "Ohio Anti-Slavery Society" and would be an auxiliary of the American Anti-Slavery Society, it minced no words when describing its purpose. "The object of this Society, shall be the entire abolition of Slavery throughout the United States, and the elevation of our colored brethren to their proper rank as men." Not limiting itself to just abolition, this society would advocate for total racial equality under the law.[98]

After approving the Declaration of Sentiments, the constitution, and the remaining matters that Rankin's committee had resolved to address, the convention selected the first officers of the Ohio Anti-Slavery Society. Leicester King of Warren County was elected as the Society's first president. Ripley's Dr. Campbell was elected as the first vice president. Mahan and Gilliland also represented Brown County as officers or managers in its first year of operation. The first convention for the Ohio Anti-Slavery Society transpired relatively smoothly. One evening during the convention, however, Rankin was exposed to a degree of violence that would only heighten in the coming years. "There was an Englishman," Rankin later recalled, "a preacher of some order, at whom (an anti-abolitionist mob) had a double hatred, because he was both a foreigner and an abolitionist." He had invited Rankin for tea after the day's sessions. Rankin agreed, and the two started walking back to his house. There, a mob had formed around the home. They tried to avoid the gathering, but as they started walking away, the mob pelted them with rotten goose eggs. One hit Rankin on his shoulder, and as he recalled, "fell before it broke, and had a gosling in it ready to come out." He wrote that he had never been able to "appreciate the feelings of Christians in the Apostolic age" as much as when he faced the anti-abolition mobs in the late 1830s.[99]

With the society formed, the convention closed, and Rankin continued his speaking tour as he started traveling back toward Ripley. Along the way, he stopped to preach in Chillicothe, Ohio. "I stayed over Sabbath at Chillicothe and preached morning and night for the colored people." During his evening services, agitators began to swarm as they "threw stones into the church and hurt some of the people who were in attendance." As he left his church service, he walked back with the individual hosting him over Sunday. Rankin described him as "a large, strong man." As they crossed the canal bridge on their way home, there were several people along the bridge. Rankin believed they intended to toss him in the canal if it weren't for his large host walking beside him. Word began to spread that a mob was forming to attack Rankin at the home he was staying in. His host's wife was not healthy, and Rankin wished to divert the mob away from them. He went to the home of a church elder, describing the situation after apologizing for knocking at their door at such a late hour. They allowed him in, but the elder's wife, annoyed, suggested that the mobs would stop following Rankin if he stopped trying to help the colored community. The night passed without incident at either home. A mob never did form, and Rankin continued his travels the next morning. This tense environment would continue to follow him as he worked for anti-slavery societies. Needless to say, Rankin didn't take the advice of his last-minute host in Chillicothe.[100]

* * * * *

By the summer of 1835, the abolitionists had graduated from being viewed as a local nuisance to a national threat. That summer, the American Anti-Slavery Society adopted a new tactic in their fight against slavery. The danger associated with sending their members to speak out against slavery in the South was far too great. After all, they attracted mobs in the northern states. They were bound to be seriously harmed or killed if they attempted the same strategy in the South. Still, many in leadership at the anti-slavery society believed it crucial to get abolitionist arguments in front of Southern slaveholders. After all, James G. Birney was a prime example of what was possible when a slaveholder was exposed to the light, so to speak. Rather than risk their members, they committed to a pamphlet campaign, in which the society would mail literature and letters, most notably Rankin's *Letters on Slavery*, to southern lawmakers, business leaders, planters, and individuals of influence. They were under no disillusion that few would be influenced, but there was an opportunity to attract more like Birney to the cause of abolition. Additionally, as they mailed pamphlets out to slaveholders, there was a strong likelihood that more slaves would encounter the arguments supporting their freedom. This awareness might motivate them to flee their masters and travel along the Underground Railroad, possibly even making it to Rankin's "Liberty Hill."

Arthur and Lewis Tappan were completely sold on the campaign, and they committed to funding the printing and distribution of whatever material the anti-slavery society deemed appropriate to send to the south. Throughout the summer, thousands of letters, newspapers, and pamphlets, including Rankin's *Letters on Slavery*, were mailed en masse across the south. Slaveholders in Tennessee, Alabama, Virginia, North Carolina, South Carolina, and Georgia were flooded with abolitionist content. The purpose was to "revolutionize the public sentiment" against slavery across the country. The public was certainly revolutionized, but not always in favor of abolition. In one incident, Amos Dresser, a Lane Rebel from Cincinnati, was traveling through Kentucky and Tennessee in July, selling Bibles and abolitionist literature to raise funds for college. He stopped in Nashville on the eighteenth, where he stayed at the Nashville Inn. His carriage needed repair, so they brought the literature inside before taking it to a repair shop, but overlooked a handful of anti-slavery pamphlets. As the repair man worked on his carriage, he caught word that Dresser was an abolitionist and discovered the literature. Shortly after the discovery, Dresser was brought before a local vigilance committee, which tried him in an extralegal manner to decide his fate. They laid out his possessions before the committee, which included "one copy of *Oasis*, one of Rankin's *Letters on Slavery*, and one of Bourne's *Picture of Slavery in the United States*," according to Dresser. After further examination, they had their verdict. Dresser was found guilty by the committee of "being a member of an Anti-Slavery Society in Ohio," and of being in possession of literature "published by the American Anti-Slavery Society." They also believed he was guilty of circulating the literature and advocating for "the principles they inculcated." Dresser received twenty lashes on his back as a verdict. Many in the South believed that the vigilance committee had done Dresser a favor. "Had it not been for the…firmness of the Committee," wrote *The Tennessean* in August 1835, Dresser's life could have been at the mercy of a lynching mob. He was forced to leave Nashville immediately. That same August, Dresser recounted his extra-legal trial in *The Cincinnati Daily Gazette*, which set the anti-slavery societies into a craze. This, they believed, underscored the importance of their work.[101]

Likewise, Southerners were on high alert. The same summer of Dresser's incident in Nashville, mobs began to form around post offices in the South. The Jackson administration was disturbed by what was being dubbed the "great postal campaign" of 1835. Jacksonian postmaster Amos Kendall took the law into his own hands as he permitted postmasters in the South to refuse delivery of abolitionist literature. This federal censorship of the abolitionists further emboldened Southern mobs. As the steamer, *The Columbia*, docked in Charleston, South Carolina on July 29, 1835, residents of Charleston discovered that it had transported abolitionist mailers from New York City. Several residents took to the streets, broke into the post office, and stole and torched the literature intended for slaveholders. Southerners across the region were infuriated by the actions of the abolitionists. Effigies of Garrison and Arthur Tappan were burned in protest. Southern localities started to offer bounties for Arthur to be delivered "dead or alive." As silk merchants, the Tappan brothers had many business ties to the south. Boycotts of products associated with the Tappans started to emerge.[102]

In December, during his annual address to Congress, President Andrew Jackson took time to make special note of the threat posed by the abolitionist postal campaign. "I must...invite your attention to the painful excitement produced in the South by attempts to circulate through the mails inflammatory appeals addressed to the passions of the slaves, in prints and in various sorts of publications, calculated to stimulate them to insurrection and to produce all the horrors of a servile war." Jackson called for "the special attention of Congress" to pass new legislation that would "prohibit, under severe penalties, the circulation in the Southern States, through the mail, of incendiary publications intended to instigate the slaves to insurrection." It soon became clear to abolitionists in the North that sending literature to the South only to be censored by the postmaster or burned by a mob was a waste of proper resources. Although the campaign didn't have its intended effect, many still considered it successful. The scales were removed from the eyes of many fence sitters in 1835. The true intentions of the slave-holding Southerners were now clear—slavery must be preserved at the expense of the rest of the Union. The president of the United States himself was openly calling for Congress to violate the civil liberties of abolitionists in the North to appease the South. Indeed, legislation was proposed to suppress the circulation of such mailers. While this failed to pass, censorship from postmasters continued in the south.[103]

Such open targeting by the federal government did wonders to help the local and state anti-slavery societies grow. By the end of 1835, there were twenty-five local societies in Ohio. That number ballooned to 120 in 1836. As Rankin returned in the fall of 1835, he ensured Ripley would be among the most active of the anti-slavery societies. On November 25, Rankin met with Campbell, Gilliland, Thomas and Theodore Collins, and several other local abolitionists (most of whom were Underground Railroad conductors) at the Red Oak Presbyterian Church. During their convention, they established a constitution for the Ripley Anti-Slavery Society. "This Society shall endeavor to convince their fellow citizens that slaveholding is a heinous sin in the sight of God." Like in the Ohio and American anti-slavery societies before it, they vowed that they would continue to lobby Congress to abolish slavery in areas of its jurisdiction, "especially in the District of

Columbia," and to prevent slavery's spread into "any State that may be hereafter admitted" to the Union. Once they agreed upon the constitution, officers were selected. Campbell was named president of the society, Gilliland was vice president, and Rankin assumed the role of secretary for the first year. They determined that they would meet annually on December 25, with their first meeting scheduled for the following month. In April, they selected their delegates to the annual Ohio Anti-Slavery Society convention set to be held in Granville, Ohio at the end of the month. They selected Rankin to serve as a delegate. Rankin had become accustomed to the threat of violence throughout 1835. Nonetheless, the Granville convention would soon test the limits and patience of all the abolitionists.[104]

* * * * *

In late April, nearly two hundred delegates from Ohio's 120 local anti-slavery societies traveled across the state to reach Granville. Not far from Putnam and Zanesville, where many of them met a year earlier to form the society, Granville was and still is a neighboring community of Newark, Ohio. It is a quaint community that, at the time, had strong anti-slavery sentiments. These sentiments were offset by fears of mob violence that would surely occur as the abolitionists opened their convention. It was out of these fears that the mayor, council members, and several other notable citizens signed a proclamation urging the abolitionists to stay away from their community. Several anti-abolitionist and pro-slavery communities circled Granville, and they were sure to come out in protest once the convention took place. Tensions had risen significantly in the wake of the great postal campaign. To avoid any unwanted violence within the community, the abolitionists gathered outside the town in a barn they christened the "Hall of Freedom." Many of the founding fathers of the Ohio Anti-Slavery Society had arrived at the barn ready to continue their work. Asa Mahan was there, as was James G. Birney, who now operated the anti-slavery newspaper he called *The Philanthropist* near Cincinnati. Many of the Lane Rebels once again gathered, including Dresser. For many in attendance, these conventions weren't just an opportunity to advance their sacred cause, they provided a rare opportunity for friends from across the state to see each other once more.

The convention got started in the morning on April 27, largely without incident. Several resolutions were read and discussed by men like Birney and James A. Thome. In contrast to the Putnam convention, however, the Granville convention had added layers of security. The road to the barn was blocked by a large gate locked with a heavy chain. In addition, there were guards to warn and protect the delegates, should any mobs begin to form. As the second day got underway, Birney and other delegates suggested the society raise $5,000 for organizational operations over the next year. Delegates from across the states started passing bills forward until they easily surpassed the goal. A new call was made for $10,000, which they raised just $500 shy of. Following a few other resolutions, Rankin delivered an address at the convention, titled "An address to the churches in relation to slavery." This matter had ached in his heart ever since he was a young minister in eastern Tennessee. "The duty of the church, on the subject of slavery," he opened his address, "must be determined by sacred Scriptures." As he spoke, he made routine arguments against the so-called biblical case in favor of slavery. "That there was a kind of servitude allowed in Israel, must be admitted," Rankin conceded. But the servitude in ancient Israel was limited and voluntary. As he provided a detailed history of biblical servitude, he resolutely refuted the notion that the oppressive system of American slavery was anything like that which ancient Israel experienced. "Whatever rights the first man had, all his children must have," Rankin proclaimed. "God created no slaves." Slavery, therefore, was a sin against God, and thus any churches that accepted slavery as a just institution are in rebellion with God's word. "It is the duty of the church to exclude all slaveholders from her communities," he proclaimed. As his writings had done a decade earlier with his *Letters on Slavery*, Rankin's speech filled the convention with a spirit of defiance against the slave powers. They were ready to vanquish this great evil spirit from the land. As Rankin closed, he looked to eternity. "Union in the great work will prepare the church for the rising of millennium glory, when liberty shall be universal, and the song of redeeming love shall ascend from every tongue, 'Glory to God in the highest, and on earth, peace, good will toward men.'" After cheers and applause, the convention voted to send a copy of Rankin's speech to every minister in Ohio.[105]

As Rankin elevated the spirits of the convention, the streets of Granville became agitated. Pro-slavery residents from nearby towns had filled many of the taverns in anticipation of the abolitionists eventually making their way to the town. As tensions continued to build, protest mobs began to form. It was at this point that the convention adjourned, and the delegates had to find a safe way home without being waylaid by the ruffians in town. Notably, there were about fifty women at the convention, many of whom lived in a boarding house on the other side of town. To protect the women from being assaulted by the mob, the delegates and attendees formed a column around them. The bigger, stronger men were placed on the ends. Once they were in position, they went into town together, as one movement. The mob was waiting for them as they passed the gated barn road entrance. They began to pelt the abolitionists with rotten eggs and obscenities. As they made their way to the boarding house, they kept a steady pace, careful not to show the mob any signs of fear. The mob noticed that they were trying to protect the women, who then became their direct target. After being targeted with eggs, the mob's violence accelerated. They started grabbing and pulling the women. The men in the column didn't tolerate this. In one instance, as a ruffian pushed one of the women into the mud, her male escort knocked him out with one punch, allegedly having a stone in his fist. Protesters and abolitionists alike began throwing punches. For the abolitionists, it was self-defense. For the protesters, it was drunken rage. After the women were delivered to the boarding house, the abolitionists scattered, trying to get back on the road as safely as possible. As the "Granville riot" concluded, Birney mounted his horse, which had since been bobbed by the protesters.

Refusing to give the mob any satisfaction, he pridefully strode through town at a steady pace as eggs and rocks were thrown at him. It wasn't until he finally reached the edge of Granville that he picked up speed and headed back to Cincinnati.[106]

* * * * *

The Granville Riot left the abolitionists in a dour mood that spring. As Rankin traveled back to Ripley with his colleagues, he had more to stress over than most. Traveling around the state had not been kind to his health. He was constantly catching a cold or running a fever in early 1836. The stress of being away from his family didn't help matters either. Money was a constant worry, and the more he traveled the less he could ensure the family farm would bring in a rich bounty that year. Many of his children were also at an age when they would most need a father figure. Moreover, he had a wife and newborn waiting for him at home. Jean had given birth to their eighth son. They named him after the abolitionist philanthropist who funded their postal campaign over the past year; Arthur Tappan Rankin was born on March 5, 1836.

As Rankin continued his journey returning to Ripley with the Brown County delegation, Birney was not far away heading toward Cincinnati. His name around the city had grown, and not in a positive light. The abolitionist and former slaveholder from Kentucky was seen as a troublemaker, especially by the business class in Cincinnati. He had recently moved his printing press deeper into the city, which meant his abolitionist rhetoric would be heard more frequently. Inspired by his activities in Granville and Putnam, Birney was animated to ensure the abolitionist message would take hold throughout his community. He would use his voice in *The Philanthropist* to shame southern slave-holders, specifically in his native Kentucky. This only escalated tensions between him and the anti-abolitionist community. Many white citizens of the city viewed Birney as a dire threat, thinking he might attract more like him and turn Cincinnati into an anti-slavery hub. This would surely sour the relations that many businessmen had with southern slaveholders. Furthermore, it may influence black residents to feel as if they should be on equal footing as whites. Before the Granville convention, a Cincinnati riot broke out targeting black families. Concerned by the perception that black community members were threatening the jobs of their white neighbors, a mob burned down a tenement building in April, killing many black people in the process. As spring turned to summer, tensions continued to grow between Birney and the anti-abolitionists. On July 5, Birney spoke to an Independence Day gathering of African Americans. His presence at the event was seen as inflammatory to many of the whites in Cincinnati, especially in wake of the April riots. Tired of Birney's growing influence, a few dozen men broke into Birney's printing press and destroyed it on July 12.

To the dismay of the men, Birney would prove more difficult to get rid of than they had expected. The destruction of his press was an unfortunate setback, but one that the Ohio Anti-Slavery Society would quickly help him overcome. The estimated damages amounted to approximately $1,500. The Executive Committee of the Ohio Anti-Slavery Society guaranteed $2,000 to ensure the continuation of the publication of *The Philanthropist*. Three days after the break-in, the paper was back in print. On July 17, matters worsened. A bounty of $1,000 was placed on Birney as a "Fugitive of Justice." Place cards scattered across city street corners stated that "the above sum will be paid for the delivery of one James G. Birney, a fugitive from justice, now abiding in the city of Cincinnati. Said Birney in all his associations and feelings is black; although his external appearance is white." Upon his capture and delivery, payment would be made without question by a man with the alias of "Old Kentucky." A well-attended meeting took place on July 23, 1836, to address the recent wave of civil and racial unrest. This meeting quickly became overrun by the anti-abolitionists. It was filled with prominent community members and city leaders who vowed to use every legal measure to prevent the spread of *The Philanthropist* and similar publications. They presented Birney with a formal request to immediately cease production of his paper and subdue his abolitionist impulses. In face of this mounting adversity, Birney stood firm, refusing to shut his paper down.[107]

As word spread of the attempt to silence Birney and the abolitionists, some citizens of Cincinnati were appalled by the abuse of civil authority and influence. Notably, a young lawyer named Salmon P. Chase reacted to the meeting by stating that "freedom of the press and constitutional liberty must live or perish together." Chase was not yet an abolitionist during the summer of 1836. Even as he became a fierce opponent of slavery, he would hesitate to use that term to describe his views. He was, however, a strong proponent of the rule of law. Chase viewed the threats against Birney from the city officials as being subservient to mob-rule. A week later, on July 30, a mob again formed and destroyed Birney's printing press. The crowd rampaged, attacking Cincinnati's black community and destroying property along the way. The riots continued the next night. As they circled the hotel where they believed Birney was hiding, Chase appeared out front and informed them, "calmly but resolutely, that no one could pass." The mob obliged, and they dispersed.[108] Chase was repulsed by the riots, and the inaction from the city officials left him with "disgust and horror." The Ohio Anti-Slavery Society refused to sit back and let riotous mobs prevent abolitionists from exercising their freedom of speech and press. The society and Birney himself hired Chase in two separate lawsuits against the leaders of the mobs for damages. Chase knew that representing them in their lawsuits would provoke the anti-abolition crowds to view him as an enemy. He knew it would likely cost him clientele. However, Chase's sense of duty overcame any worry of personal loss. "A man must perform his duty and leave consequences to Him, who requires the duty." Chase won the case for Birney and the owners of *The Philanthropist*. More importantly, a long and fruitful friendship formed between the two, which would be incredibly beneficial to the anti-slavery cause.[109]

James G. Birney was often the target of mob violence, but he wasn't deterred. John Rankin would frequently contribute editorials to *the Philanthropist*, Birney's Cincinnati paper.

* * * * *

News of the riots targeting Birney was met with outrage by the Ripley Anti-Slavery Society. During an August 11 meeting at the Red Oak Church, the society voted on resolutions that "would take into consideration the alarming state of things occasioned by the spirit of mobocracy that is abroad in the land and especially the late proceedings of the mob at Cincinnati." Led by Gilliland and Campbell, they resolved that "the origin of this disgraceful affair" is the result of "the nature and system of slavery," not abolitionist rhetoric, as many anti-abolitionists claimed. They also placed the violence at the feet of Cincinnati's high society. As they continued, they resolved that "we do not view the getting up of the late mob in Cincinnati to be the act and doing of the honest industrious, and laboring class of our fellow citizens; but the deliberate working of a few wealthy aristocrats combined with a few Orlean traders and principle mechanicks who are interested in trade with slaveholders." It was a handful of business leaders who financially gained from trade and cooperation with slaveholders who instigated the riots, they declared. It was those who instigated that must be held most responsible. In the Cincinnati riots, the Ripley Anti-Slavery Society found a real-time example of one of Rankin's earliest arguments against slavery. "The love of gain first introduced slavery into the world, and has been its constant support in every age." Since Rankin first wrote these words to his brother in 1824, the abolitionists believed these words to ring truer than ever. Before closing the meeting, the society agreed to a resolution of approval in favor of the Ohio Anti-Slavery Society's lawsuit, "refusing to surrender the right to publish the Philanthropist." They then raised $156.50 supporting the re-establishment of the paper.[110]

While Rankin's spirit and influence were present during the August 1836 meeting of the Ripley Anti-Slavery Society, he was physically absent. In July, Rankin joined a group dubbed "The Seventy."[111] Taking inspiration from the Great Revival that influenced Rankin when he was just a boy, this group of speakers sought to ignite the same kind of fever in opposition to slavery within local communities. Sparking this kind of abolitionist revival in 1836 was dangerous for those involved. In the wake of the "mobocracy" that had gripped the country, Rankin yet again risked his health and potentially his life to support the abolitionist cause. The election of 1836 heightened political tensions. President Jackson had decided not to run for a third term, and onlookers wondered how long Jacksonianism could continue without him. Many Jacksonians, especially in states that bordered slavery and freedom, began to worry that abolitionists may start securing political power in such a transitory phase of American politics. As Rankin continued to speak throughout Ohio, mobs were never far behind. On several occasions in neighboring Adams County, mobs formed around the venues as he spoke. Horses were bobbed as he lectured, in hopes that one of them would be his. Now familiar with mob tactics, Rankin kept his horse on the other side of town to protect them. Still, as he tried to travel to and from his lectures, he was met with resistance. On one occasion, after being imbued with drunken confidence, a pro-slavery protester armed with a club attempted to hit him. Rankin later wrote that "a gentleman rose up between us and gave him to understand he must strike over him. This prevented any violence to me."[112] For all these reasons, many community members in Ripley opposed his activities in the anti-slavery society. They believed that it opened Rankin to unnecessary safety risks when he was also needed in their community. His responsibilities still included his church, his school, and his family. For many, Rankin was the soul of Ripley. He provided a much-needed center of gravity to a town that just a decade ago was soiled with scoundrels. If something happened to Rankin, what would happen to their community?

Rankin was cautious of the ever-present threats, but he continued to press on in service of the anti-slavery cause. He had a sense of duty driven by his belief that God was calling him to lend his hand toward the annihilation of slavery from the land of the free. His speaking tour paused in October of 1836. He returned to help his son, Adam Lowry Rankin, settle into his first semester at Lane Seminary. Lowry's first choice was Andover Theological Seminary in Massachusetts but his father's anti-slavery activities meant that money was tight. Lane was a much more affordable option. Rankin and Lowry agreed that Lane would be the best option, despite the controversy over the Lane Rebels a few years before. Rankin moved beyond the controversy over the Lane Rebels in part because of his friendship with the president, Lyman Beecher. Lyman's daughter, Harriet Beecher, had married a professor at the school, Calvin Stowe. Rankin joined his son to meet with President Beecher and Professor Stowe in the fall of 1836, going over his classes. Benjamin F. Templeton, the student Rankin personally tutored in his home to ensure his continued enrollment at Ripley College, had also enrolled at Lane for the semester. Rankin instructed his son to keep a watchful eye out for Templeton, fearing what his presence might incite in a city already ravaged by anti-abolitionist and anti-black mobs.[113]

Lowry assured his father he would not only look out for Templeton, but also for runaway slaves from Kentucky on their journey north toward Canada. During his time at Lane, motivated by his vow to fight slavery and inspired by the abolitionist history at the seminary, Lowry followed in his father's footsteps. He was active in the Underground Railroad early on in his time at Lane. Not a month went by before Lowry was contacted by an agent of the Underground Railroad to assist a slave escape to a safehouse twenty-five miles away. The home was the property of an anti-slavery Quaker, William Butterworth. The transfer required expediency. There was a $500 bounty for the slave's capture, and several parties were on the hunt around Cincinnati. The longer the slave remained, the more at risk he was. The young Rankin took on the challenge. Under the veil of night, Lowry transported the fugitive slave to the safehouse twenty-five miles out, then rode twenty-five miles back to return the horse. Upon completion of the mission, he walked an additional two miles back to his dorm at Lane. He started and completed the herculean transport mission by himself, all on the same night, making it back to his bed before dawn. Nobody at Lane knew any better. He wouldn't always be so lucky.

Many at Lane Seminary grew suspicious of Lowry's activities. They began to conclude that he was involved in the Underground Railroad, but lacked evidence. One professor, Reverend Baxter Dickinson, was a pro-slavery member of the faculty at Lane. As Lowry was increasingly absent, Dickinson took note. Lowry's father's reputation was strong, it wasn't impossible to believe Lowry's absences were related to the Underground Railroad. Despite Dickinson's suspicion and bias against Rankin, he could never find definitive proof of Lowry's activities. This would not be the case for Stowe. Lowry suspected that both Stowe and his wife, Harriet, were aware and, to some degree, supportive of his work on the Underground Railroad. An encounter in early 1837 confirmed these beliefs. In April, Lowry again agreed to help a fugitive slave flee to safety further north. It was a much damper night than his first mission in October, and he could feel sickness setting in. This time, he also had no support system. Lowry was entirely by himself, without even a horse to hasten his journey. Desperate, he took a gamble that Stowe knew of and supported his anti-slavery activities. Lowry knocked on his door and "frankly told him" the situation he was in.

After some initial back and forth, Lowry recounted their conversation. Stowe looked at him and said, "'Brother Rankin, you ought not to be out in the night air; it is too damp for a man as unwell as you are. It is equally true you cannot keep the poor fellow in safety this close to the city.' 'What can I do,' I asked, 'but venture the going afoot? The risk would be less. I might not be disturbed so early tomorrow morning if I kept to the wood. The Miami River we will have to wade.' After some reflection, Professor Stowe replied, 'No, you must not do that. I see no other way out of the difficulty but for me to take my horse and carriage and go myself. If you will give me specific directions as to the way, I will try and make the trip.'"

After he received some much-needed rest, Lowry awoke to see Stowe return near daybreak. He was drenched. As he rushed over to check on him, Stowe lectured the young Rankin out of frustration. "If it had not been for the efficient assistance of your colored friend, Lane Seminary would have had one professor less today young man," Stowe remarked as Lowry stood silently. "Just think of you being the cause of my death. And think how this community would be horrified when it learned a professor in Lane Theological Seminary was drowned while 'stealing niggers.'" Lowry didn't say a word as Stowe forced him to confront the dangers of this business, and how many people it affected. "Just this of the scandal you would have brought on me and the institution I represent. Do you think the city rabble would have in the present temper of popular feeling have left one of the seminary buildings standing?" Then, having burned through his frustration after his first dangerous night on the Underground Railroad, Stowe's temperament turned from irritation to satisfaction. "Well," he confessed, "I'm glad I only got a good ducking. Also that I got the fellow safely to your station." The young Rankin was relieved. Stowe was safe and the mission was a success. Just as importantly, he was comforted to know that he had a key ally in the faculty at Lane. "I was grateful to know that I could depend upon Dr. Stowe in any future emergency," Lowry later wrote. He would be careful to seek his assistance sparingly. During his time at Lane, Adam Lowry Rankin would assist in more than three hundred missions on the Underground Railroad.[114]

Professor Calvin E. Stowe, husband to Harriet Beecher Stowe, was a cautious yet indispensable ally to Adam Lowry Rankin during his time at Lane Seminary.

* * * * *

A few months later, Rankin had completed his year-long tour as part of "The Seventy" and returned to Ripley. The community, his congregation, and his family all celebrated his return. By all measures, it was a success. New societies were popping up all over the state—but it came with a toll. Rankin had little rest during his tour and was experiencing a severe cough, so bad that many became very worried for him. Thankfully, he was able to slow down after returning to Ripley and recovered shortly after. In August, a terrible discovery was made. A free black woman and member of the Ripley Anti-Slavery Society named Eliza Jane Johnson was kidnapped from her cottage in Brown

County, Ohio. Arthur Fox, the sheriff of Mason County, Kentucky, had sent out slave hunters to reclaim a woman who had run away from him. Johnson had been in Ohio for at least three years, but she was not a runaway from Fox. However, it would be nearly impossible for a kidnapped black woman to prove her freedom in a slave state like Kentucky. Johnson was an easy target. As a group of neighboring residents of Sardinia, Ohio discovered the scene of Johnson's kidnapping, they sprung into action, hoping to intercept the kidnappers before they crossed into Kentucky. John B. Mahan was among the rescue party, and soon, Lowry would also join the pursuit. The kidnappers took the long route to the river in hopes of avoiding the abolitionist hubs of Red Oak and Ripley. This gave the rescuers an advantage. The head of the party, William G. Kephart, was set to reach the river first and intercept them before they crossed. There were only four kidnappers, but six rescuers, so the odds were favorable that Johnson could be saved. Before he could intercept them, Kephart's horse caught on a tree root. As the horse fell, Kephart was flung off, injuring him badly after falling on a rock. Two of the kidnappers seized the opportunity. They grabbed Johnson and jumped on the ferry after they "raised a shout of victory." There was a brief standoff between the rescue party and the remaining kidnappers on the banks of the Ohio River. The rescuers had a writ of authority from Ripley to arrest the kidnappers once intercepted. The kidnappers weren't keen on being arrested and threatened to shoot the first person who tried. After some tense moments, the remaining members of the rescue party arrived, after ensuring Kephart's health and safety. Seeing that they were outnumbered and outgunned, the kidnappers surrendered. They were arrested and sent back to Ripley for trial. As Lowry returned to Ripley, several "ruffians" who had observed the pursuit at a distance approached him. "She was a runaway nigger," one shouted at him. They began to form a crowd around him as their irritation by Lowry's part in the pursuit accelerated. Putting on a bold face, Lowry confronted them head-on. "That only makes the meanness more apparent," he countered. "There is a legal way to return runaway slaves. That you know would not be successful so you would steal a poor, helpless woman and sell her. All woman thieves are cowards." As the man prepared to strike at Lowry, some of his friends intervened and gave him a ride back, removing Lowry from the situation[115]

Johnson's kidnapping set the abolitionist ablaze with outrage. Many wondered openly how harmony between the states could be preserved as residents of one state, supported by the law, could blatantly kidnap residents of another without repercussions. "Can friendship between the States be maintained," asked the *Cincinnati Journal* and *Luminary,* "while such outrages are perpetrated by private citizens, and then sustained by the civil authorities?"[116] Johnson sat in a jail cell in Mason County, waiting for Fox to claim her. As Fox arrived, he realized that his slave hunters had made a mistake. Still, there was an opportunity. If nobody claimed her within a year, he could sell her into slavery and use the proceeds to cover the cost of her incarceration. Johnson had much to worry about. Fortunately for her, the Ripley conductors and members of the anti-slavery society knew of her status and were prepared to fight for her freedom.[117]

Rankin joined several colleagues from Ripley and Sardinia to travel to Mason County and demand a *habeas-corpus* hearing. Rankin's presence in Mason County with his colleagues created controversy. Many in the region viewed Rankin as the thief, trying to take a slave away from her master. His effort to bring Johnson back to freedom would bring about new enemies, the likes of which would make the northern mobs appear tame in comparison. They successfully secured the hearing, and after receiving testimony, Mason County Judge Walker Reid made his decision. "For the present, Eliza Jane Johnson is remanded to the jail as a runaway slave. The law will not justify me in discharging her."[118] This was a blow to Rankin and the Ripley abolitionists. However, there was still time to turn things around. Johnson had to remain in her cell in Mason County for the remainder of the year before she could be sold into slavery. They now sought the assistance of the Ohio legislature.

In the eyes of many, the Johnson case was more than a kidnapping. It could ignite an open state of warfare between Ohio and Kentucky. Some welcomed the prospect, including those in high positions of authority. Senator Thomas Morris of Ohio visited Alexander Campbell in Ripley a few months after Judge Reid's decision, and he was irate. He was alleged to have claimed that "war ought to be immediately declared against Kentucky and that every Kentuckian should be shot down so soon as he set his foot on the Ohio side." Hoping to clarify his position, he had a letter to Campbell printed in *The Philanthropist* detailing his official thoughts on the matter. "It would by the nation whose sovereignty was thus violated be considered just cause of WAR and I am well convinced that if the scene in Ripley is to be enacted over again…it would eventually lead to a nonintercourse between states…."[119] Over the fall and winter, more people speculated war between Ohio and Kentucky, so long as slave hunters were permitted to kidnap Ohio residents without consequence. The only reasonable course of action was for the governor of Ohio to open negotiations with the governor of Kentucky for Johnson's release. The Ohio legislature passed a resolution urging just that. "Resolved, that His Excellency the Governor be, and he is hereby requested to open a correspondence with the Governor of Kentucky, in relation to the illegal seizure and forcible removal of said Eliza Jane Johnson from Brown County, Ohio to Mason County, Kentucky…and that he respectfully insists on the restoration of said Eliza Jane Johnson to the enjoyment of freedom and friends."[120] By March 1838, the circuit court of Mason County issued an order, stating, "It is now considered by the court that there being no just grounds that the said Eliza Jane Johnson is a slave, it is ordered that she be released and discharged from the custody of the jailer of Mason County." The next day, Johnson was back on the Ohio side of the river, celebrating her freedom with her friends and family in Ripley.[121]

Despite the victory, Rankin was not in a celebratory mood. While he was relieved that Johnson was back in Ohio and saved from the clutches of slavery, the fact that it took threat of warfare between Ohio and Kentucky fiercely concerned him. Had slavery truly blackened the souls of his southern brethren so much that further bloodshed was the only way to force them to release a woman who should by all accounts be considered free? He wrote about his concerns in *The Philanthropist*.

If Johnson was released before her case was brought to the Ohio legislature, he wrote, "We should have a higher sense both of their justice and humanity. Ought not the state of Ohio…demand full justice? Can the people of Mason County sustain a character for honesty, if they refuse to pay reasonable damages?"[122] Rankin didn't believe that the case was truly closed until she was compensated for the violation of her liberties. Compensation never came. The people of Mason County remained bitter over Rankin and the other Ripley abolitionists for threatening the stability of the slave system in their state. In their view, they were the ones who deserved compensation. If Rankin and the Ripley abolitionists were allowed to get away with this, they might threaten the stability of slavery, not just in Kentucky, but everywhere. By April, notices were made throughout northern Kentucky for the apprehension or assassination of several Brown County abolitionists. John B. Mahan, Dr. Alexander Campbell, Dr. Isaac Beck of Sardinia, and of course, John Rankin, were wanted dead or alive in return for rewards up to $2,500.[123]

* * * * *

By the time Eliza Jane Johnson was released from her Mason County jail cell, the abolitionists had made their impact on the trajectory of American politics. No longer were they a small group of irrelevant moralists relegated to church pulpits. Now, they were organized. Members of the American Anti-Slavery Society and its several state and local auxiliary societies held office in state legislatures and even in Congress. Joshua Giddings, a founding member of the Ohio Anti-Slavery Society, was elected to the US House of Representatives in 1838. In Congress, he repeatedly joined former president and now congressman John Quincy Adams in opposing the infamous "gag rule," which prevented the reading of petitions dealing with slavery. Both men viewed this as a blatant violation of the freedom of speech and the right to petition. After the "Great Postal Campaign," petitions to Congress concerning slavery exploded in quantity. Many of them demanded slavery's abolition in the District of Columbia and areas where it had direct jurisdiction. This was through the direct influence of growing anti-slavery societies, which committed to drafting petitions "for the abolition of slavery, and the slave trade, in the District of Columbia…." By 1835, Congress had received over 34,000 petitions related to slavery. By the time Giddings arrived in Congress, the number had exploded to more than 300,000 petitions. Adams, an anti-slavery man himself but cautious not to fully embrace the label of abolitionist, was determined to have these petitions received, even if he stood alone. Rankin and the Ripley abolitionists profoundly counted themselves among the thousands who flooded Congress with appeals to abolish slavery where it had the jurisdiction to do so.[124]

As the abolitionists rose in influence, the anti-abolitionists rose in anger. Mob violence continued as a staple of the late 1830s, and few incidences were worse than the murder of Elijah P. Lovejoy. In 1836, Lovejoy, who was a Presbyterian minister and printer, had his printing press ransacked and destroyed by a group angry at his anti-slavery editorials, similar to the destruction of Birney's press in Cincinnati. Lovejoy moved from St. Louis, Missouri to Alton, Illinois, where he reopened his press. Illinois was a free state, similar to Ohio, and Lovejoy had hoped it might allow him more freedom to express his anti-slavery beliefs than he had in Missouri. He was mistaken. There was strong anti-abolitionist sentiment in Illinois, and they were determined to silence Lovejoy, no matter the cost. Lovejoy would not be intimidated, stating on November 2, 1837, that "as long as I am an American citizen, and as long as American blood runs in these veins, I shall hold myself at liberty to speak, to write and to publish whatever I please, being amenable to the laws of my country for the same." Four days later, a mob formed around the warehouse storing his printing press with the intent to destroy it. Lovejoy was determined to defend his press and his right to speak against the mob, no matter the risk. A standoff ensued, and before long, a firefight erupted. The mob began shooting into the warehouse, and Lovejoy returned fire with the men helping him protect the press. During the firefight, Lovejoy was struck by five bullets, killing him in the early hours of November 7.[125]

It was a somber reminder of the risks associated with involvement in the abolitionist movement. What happened to Elijah Lovejoy could have easily happened to James G. Birney in Cincinnati, or Theodore Weld as he went about his speaking tour, or even John Rankin. As the Ripley Anti-Slavery Society met for their annual meeting, they issued a resolution declaring Lovejoy a "Martyr to liberty," the city of Alton "a disgrace to the nation," and that "the freedom of the press and of speech is the inalienable right of all classes of human beings…." Furthermore, they asserted that "slavery has abolished both the liberty of speech and of the press in the slave states, and is attempting to do the same in the free states."[126] Rankin grew in despair and anxiety over the direction the country was headed. The writing seemed to be on the wall that only a violent conflict would result in slavery's abolition. As much of an abolitionist as he was, he was horrified by this notion. Not even six months after Lovejoy's murder did Rankin find an assassination bounty on his head. Because of his commitment to the cause of abolition, Rankin took extra precautions to protect himself and his family. The people of Ripley were on the frontlines of a local war over slavery that predated the Civil War by nearly three decades. Rankin and his fellow conductors weren't going to be intimidated into submission, but they would have to look out for one another like never before. Knowing the dangers of the days ahead, Rankin sought guidance from the Almighty, praying for strength as he faced the worsening conflict against slavery.

FRONT LINES
1838–1840
VII.

I t was late in the evening when John Thompson Rankin (or John Jr.) heard his father call for him downstairs. He knew it was urgent by the way he was called, both he and his older brother, Richard Calvin Rankin, were needed promptly. As they hurried downstairs, the situation became clear. There, sitting around the fire, was a black woman, drenched and shivering, baby in her arms. It was February 1838, and while the Rankin boys were accustomed to fugitive slaves coming to their home for help, they were nonetheless surprised to see the woman and her baby in their living room that evening. John Rankin looked at his boys and explained that she had "crossed the river on the ice!" The boys were stunned to the point of disbelief. "She couldn't have," one of them replied. "But she did!" insisted their father.[127]

In modern times, it can be difficult to imagine the Ohio River in such a state. Rarely does it remain cold long enough for ice to form, let alone grow to such an extent that someone could cross the river by foot. In 1977, twenty-eight days of negative temperatures froze the river from bank to bank, up to twelve inches thick.[128] There have been a handful of similar occurrences throughout the twentieth century. In one particularly dramatic instance, navigation was suspended on the river for 64 days from December 10, 1917, to February 12, 1918.[129] In the nineteenth century, though, ice clogging the river was a more common occurrence. Earlier in the winter of 1838, the river had frozen for almost ten days. The youth of Ripley seized the opportunity to go out and skate on the ice. It was so thick that a horse and sleigh were brought out for enjoyment. As fun as it could be for the ambitious skaters, it was also risky. The ice could break at any moment, consuming anyone who dared to venture out too far. By the time Rankin had opened his home to their guest, the river had already started to break up. No longer a continuous plane, the woman would have crossed the icy river by jumping from ice sheet to ice sheet with her child in her arms. If the woman and her child hadn't been curled up by the fire in their own house, the Rankin boys wouldn't believe it. How bad must her situation have been to attempt what under normal circumstances would be considered a suicide mission?

Winter brought about anxiety for slaveholders and conductors alike. As the river froze, fugitives were emboldened to cross the divide, reach Ohio, and begin their mad sprint to Canada in pursuit of freedom. For conductors in Ripley, it meant a season of danger. Fugitives would often show up to their doors in the dead of night seeking help. Involvement in the Underground Railroad carried severe risk and demanded the utmost secrecy. The longer a fugitive slave remained at a conductor's home, the more likely they would be caught. On the other side of the river, slaveholders worked against the clock, moving quickly to intercept runaway slaves before they made it to Ripley. The town was infamous as the location where slaves went to never be found by their masters again. Often, hunters would already be on the Ohio side of the river, waiting to snatch fugitives and return them to bondage. For slaves, however, winter, ice on the river, symbolized the only window for freedom they could hope for.

* * * * *

As the woman sat by the Rankin's fireplace, she recounted her story to them. Rankin, Jean, and their sons listened attentively with astonishment.

The woman fled from her master near Dover, Kentucky, upon discovering that he had planned to sell her and her two-year-old. Any dream of escape, she believed, would evaporate if they were sent further south. As the river froze solid, she realized she had a small but meaningful window to cross over to Ohio and become lost through the network of conductors on the Underground Railroad. She seized her moment, escaping from her master's farm in the dead of winter. The threat of death was never far away, but the hope of freedom gave her the motivation to push through. She reached the cabin of an old man on the Kentucky side of the river, where she stopped after her escape. There, the old man sheltered her and allowed her to eat. He explained to her that the river was starting to thaw and that crossing it was perilous, both for herself and her child. Even if she didn't fall through the ice, he explained, they may still freeze to death under the harsh condition. This, of course, was assuming she didn't get caught first. Suddenly, dogs barking in the distance interrupted their conversation. Slave hunters were tracking her, not far behind. They both knew that she would confront the risk of crossing the river if it meant securing her freedom. The man gave her a blanket to wrap her child with and sent her on her way.

As she reached the river, the gravity of her situation began to set in. The sound of ice cracking and grinding along the riverbank against the backdrop of darkness was haunting. As the barking dogs intensified, she knew she must commit to her plan. Stepping on thin ice, her foot broke into the cold, harsh waters of the Ohio River. Terrified, she looked to the hilltop behind Ripley and saw Rankin's house. On that hilltop, she knew she would find her salvation. She picked herself up and continued across the river, stumbling frequently as the ice buckled beneath her. Rankin's home on Liberty Hill inspired her to keep going. She dashed quickly yet carefully across the thawing river. Abruptly, the moment she feared finally came. The ice broke beneath her as she plunged into the freezing river. She let out a scream easily recognized as that of a fugitive attempting their luck across the ice. Acting quickly, she tossed her infant on the ice as she climbed out of the water. Both were alive, but time was of the essence before more ice gave way. She stumbled three times as she crossed, shivering, before she finally leaped onto the Ohio side of the river, instantly collapsing with relief and exhaustion. She should be dead, but both she and her child had made it to Ohio's frozen but free soil. As they laid on the ground, the woman was overcome with emotion. But she was still in great danger. She couldn't remain on the banks of the river; she must make the climb uphill to Rankin's house.

ELIZA CROSSES THE OHIO ON THE FLOATING ICE.

A fugitive slave woman, later dubbed "Eliza," crossing the ice-covered Ohio River with her child in her arm. Though slave hunters were in hot pursuit, she was determined to reach Ripley and escape to freedom.

As she tripped and trembled, trying to get up, a man's hand was extended to her. She looked up in terror, gripping her child close to her breast as she cowered away from the mysterious man. This was a slave hunter, she thought to herself. She had risked her life across the river only to be caught on the other side. After crossing, she had hardly the energy to finish her journey, let alone run away or fight. She sat and waited for her capture with great anxiety, until he spoke up. "Any woman who crossed that river carrying her baby has won her freedom," he said. She was stunned but relieved. The gruff man that stood before her with his hand extended wasn't capturing but helping her. He brought her through the back alleys of Ripley, careful not to risk discovery while helping a fugitive slave escape. At the foot of the hill, he pointed her up to Rankin's home, where she found the door unlocked and Jean Rankin ready to help the moment she walked through.

Little did this woman know, the man who helped her find her way to Rankin's home was indeed there to capture her, as she suspected. Skilled and experienced in hunting fugitives, Chancey Shaw was the perfect stereotype for an American scoundrel. He had been arrested no fewer than two times and had a reputation for enjoying his whiskey a little too much. He faced no moral dilemma in snuffing out the hope of freedom from a runaway slave. He had returned fugitives back to the South several times before. As he patrolled the banks of the Ohio River on that cold night in February 1838, it was just another job for him. But as Shaw witnessed the spirit of this woman risking not only her life, but the life of her infant child, over the mere chance that she might make it to freedom, something stirred in him. He was likely alerted to her presence when the ice broke from underneath her. Certainly, nobody would survive such a foolish trek. But as the minutes passed, he witnessed her complete her journey all the way to the Ohio side of the river. After seeing her do this impossible task, he decided that if anyone had earned the right to be free, it was this woman who collapsed at his feet.[130]

Rankin was particularly moved by this woman who now huddled in front of his fireplace. Such courage in pursuit of freedom had rarely been displayed. He helped hundreds of runaway slaves escape along the chain of the Underground Railroad. "Whole families, parents and children, were sheltered under my roof on their way to Canada," he later wrote. But it was this woman who seemed to have left a special impression on him. "While she was safe enough for the moment," John Jr. later wrote, the danger was "imminent as long as she remained with us." They made sure both she and her child were fed, dry, warm, and somewhat rested, but acted quickly. Before daybreak, the two Rankin boys helped her and her baby move further inland, away from the river where slave hunters swarmed. They took them to the home of James Gilliland, where they could stay the next day before being pushed further up the chain at night. As Calvin and John Jr. returned to their home, they crossed paths with a local man they knew was a slave hunter. When the boys asked him what he was doing, he replied that he was "jes coon huntin'." It was a close call.

When they returned home, the boys found both their parents still up. Their father was overcome with severe anxiety over the woman's safety. Developing a nervous tick, Rankin repeated to himself over and over, "I hope she gets away, hope she gets away." Fortunately, she was in good hands. The conductors at each station moved rapidly and efficiently to ensure that the woman and her child were safe. Eventually, she made her way to the home of Levi Coffin in Newport, Indiana, not far from the Ohio border. Coffin sheltered and fed her and her child before again moving her up the chain.[131] Her journey north continued into the spring when she and her infant finally reached Ontario. Rankin thought often about the woman who huddled around his fireplace in the winter of 1838. His friendship with the Stowes strengthened during this period, no doubt due to his son's attendance at Lane Seminary. When they got together, Rankin shared the story of the slave woman's perilous trek across the river. Calvin Stowe sat in astonishment, and his wife Harriet even more so. On several occasions, Harriet interjected Rankin's story with exclamations. "Terrible!" she would gasp. "How terrible!"[132]

* * * * *

While Kentucky and Ohio avoided outright war in the wake of the Eliza Jane Johnson case, Ripley often felt like the front lines of a great battle. Fugitive slaves passed through the town with roaring fervor. With them came an uptick of slave hunters, hoping to capture them before they were lost to the Underground Railroad. With a bounty on many of their heads, the Ripley conductors were especially careful. It was common for the occasional anti-abolitionist heckler to shout at Rankin, Dr. Alexander Campbell, or John B. Mahan when they were in public, eager to remind them and anyone in earshot that there was a reward for their capture or death. When a knock came in the night, there was as strong of a chance that bounty hunters, rather than fugitive slaves, stood waiting on the other side of the door. Conductors would often answer these knocks with a rifle in hand, or at least at an arm's length away. Rankin's hung just above his door.

Later that summer, Mahan faced the full fury of the slavocracy. A slaveholder by the name of William Greathouse had come to Ripley with a hoard of hunters by his side. Greathouse was certain that the abolitionists of Ripley knew where his slave was, and he was willing to use any and all means necessary to get him back. His suspicions weren't off base. Indeed, Adam Lowry Rankin, who was home from school for the summer, had pushed the slave up the chain to Mahan's station in Sardinia.[133] Rankin later recalled how Mahan agreed to harbor him, but "did not conceal him as closely as he should have done."[134] Rather than sending the fugitive up the chain the next night, Mahan felt it better to shelter him until Greathouse left Ohio. After some days, feeling as if the coast was clear, the fugitive walked around a little more publicly. Mahan hoped he would have the opportunity to relax before being sent to Canada. However, not only did Greathouse remain in Brown County, he was headed for Mahan's home. When word got out that Greathouse was heading to Sardinia, Mahan moved swiftly and pushed the fugitive up the line to Canada. By the time Greathouse arrived at Mahan's home, the slave Greathouse was after was on his way north. Though he was certain that Mahan knew of his whereabouts, he couldn't prove it. Hoping to secure evidence, Greathouse solicited the assistance of a colleague. The colleague was to disguise himself as an abolitionist and get the truth from Mahan. He went to Mahan's house in August with a black woman under the guise of trying to reunite her with her husband. Believing the man to be sincere, Mahan mentioned two fugitives who came through the area in the summer who might be the woman's husband. He wrote a note with instructions on where to go in hopes of reuniting the couple. "Send her to Mr. Johnson's, brother of the Rev. Hezekiah Johnson, ten miles north of Hillsborough, or Thomas Hibbens, at Wilmington," it read. He signed it "Yours, John B. Mahan[135]   The two visitors then rode off in the moonlight. Mahan believed they were off in search of the woman's husband. Instead, they rendezvoused with Greathouse, note in hand. He had exactly what he needed. Rankin later remembered that "by false swearing, [Greathouse] got in Kentucky an indictment against Mahan, and demanded him of the governor of Ohio." To the anger of abolitionists everywhere, the governor approved of the [136]

Mahan was arrested and extradited to Kentucky on September 17, 1838. His family and community hoped and fought for his safety and release, but there was much more at stake. His capture threatened to expose the entire chain. Every conductor from Ripley up all the way to Canada was in danger of being exposed. They could all be arrested for helping to aid and abet fugitive slaves. Rankin, Campbell, and the rest of the Ripley conductors faced the greatest risk.

John B. Mahan was a fellow conductor and friend to John Rankin. His imprisonment horrified abolitionists across the country, but especially in Ripley. His trial threatened to expose their entire underground railroad operation.

Rankin picked up his pen and wrote a letter urgently to *The Philanthropist*. "This is more alarming than even the case of Eliza Jane Johnson," wrote Rankin, keenly aware that this extraction took place almost a year to the day of Johnson's abduction. "It has occasioned no little excitement among the citizens of Brown County. They begin to feel that no one is safe any farther than he may have physical force to defend himself. What shall the end be? What protection of slavery lead men to do!!"[137] After running the story in *The Philanthropist*, news of Mahan's arrest and extraction spread like wildfire. *The Liberator* considered his imprisonment to be "even more alarming than the assassination of Lovejoy."[138] Lovejoy, after all, was murdered at the hands of a mob. Mahan, in contrast, was betrayed by the law itself. "MAHAN IN IRONS," wrote the paper a few weeks later. "Irons on a citizen of Ohio, the victim of perjury! What say our fellow citizens? Have they any regard for the sovereignty of their State?"[139] Once *The Liberator* got ahold of the story, it was the news across the country.

The Mahan trial commenced on November 12th, and Judge Walker Reid sat over the courtroom. About a year earlier, Reid ruled that Eliza Jane Johnson was to remain in jail as a fugitive slave. His ruling nearly brought about open warfare between Ohio and Kentucky. Now, he would determine the fate of yet another Brown County abolitionist. Mahan was charged with "the abduction of a negro, the property of William Greathouse from the State of Kentucky...." A charge of abduction, Mahan asserted, was absurd. Never once did he come to Kentucky trying to liberate slaves and send them to Canada. Furthermore, the evidence they held (Mahan's note) hardly proved his involvement in helping fugitive slaves. He pleaded "not guilty." The trial lasted about a week. After hearing arguments and testimony on both sides of the matter, Reid gave his opinion on the case. He believed that "the prisoner has not violated the law of Kentucky, unless he aided and assisted the slave in making his escape from the owner and possessor *here* (in Kentucky), to another state or foreign country." Just a few minutes after hearing the opinion, the jury issued their verdict: not guilty.[140]

Despite the verdict, Mahan was not yet free. Greathouse had also filed a civil suit against Mahan so that he would be compensated for the loss of his slave. Mahan couldn't be released until either Greathouse lost the suit or he paid the compensation, which amounted to $1,600. That was money that Mahan didn't have, so he waited in his jail cell. Relief finally came when a wealthy Brown County farmer, William Dunlop, posted Mahan's security, allowing for his release. Dunlop would pay Greathouse the compensation if the verdict was in his favor, and Mahan would pay Dunlop back by forfeiting all the property that he owned in Brown County. Dunlop assured him, however, that the Mahan family could still live on the property so long as he lived. The civil case would drag on for several years, and pulled the other Ripley conductors into the legal battle. The matter proved to be financially draining for Mahan, victory or not. Caring little about the justice of the case, this drain was what Greathouse truly hoped for—vengeance. Rankin later noted that while the criminal lawsuit was straining Mahan's health, the civil suit reduced him "to utter poverty."[141]

As the lawsuit stretched into 1839, all eyes were on the Ripley conductors. Rankin's hilltop home transformed from a beacon of hope for fugitive slaves to an open target. The Mahan trial may not have ended with him rotting his days away in a jail cell, but it did bring a significant amount of unwanted attention to the activities of all Ripley conductors. In the court of public opinion, Rankin and his allies didn't have the luxury of being considered innocent until proven guilty. In the eyes of hundreds of northern Kentucky slaveholders, Greathouse had provided all the evidence they needed. Conversations about the trial and abolitionism in general would intensify both locally and nationally. Rankin, Mahan, Campbell, and the others around Ripley threatened the southern way of life. A conflict with bloody potential brewed between Ripley and northern Kentucky.

In response to the rising stress over runaway slaves, the Ohio legislature passed the Ohio Fugitive Slave Act on February 26, 1839. This law included the penalty of up to six days in jail and a $500 fine for anyone who interfered with the capture of a fugitive slave or for anyone who aided a fugitive slave in their escape. Certainly, the Mahan trial was on the minds of many legislators who voted for this, especially as the civil case was ongoing. Southern slave forces did all they could to crush abolitionist efforts in Ripley. The conductors now understood that the law in Ohio would be against them as well.[142]

* * * * *

Although Rankin continually faced the threat of exposure, he proceeded in both his personal and professional life in 1839 and returned to teaching at Ripley College. Among his students at the school, in the winter of 1838/39, was a teenage Ulysses S. Grant. Born in nearby Georgetown, Ohio the same year Rankin crossed into Ripley, Grant later admitted to not being very "studious in habit" while at Ripley College. Still, he attentively listened as Rankin spoke, and would also hear him preach on many occasions. Rankin had become friends with Grant's family since before 1825. When Rankin's *Letters* were released in book form in Maysville, he could count on the support of Peter Grant, Ulysses' uncle. Peter, unfortunately, drowned in Wheeling, Virginia in 1829. It's likely that Peter's abolitionism had an influence on Grant's attitude toward slavery. Grant stayed with Peter's widow as he went to Maysville Academy in the winter of 1836/37. During his winter in Ripley, Grant had the unique opportunity to listen to one of the movement's most influential abolitionists teach and preach at the epicenter of Underground Railroad activity. It was that same winter that his father, Jesse Grant, revealed to him that he had applied for an appointment to West Point on Grant's behalf. There was little at this point to suggest that Grant would go on to lead the Grand Army of the Republic to victory against rebel forces in the bloodiest conflict in American history. In fact, he had no interest in pursuing a military career at all. When Jesse revealed that he obtained the appointment for his son, Grant's initial reaction was to protest. "But I won't go," he declared. His father insisted otherwise. Grant was to attend the academy in the fall. Although his time at Ripley College was short, Rankin would later take immense pride in the small role he played in Grant's formative years.[143]

Ulysses S. Grant as a 21-year-old man graduating from West Point. Just a few years earlier, in 1839, he was a student of John Rankin's at Ripley College.

* * * * *

In May 1839, Rankin made his way to New York City for the annual meeting of the American Anti-Slavery Society. The Ripley abolitionists were the talk of the town. The Mahan trial was fresh on everyone's mind, and Ohio's recent Fugitive Slave Act further enraged attendees. For many, Rankin was the godfather of abolitionism itself. His perspective was invaluable. As the meeting kicked off on May 7, 1839, Arthur Tappan took his seat as president of the society. Once the convention officially began, Rankin rose to address the events in Ripley over the past year. He opened by reflecting on his upbringing, how he was "brought up in the midst of slavery," and now resided "on the borders of a free State," where he looked "over upon the land of oppression" any time he gazed across the river.

"All my life, except seventeen years, has been spent in the slave States, and no person has more kindly feelings towards the slaveholding States than myself," he said. Unlike most of those at the convention, he came of age with southern neighbors, southern teachers, and southern ministers. "There (is where) my friends and kindred dwell." It pained Rankin still to see his southern brethren driven astray by the institution of slavery. They weren't evil as much as they were lost, in need of someone to show them the light. "I speak the language of kindness," Rankin told the convention, "and would do the utmost in my power to persuade them to put away an evil which threatens their destruction." These were the same sentiments that he possessed as he wrote to his brother Thomas about fourteen years earlier. Rankin was originally a southerner. He was proud of his heritage. He found God in the hills of eastern Tennessee, not Boston. He found his voice in the bluegrass fields of Kentucky, not Ohio. He became an abolitionist in the south, not the north. Rankin had a perspective that few in the convention possessed. He was uniquely qualified to speak out against the destructive nature of slavery because he was surrounded by it during the most formative years of his life. "I rejoice in the triumph of the principles of immediate emancipation, because I know, from long observation, it is the only thing that can relieve both master and slave from inevitable ruin." Perhaps only James G. Birney, who also attended the convention, could speak with equal authority on the corrosiveness of the institution.

"We feel the hand of oppression not only upon the slave," Rankin continued, "but upon ourselves. Where I live, my soul is harrowed continually with the cruelties committed in sight of my house, where slavery exists in its mildest form. There, slavery has sometimes caused our town to go in mourning. While I continue to be a husband and father, I must stand up and protest against this evil." He then set his sights on Ohio's new Fugitive Slave Act. "Laws have lately been passed in Ohio, imposing a fine of $500, or imprisonment, on any person who shall knowingly assist a slave to escape." To Rankin, this ran counter to the core of his faith. "I am forbidden to do an act of charity—I am commanded to do the very thing which the Bible forbids me to do—to deliver the fugitive servant to his master. I should be bound to take this sister into my house, if she comes there; and yet such is the effrontery of slavery, that they have come over and demanded that we, who assist our brethren, according to the requisitions of God's word, shall suffer bonds and imprisonment." As he concluded, Rankin's speech shifted in tone. He celebrated the impact of the American Anti-Slavery Society over six years. "I cannot, therefore, but rejoice in the success of this Society; and it shall have my prayers day and night."

Other society leaders spoke following Rankin, then the executive committee for the next year was elected. Rankin was selected along with Birney, Arthur and Lewis Tappan, and others to join the committee. Arthur assumed the position of president for the next year, and Rankin became the society's treasurer. As the convention proceeded in the following days, the subject that provoked the most significant controversy concerned the role that abolitionists should take in the political process. They were one year away from a presidential election, and the Democrats were in a place of vulnerability. Andrew Jackson's successor, Martin Van Buren, disappointed many Jacksonians across the country. The economic bust in 1837 severely weakened the influence that Democrats had on the electorate. The Whigs, formed by Henry Clay in opposition to what they viewed as Jackson's abuse of executive authority, saw an opening. For many abolitionists the Whigs were subservient to the slavocracy. Whereas the Democrats actively advanced slavery across the country, the Whigs did so passively. This, they believed, was on no account a choice. Birney led the charge at the convention in favor of political action, believing that if they hoped to witness the end of slavery in their lifetime, they must use the political structure they found themselves in. William Lloyd Garrison, and most of the Massachusetts delegation for that matter, disagreed.

The Business Committee presented the following resolution on the subject of political participation: "Resolved, That this society still holds, as it has from the beginning, that the employment of the political franchise, as established by the constitution and laws of the country, so as to promote the abolition of slavery, is of high obligation—*a duty*, which, as abolitionists, we owe to our enslaved fellow-countrymen groaning under legal oppression" (emphasis added).

Garrison and most of the Massachusetts delegation voted in opposition. But most of the convention joined Birney in voting in favor. The motion passed, 84 to 77. Rankin joined the *yeas*.

This hardly settled matters on political engagement. Birney was just getting started in his advocacy for political abolitionism, which he believed was the most practical method for immediate emancipation. Garrison, likewise, would only further dig his heels in with his opposition to participating in the political process. Rankin, on the other hand, remained flexible. He was disappointed in the political system, which allowed the slavocracy to seize a disproportional amount of control. However, as he mentioned earlier in the convention, he witnessed the atrocities of slavery from his hilltop home every day. He simply desired to find the most practical route to bring an immediate end to slavery as they knew it. The methodology mattered little to him. In the sixth annual report of the American Anti-Slavery Society, the Executive Committee pointed to the "case of the Rev. John B. Mahan" as evidence of the "necessity of political action." Ohio Governor Joseph Vance served Mahan up to Kentucky without taking any "time or pains to inquire whether the crime with which Mr. Mahan was charged, came within the constitutional category of 'treason, felony or other crime;' whether he had actually fled from justice, or whether he was likely to have a fair trial." Vance was Ohio's first Whig governor and was known for his favorable attitude toward abolitionism. After the Mahan extraction, abolitionists believed his true colors were revealed. In the gubernatorial election of 1838, the Executive Committee reported that "the Abolitionists of Ohio had defeated" the governor's reelection bid. "Had it not been for the value of Abolition votes," reported the committee, "there is no reason to believe either that Gov. Vance would have interested himself to send a deputation to [Kentucky] Gov. Clark to rectify his blunder, that the latter would have used his influence with the court, or that Mahan would have been acquitted." The sensational events in Ohio demonstrated the influence of abolitionists when they took political action and provided a template for future political impact.[144]

The abolitionists held a strong position as they approached a new decade. Their influence continued to grow, and the political class in Washington took special notice. The abolitionists seized the moment, making a point to emphasize how the "fierce fanaticism of John C. Calhoun" and the "hypocrisy of Henry Clay" allowed the society to present abolitionism to new audiences. Now a United States Senator from Kentucky, Clay made an impassioned speech against the influence of the "ultra-abolitionists" a few months prior on the Senate floor in February. Clay pointed fingers, stating that these individuals "are resolved to persevere in the pursuit of their object at all hazards, and without regard to any consequences, however calamitous they may be." Clay suggested that the momentous influence of the abolitionists threatened the stability of the government and the rights of the states where slavery existed. Clay was a very vocal supporter of colonization. He had even served as the president of the American Colonization Society. The single issue that dominated his political career was the preservation of the Union. In Clay's view, the abolitionists presented a great threat to that cause. Clay had long held the position that slavery's end would need to be gradual and paired with colonization efforts. "I am…no friend of slavery," Clay proclaimed. "The Searcher of all hearts knows that every pulsation of mine beats high and strong in the cause of civil liberty." However, Clay prioritized the safety of white Americans over the liberties of enslaved Africans. "I prefer the liberty of my own country to that of any other people; and the liberty of my own race to that of any other race. The liberty of the descendants of Africa in the United States is incompatible with the safety and liberty of the European descendants." In this statement, Clay summed up the starkest divide between the abolitionists and Whigs.[145]

* * * * *

The convention lasted four days in New York. As Rankin returned to Ripley, he returned to the front lines of conflict. Mahan's civil suit continued to drag on, and Rankin was roped into the dispute. Greathouse remained hellbent on exposing the activities of Ripley conductors, and believed that Rankin transported fugitives via carriage. Rankin didn't own a carriage, and because Greathouse fixated on his carriage theory, Rankin could truthfully deny involvement in the Underground Railroad in such a manner. "I have not owned any carriage since I have been a resident of this state, nor have any slaves ever been conveyed to Sardinia or anywhere else in any carriage or other wheeled vehicle, either owned or in any way procured by me." To Greathouse's frustration, nothing Rankin said was a lie. Even though Greathouse couldn't prove Rankin's involvement in the Underground Railroad, speculation about Rankin's activities deepened. In the early months of 1840, that curiosity brought unwelcome visitors to Rankin's hilltop home.[146]

On February 17, Rankin was in Adams County, leaving his wife, Jean, to watch over the property and children. David and Richard Calvin Rankin were also out of town, but heading back after aiding in a fugitive slave's escape. The oldest son with Jean that morning was seventeen-year-old Samuel Rankin. Suddenly, Jean overheard the voices of several men making their way to the house. She proceeded to the front porch with Samuel at her side and her toddler, Thomas Lovejoy Rankin, on her hip. Five men, armed with pistols and two bulldogs, approached. A store had been broken into in Dover, Kentucky by a slave, and the men believed he was currently harbored in the Rankin home. At the very least, they believed, Jean was aware of where the man was heading. Jean wanted no trouble with the hunters. Sensing the men meant her harm if she didn't comply, Jean told them there was "no slave here; we neither harbor thieves nor conceal stolen property and you are welcome to come and look through the house." As the men marched forward, ready to ransack the Rankin property, Samuel abruptly stepped inside the house, grabbing his father's shotgun. "Halt!"

he shouted as he stepped back outside, pointing the firearm directly at them. "If you come one step farther I will kill you." The senior Rankin's fearlessness had been passed on to his sons. The men stopped, but they called Samuel's bluff. "We're all well armed," one shouted back, "and we know you're alone. I reckon we'll search your house with or without your say so."

Samuel stepped forward and cocked his gun. He summoned his courage and accepted he'd shoot if they made a move, come what may. Jean stood her ground in silence, careful not to create further agitation, but refusing to back down. She would stand with her son and defend their hilltop sanctuary. A dreaded silence fell upon the group. The tension was unbearably thick. With one wrong step, Jean and Samuel could be killed in an instant. Rankin's entire operation would be ruined on a day he wasn't even home. Suddenly, a commotion broke the silence. All parties involved whipped their heads around, confused. Men and horses approached from all sides, rushing the hilltop with urgency. Calvin's voice broke through, commanding the hunters to stay where they were. He and his brother, David, had returned from their mission the night before when they learned that several men planned to confront the Rankin house. Nearly a dozen men joined the Rankin boys up the hill, rifles and pistols in hand, ready to protect the matriarch of the Ripley underground rail line.

Outnumbered but persistent, the hunters remained on the property until they could verify the slave wasn't harbored in the house. The Rankin boys refused entry to the men, but they allowed two men from Ripley who rushed the hill by their side to check on the men's behalf. This seemed to be agreeable to all parties involved. The two men searched the house while Rankin's sons kept their guns raised, ready to shoot if the hunters made a wrong move. The two men confirmed that no black man was inside the house. As the search concluded, the slave owner who hired these hunters arrived on site, demanding to search the home himself. Neither Jean nor the Rankin boys would allow this. Frustrated, the slave owner lashed out, shouting at them that slaves all along the river knew to head to Rankin's hilltop home to make a successful escape. He warned that more slave hunters would come, making Ripley a battleground. Rankin's house, he believed, would need to be "broken up or destroyed" because of this. This struck a nerve with Jean. "I give you fair warning," she barked back with stern confidence, "that if you do not hereafter keep away you will feel the force of powder and lead upon you and if no one else would shoot you I would do it myself." With that, the slave owner and his hunters finally relented. The standoff concluded without a shot being fired as the Rankin boys escorted them down the hill. They were safe, but the town was reasonably shaken up. For how long could conflict be avoided? So long as Rankin and his family sat on that hill, danger was ever present. Neither Rankin nor Jean, nor any of their children for that matter, were willing to back down.[147]

* * * * *

Rankin returned to Ripley unsettled by the events that had transpired and grappling with the reality that it was now unsafe to leave his wife and children alone in their own home. Rankin understood his duty to his family and was prepared to do what was necessary to protect them. Still, the prospect of violence, even as a last resort, left Rankin distressed. Making matters more complicated, the abolitionists descended deeper into division, with more believing it necessary to participate in the political process. Rankin would need to navigate the political arena with caution. He agreed that the abolitionists must work within the political process to achieve the change they were hoping for. However, Birney believed this should result in the formation of a new political party driven by abolition. The Liberty Party, as it was called, nominated Birney as their candidate for president in the 1840 election. Salmon P. Chase, who had become good friends with Birney after representing him following the 1836 Cincinnati riots, was fully supportive of the Liberty Party. Notably, their platform included advancing the "absolute and unqualified divorce of the general government from slavery." They also endorsed the idea that the Constitution was an anti-slavery document, and could be used to drive abolition.[148]

Adam Lowry Rankin was ecstatic regarding the prospect of a new party. He graduated from Lane Seminary in June, now licensed to preach by the Presbytery of Cincinnati. In January, he became a publishing agent for the Ohio Anti-Slavery Society. Lowry felt ready to take on the world and the Liberty Party would be his vehicle. His father was skeptical. Rankin feared the creation of the Liberty Party would incite further conflict. Lowry may have been itching for a fight, but Rankin knew such a fight would bring hardship. Because of this, Rankin thought it better to support the Whig nominee, William Henry Harrison. Lowry had no problem with Harrison himself. "I had become personally acquainted with Mr. Harrison," he wrote, "and admired the manly stand he had publicly taken in favor of the use of the Bible in the public schools." Harrison's nomination was "very acceptable" to Lowry, but John Tyler's nomination for Vice President was another matter altogether. "The tacking on the ticket of a man who had never been in sympathy with the Whig party and who was a slaveholder simply to enable the party to carry Virginia in the coming national election was a selling out to catch votes and was very repugnant to my ideas of manliness and honesty." John Tyler had spent much of his early political career as a Democrat, but had earned a reputation as a bit of a political maverick. On several occasions, he broke with the Jackson administration, often over constitutional concerns of executive authority. By tagging Tyler on the ticket in 1840, the Whigs hoped he would attract southern Democrats disillusioned with Jacksonianism. This, paired with Harrison's status as a war hero during the War of 1812, they hoped would help them secure enough southern and western votes to win the election. In doing so, the Whigs would finally break the grip of Jacksonian thought over the country. While Rankin saw value in this, Lowry believed this only further demonstrated the Whigs' subservience to slaveholding influence. The difference in perspective between Rankin and his firstborn "caused friction" within their household.[149]

The political differences between Rankin and his son are a familiar story for many. On one hand, a young, ambitious son, ready to take on the world and change it for the better, is disenfranchised by the world the prior generation left for him. On the other hand, there's a father who agrees in sentiment and principle, but errs on the side of caution in temperament, understanding the consequences of brash, unregulated action. Rankin didn't allow his relationship with Lowry to sour over these differences, but he was firm in his conviction that supporting the Whig ticket was the most practical path forward. Lowry, likewise, distanced himself from the Ohio Anti-Slavery Society, careful not to tie the Liberty Party too closely to the state auxiliary when the subject of political abolitionism still greatly divided members. He resigned from his position as publishing agent in September. Throughout the fall, both Rankin and Lowry proceeded to advance the political cause they believed would achieve the most effective means to abolish slavery. In Ripley, a Whig rally was held, with Harrison and Clay both present as speakers. To ensure that abolitionism wasn't forgotten by the Whigs, Rankin was present for the event. It likely wasn't lost on Rankin that Clay, the face of colonization, was declared a hypocrite just a year prior by the American Anti-Slavery Society.[150]

Rankin attempted to further clarify his position in a series of letters in *The Philanthropist* throughout the summer and fall of 1840. "I deem it my duty so to cast my vote so as neither to injure the slave nor anyone else," he wrote in September. "I have always voted on the principle for which I now content." He thought the Harrison ticket to be the lesser evil, so to speak, compared to Van Buren. "One of these two men will be president," Rankin wrote, "unless death prevent it. All that can be done now is simply to say which of them shall be president." Rankin believed Harrison was the candidate more likely to support anti-slavery efforts, even if only slightly. Others, however, believed Rankin to be dripping with hypocrisy. In *The Philanthropist*, Birney supporters voiced their frustration with the man many considered the father of abolitionism. They expressed, "Our wonder still increases, that such a man as Mr. Rankin should devote his talents to the support of a ticket pledged to slavery." Rankin's commentary on the election drew significant controversy in abolitionist circles. His "highest interest," he explained in a prior letter, was "the anti-slavery cause." His critics were quick to point out the flaws in Rankin's rational. "Mr. Rankin, by some legerdemain of logic would come to the conclusion, that though it was wrong for the people to put [pro-slavery] men in office, yet it would not be wrong for him to help put them there!" They were particularly drawn to his comments stating "all that can be done now is simply to" select between Harrison or Van Buren. "Admirable logic truly!" his critics wrote in rebuttal. "Because other people will do evil, [Rankin must] go along with the multitude. And it will be no wrong in [him], since the evil would be done any how!"[151]

Despite the grumblings and harsh criticism, most anti-slavery men in Ohio sided with Rankin. The Ripley Anti-Slavery Society passed a resolution during a special meeting, noting that "while we recognize the duty of abolitionists to carry their principles to the polls we deem the formation of a distinct political party, in reference to the Anti-Slavery cause inexpedient & uncalled for at the present time."[152] In other words, the newly formed Liberty Party would receive no official support from one of the most influential anti-slavery societies in Ohio. Still, it would pull support from some of its members, despite Rankin's position. Both Dr. Alexander Campbell and Thomas Collins supported Birney in the 1840 election, as did three other Ripley residents, including Lowry. Unlike his father, Lowry "was not prepared to accept" the concept that when "two evils confront a man it is his duty to choose the lesser."

As it came time to vote, Rankin wasn't the only one confident in "Tippecanoe and Tyler, too." The Harrison campaign had just about everyone wearing coonskin caps and drinking hard cider. In 1840, they capitalized on American frontier iconography in a way rarely seen. Harrison was the man of the moment. As the results came in, the Whigs swept the election. Even Van Buren's home state of New York, as well as Jackson's home state of Tennessee, went to Harrison. In all, Harrison carried nineteen states and secured 234 electoral votes. Van Buren secured only seven states and sixty electoral votes. Birney captured none. Ironically, Birney wasn't even in the country during the campaign. He found his time better spent in London serving as a delegate for the gathering of the World Anti-Slavery Convention earlier that summer, and didn't return until November.[153]

Despite their best efforts, the Liberty Party was never going to secure victory in 1840—even its biggest supporters recognized that. With anti-slavery circles divided on the issue of political abolitionism, there wasn't nearly enough support to carry Birney over the finish line. However, the groundwork was laid. They would continue to build upon it over the next four years, turning the Liberty Party into a formidable third party.

After more than a decade of Jacksonian Democrats enabling mobocracy and gagging the reading of petitions concerning slavery in Congress, abolitionists felt as if some political advances might finally be made. Harrison was sworn into office on March 4, 1841. During his long-winded inaugural address, he spoke at length on constitutional issues. Although he left slavery untouched, he did address the importance of a free press. The maxim "that 'the freedom of the press is the great bulwark of civil and religious liberty' is one of the most precious legacies which [our ancestors] have left us." The attack on Birney's press in 1836 and the murder of Elijah Lovejoy in 1837 were still top-of-mind, signaling that Harrison would take these matters more seriously than many believed his predecessor had. He gave the longest inaugural address in American history, lasting roughly an hour and forty-five minutes in the cold open air. At sixty-eight, he was also the oldest president in American history, a record he would maintain until Ronald Reagan won the presidency 140 years later.[154]

* * * * *

On Wednesday morning, April 21, 1841, a headline in *The Philanthropist* read, "DEATH OF GENERAL HARRISON." According to the paper, "At thirty minutes before one, on the morning of the 4th [of April], just one month, after his inauguration, died

William Henry Harrison.—a singular and mournful event." Three weeks after his inauguration, Harrison began to develop a cold. It is believed that this evolved into pneumonia, but the exact cause of death was, and remains, unclear. Never before had a sitting president died in office. As news swept the nation, Whigs and Democrats alike were stunned. As Americans mourned the loss of their ninth president, abolitionists quickly grasped that their worst fears were realized. "One of these two men will be president," Rankin wrote seven months earlier, "unless death prevent it." Harrison wasn't prevented from obtaining the presidency, but now his vice president, John Tyler, would finish his term. As *The Philanthropist* continued to report on Harrison's death, they shifted their attention to the new president. "Mr. Tyler, by the constitution and the voice of those who voted for General Harrison, becomes virtually the President of the United States." Time would tell whether Tyler would advance the policies set out by the Harrison administration or set his own course. "For ourselves, we do not feel comfortable under a slaveholding president," they wrote. In an apparent dig at Rankin and the abolitionists that backed the Whig ticket, they added that it provided them with "some consolation" in knowing "that we did not aid in placing him where he is." As many predicted, the election of 1840 marked a new era for the country, but it's unlikely anyone could have anticipated this predicament.[155]

CRISIS & SCHISM
1841–1849
VIII.

O ver the past five years, slaveholders in the region came to know John Rankin as their most serious threat. John B. Mahan's trial all but confirmed their worst suspicions. Although the specifics were foggy, the Underground Railroad was an open secret by 1841, and Rankin was its most important conductor. More than any other home in Ripley, Rankin's house represented the freedom that awaited fugitives on the other side of the river. To those who knew of his work, mention of Ripley in conversation evoked images not of town, but of the red brick safehouse sat atop the hill, lantern shining brightly in the night. Rankin owned a sizable property, especially compared to the other conductors in town. To accommodate the rising number of family members the Rankins hosted, they built more structures surrounding the main house. There was also a large barn, where fugitive slaves would sometimes hide until nightfall. In many ways, the Rankin property had become a fortress. To Adam Lowry Rankin, it was still home.

Despite the 1840 election causing a rift in the abolition movement and differences in the Rankin household, Lowry maintained a positive relationship with his father. Rankin had recently returned to book writing. He wrote two books that attempted to address the root of America's moral dilemma, communicating that slavery's influence in the United States was a symptom of a greater moral degradation. The first, *A Present to Families*, was meant to serve as a guide for parents to raise their children in righteousness. "The book was designed to be practical and propagate family religion," Rankin wrote. "It was not written in a controversial spirit. There is nothing in it to offend the most pious person." The other book, *An Antidote for Unitarianism*, was more confrontational. It was meant to be Rankin's "comprehensive defense of the doctrine of the Trinity, the Divinity of Christ and the personality of the Holy Spirit." Recognizing the nation's appetite for change, Rankin opens with cautious optimism. "The present is pre-eminently a time of moral revolution," read the first line of the preface. "Long established systems are rapidly breaking up, and the cords that for ages bound great masses together are sundered, and new combinations are daily forming." This presented a great opportunity, Rankin argued, especially in the fight against slavery. However, he warned, during "such a period there is, through the pride of intellect, and the love of novelty, peculiar danger of departing from long established truths, and embracing the grossest errors." He found it immensely painful that "great numbers calling themselves Christians, deny the doctrines of the Trinity, the divinity of Christ, the personality and Deity of the Holy Spirit, the original and total depravity of man, the necessity of the agency of the Spirit to renew the heart, the substitution of Christ for his people, and justification by his righteousness." This echoed many of the concerns he raised about the Great Revival from his childhood. A lack of biblical literacy and rise in doctrinal inconsistency, Rankin thought, would only lead to a twisting of scripture into whatever suited the will of men. A biblical defense of slavery, after all, could be traced back to misapplied theology. "Unitarianism is advancing under different forms," he wrote, "and in various denominations; and in all its forms, it is a spiritual poison that pervades the head and the heart, produces derangement in all the moral system, and sooner or later, it will bring on the chills of the second death, unless its progress be arrested by the application of the truth—by the power of the Holy Ghost."[156]

When *An Antidote for Unitarianism* was released, Rankin was again struggling financially. His work only paid an annual salary of $350. Book writing offered him an additional influx of funds when times were difficult. Conveniently, Lowry was also in need of more disposable income. After graduating from Lane Seminary, he considered traveling as a missionary in the West Indies or Africa, but without funds to support the trip, Lowry was forced to consider other options. Rankin needed to sell his books and Lowry needed something to occupy his time, so Rankin asked his son to serve as his sales representative. Into the early winter months of 1841, Lowry traveled across southern and central Ohio, and eventually parts of Indiana, selling his father's most recent books. He went to Presbyterian churches in the region and called upon their pastors. He found many to be very receptive. He managed to sell over 500 copies of *An Antidote for Unitarianism* and more than 1,000 copies of *A Present to Families*. "I succeeded [in selling the books] beyond [Rankin's] and my expectations," Lowry later wrote.

* * * * *

The verdict of *William Greathouse v John B. Mahan* was released in the summer of 1841. This time, Greathouse's persistence paid off.[157] The Mason County court ruled in his favor in this civil dispute, meaning Mahan owed Greathouse $1,600 for the loss of "property" (his slave). William Dunlop had already guaranteed he would cover this cost, but the damage to Mahan and the Ripley line was done. The precedent set meant blood was in the water, and the slaveholders in Kentucky swarmed like sharks. Mahan would never financially recover from the lawsuits, and his time in the Kentucky jail seriously deteriorated his health. Greathouse immediately filed a new lawsuit seeking the collection of security funds from Dunlop. All of Ripley was tired of Greathouse's unrelenting presence, and Dunlop paid him immediately to be rid of him. The case was thus dismissed, and Greathouse returned to Kentucky. Mahan was, for all intents and purposes, neutralized as a result of the drawn-out trial. With the Mahan matter settled, Kentucky slaveholders concentrated all their efforts against Rankin, and the bounty on his head was raised. Posters began to appear across Mason County and northern Kentucky for Rankin's delivery, dead or alive, in return for a $3,000 reward.[158]

Rankin was keenly aware of the danger he faced. At any moment, a gang of slave hunters may confront his house demanding he hand over fugitives. How could he forget the standoff his wife and children faced while he was away the year prior? And now, the heightened reward had piqued the interest of local scoundrels. "Men lay around my house at night to murder me," he later wrote. His daughter, Isabella, noticed a man one night coming into their home "to find where I slept, but I was not at home and he left without doing any mischief."[159] The whole family was on edge, ready to spring into action against any would-be assassins at a moment's notice. Thus, they were caught by surprise when a familiar visitor found her way to Rankin's hilltop fortress in July. This was not a fugitive slave or bounty hunter that arrived at Rankin's door as he was tending to his crops on a hot summer day. It was the very woman who made her daunting escape across the Ohio River in the dead of winter just a few years ago. "What has brought you back?" Rankin asked, looking on. She was wearing a disguise, dressed in a waistcoat and pants. Surely, Rankin thought, she wouldn't have returned to the point of her escape if it weren't for something truly urgent. "I want my daughter and her children," she explained to Rankin. "She belongs to Mr. Thomas Davis, over back of Dover. I've come back, just as I said." Rankin, understanding the danger better than anyone, gave her fair warning of what awaited her as soon as she crossed back into Kentucky. He looked at her and the man who accompanied her, predicting "they will catch you and they will sell you down river, and they will hang him. Slavery will be your partner and death or the penitentiary will be his." This was not the first time Rankin had to explain the risks associated with remaining in Ripley or the surrounding area. Many slaves, as he helped them escape, wished to return to Ripley and visit him.

They felt an overwhelming gratitude toward him. "Oh, how good to find friends," one fugitive exclaimed during his escape. "Can't I come back from Canada and see you all?" Rankin was unwilling to risk his freedom. "The laws are against you," he explained. "You cannot come back."[160] Rankin felt obliged to make the dangers known to her, but he could also sense that nothing was going to prevent her from trying to rescue her daughter and grandchildren. Rankin invited them for dinner that night, and afterward, they hatched a plan to reunite her with her family. The man who accompanied her was a French Canadian who could speak English without an accent. He was to hire himself out on the same plantation where her daughter was kept. At night, he worked toward their escape. It took some time, but by the end of August, they were back on their way up to Canada, reunited as a family unit.

* * * * *

Runaway slaves had flooded the river cities in the summer of 1841. The Ohio Supreme Court ruled in June that any slave that accompanied their master from a slave state into Ohio would legally be considered free. In places like Cincinnati, many white residents felt threatened by the influx of slaves claiming their freedom. They believed these slaves would threaten their jobs and livelihoods. The spirit of mob violence was reinvigorated, and riots broke out in the city in late August and early September, fueled by anger at black residents and abolitionists. Free blacks in the community, many of whom had lived in Cincinnati for years, were beaten by the mob, some were even stabbed. Buildings were destroyed. The mayor tried to calm the crowd, but they refused to be tamed. Troops were called in to suppress the riot, which had limited success, but by the next night, the mob had grown and set its sights on abolitionists as well as blacks. *The Philanthropist* was a primary target; the mob broke in and carried the press down to the river. It was yet another setback for Ohio's premier abolitionist paper. Many blacks in the city even volunteered to be arrested to find protection against the mob. Many were wounded, and some were killed. As the mob dispersed around dawn on Sunday, about forty were brought into custody. The spirit of mobocracy had made a startling comeback.[161]

Slaveholders in Kentucky and slavery sympathizers in Ohio felt emboldened in the first few weeks of September 1841. As the abolitionists grew in popularity, the slavocracy diminished in power. Papers like *The Philanthropist* certainly contributed to the anti-slavery sentiment spreading across the country, but it was merely a branch. Rankin was continuously identified as the root of all their troubles. If only they could destroy this powerful symbol of liberty, that inspired thousands of slaves to flee their masters, surely abolitionism itself would begin to crumble.

The week following the Cincinnati riots, men were seen coming and going around Rankin's property. His sons were anxious and stood ready to fight. It was Rankin's wish for no violence to occur on his property, unless no other option remained. He understood that slaveholders and sympathizers would rejoice if such a prominent abolitionist like him turned one of their own into a martyr. If Rankin's opponents fired the first shot, however, Rankin was prepared to unleash a firestorm upon them. "Father had positively forbidden them to be molested unless seen to commit some act of depredation," wrote Lowry, "we only kept a watch on their movements."[162] September 12, 1841, was on a Sunday. Rankin had preached that morning, as he had time and again on the Sabbath. Richard Calvin Rankin was in town that afternoon and felt an overwhelming, unshakable discomfort. There were an unusually high number of young men from Kentucky in town, glaring at him as he walked by. After the evening service, Calvin escorted a young lady home. As he returned, the number of young men in town seemingly grew. As they glared, Calvin predicted "there would be trouble before morning." The rest of his family brushed it off, feeling this night was no different than the nights before. "We had gotten accustomed to such things," explained Lowry. Still, they took what they believed to be the necessary precautions for their security, as they had all week. John P. Rankin, a cousin to the Rankin boys, was staying on the hilltop home at the time. Unlike the rest of his family, he didn't think Calvin was paranoid. As they all went to bed, Calvin and John P. Rankin remained dressed in case the need for a quick reaction arose.

Calvin was startled around two thirty in the morning at the sound of a low whistle outside. There was little mystery as to what this meant. He and John P. Rankin sprung from bed, grabbed their guns, and rushed to the back door. Searching for the source, they swept opposite directions. John P. Rankin searched the south end of the property, and Calvin went north. Suddenly, he discovered an armed man standing in front of him. Both Calvin and the intruder were surprised by each other's presence. Calvin demanded that the man explain himself, but as if by nervous reaction, the intruder shot at Calvin without thinking, grazing his shoulder and putting his shirt on fire. Calvin dropped to the ground and the man fled into the woods behind him. Around this time, John P. Rankin had come across another man in the south corner of the property. Like Calvin, he was surprised by the presence of the intruder, and before he could react, the man shot at him and fled into the woods, just as his partner did. He missed, but John P. Rankin returned fire and hit the man's shoulder, causing him to let out "an unearthly scream."

John Rankin's home on Liberty Hill. This photo shows the back entrance of the house. Richard Calvin and John P. Rankin burst through this entrance, guns in hand, to face off against the midnight assassins in September 1841. (Photo circa 1900. Ohio History Connection)

The screams and gunshots jerked the rest of the Rankin family out of bed. Jean Rankin ran to the door before anyone else and locked them in. She was certain they had killed Calvin and John P. Rankin, and refused to lose another child. Arguments between the Rankin boys and their parents erupted. They were determined to fight back and defend the family. Rankin and Jean believed they would shoot the first person who walked out the door. They told the boys they "could do the dead no good so our next duty was to preserve our own lives." Lowry wouldn't have it. He forced a window open that his father had nailed shut and escaped, his brother Samuel following close behind. The firing outside had ceased for several minutes, but as they dropped from the window, they heard it resume. It wasn't aimed at the house, but in the orchard. Lowry quickly recognized Calvin and John P. Rankin's voices amid the firefight. Indeed, they had survived and were together pushing the intruders off the property. As Lowry and Samuel ran to the orchard to provide reinforcement to their family, they noticed someone had set fire to the barn. They rushed to put it out. Fortunately, it was damp, and the fire struggled to spread. "Had we been three minutes later," Lowry explained, "the fire would have reached the unthreshed wheat stored in the barn and then we should have lost our entire crop of wheat, oats, and hay with the barn, 125 x 80 feet in size and our house also for a strong wind was blowing from the barn to the house."

Still inside the home, Rankin and Jean finally relented to the protests of their children. They opened the door for the rest of the family to support Lowry, Samuel, Calvin, and John P. Rankin. The firing continued but grew more distant. Calvin and John P. Rankin demanded the men surrender as they pushed them back. As Lowry continued to extinguish the barn fire, he glanced over the hill to find a welcome sight. The townspeople of Ripley were charging the hill to aid the Rankin family. Lowry estimated that "a hundred young men and older ones, having heard the shooting, had hurried up from the town." They joined Calvin and John P. Rankin in the pursuit of the Kentucky intruders. It was a relief that the two barefooted boys sorely needed. The firefight on the hilltop had drawn nearly everyone in town, it seemed. The would-be

Kentucky assassins retreated to their boats as an army of Ripley conductors and townsmen pursued them. While they made their escape, many were wounded, and the Rankin's fortress on Liberty Hill gave an appearance of strength like never before. "Before those in pursuit got back," explained Lowry, "full three hundred more men from town arrived." It was hard to determine exactly how many came to the aid of the Rankins on that night, but to the Kentucky slaveholders, the Ripley community was unified. They would need an army if they hoped to take out Rankin. "The Lord preserved me from all harm," Rankin later graciously explained.[163]

In the aftermath, Rankin determined that the fire was set in the hopes of drawing the family out, where they would be assassinated one by one. With passion dissipating over time, Rankin made only a brief, matter-of-fact account of the incident in his autobiography years later. The morning after the attack, however, he was filled with righteous indignation. As if the strong showing of unity by the Ripley community weren't enough to deter assassins from making any further attempts on Rankin's life, he picked up his pen on the Monday following the attack and wrote an open letter to *The Ripley Telegraph*: "As various false reports are in circulation respecting the recent attacks made upon me and my family by midnight assassins, perhaps it may be interesting to the public to have a series of the facts in the case, and such I shall now give." Full of passion, he described in detail what happened on the night of September 12th, as he recalled it:

> Thus, I have been attacked at midnight with fire and weapons of death, and nothing but the good providence of God has preserved my property from flames and myself and family from violence and death. And why? Have I wronged anyone? No, but I am an ABOLITIONIST. I teach the doctrine that "all men are born equally free and independent, that we must love our neighbors as ourselves, that to buy, to sell and hold human beings as property is sin." I do

not recognize the slaveholder's right to the flesh and blood and souls of men and women. For this I must be proscribed, my property burnt, and my life put in jeopardy!! I am charged with feeding the hungry and clothing the naked; poor man, white or black, has never been turned away empty from my door. And for this I must guard over my property and family while others sleep in safety.

Have I ever merited anything but good from the community in which I live? Can any person say that I have not labored to promote the best interests of all classes of men? Why then am I beset with armed men around my house at midnight? Because I am an ABOLITIONIST! These men came to sustain the slaveholders' claim to human beings as property. Such defense becomes the dark system of slavery.

As Rankin concluded his letter, he didn't want to leave any doubt as to the lengths he would go to should such an incident happen again. He wrote,

Now I desire all men to know that I am not deterred from what I believe to be my duty by fire and sword. I also wish all to know that I feel it my duty to defend my HOME to the very uttermost and that it is my duty to shoot the midnight assassin in his attacks as it is to pray.

I therefore forewarn all persons to beware lurking about my house and barn at night. When I am put upon the necessity of standing guard over my family and property, I shall not do so in vain.[164]

Rankin's letter ran in *The Ripley Telegraph* on September 14, 1841, not two days after the attack. Lowry further detailed his father's feelings following the attack. That "while he was a man of peace, he felt it as much a duty to shoot down the midnight assassin as to pray. Those hereafter seen prowling about his premises after bedtime did so at their own risk for they certainly would be shot at. Never was a man seen prowling on our premises after that warning...." The night of September 12 was a turning point for Rankin's outlook. While always committed to immediate abolitionism, Rankin had long believed in peaceful means to obtain that end. He would continue to strive toward a peaceful resolution, but this was perhaps the first time he realized that violence may be the only language that the slaveocracy would listen to. This train of thought was a troubling one, but if slaveholders were openly attempting to assassinate those who threatened them, what other conclusion could there be? Rankin wouldn't be provoked into proactive violence, but he made it known that if death is what they sought, they would certainly find it on Liberty Hill.

The 1840s were turbulent for Rankin. He experienced many ups and downs as the nation marched toward widening discontent over slavery. The siege on his home was certainly a crisis he couldn't have fully anticipated. However, many days brought him smiles and laughter, not the least of which included the weddings of his first three children. Lowry, upon returning from Lane Seminary, married his hometown sweetheart, Amanda Kephart, on October 10, 1840. As Lowry argued with his father and mother during the attack on their home, Amanda was with him, begging him to stay inside, worried, like Rankin and Jean, that he would be shot as soon as he stepped out. Rankin's first daughter, Isabella Jane Rankin, married John Wilson Humphreys just two days earlier. The following February, David Rankin married Mary Ann Wiley. Rankin played a special role in David's marriage to Mary Ann, serving as the minister who married them. Despite the turmoil surrounding Rankin over slavery and abolitionism, his family life had never been stronger.

After the attack on the Rankin home, Lowry and Amanda prepared to head west. Rankin's brother, Reverend William C. Rankin, was visiting Ripley before he embarked on a new pastorate in the Iowa territory.

He needed another minister to help him, and his nephew, Lowry, had a new ministry license, a new wife, and few career prospects. He asked Lowry to join him out west. Eager to finally find his direction in life, Lowry was happy to accept. The attack on the Rankin house likely reinforced his decision. William told Lowry to seek an appointment from the American Home Missionary Society of the Presbyterian Church as "Home Missionary for the County of Van Buren, Iowa Territory, with headquarters at Keosauqua." The Missionary Society agreed to the request and agreed to a travel stipend of seventy-five dollars on top of a $300 annual salary. Lowry left for Iowa with his wife and his brother, John Thompson Rankin (John Jr.), in November.[165]

They arrived in Iowa in the spring of 1842. Rather than joining an established, local church, Lowry formed his own, believing it easier to start anew rather than try to navigate the established church politics of a foreign land. His wife, Amanda, was instrumental in helping him come to this conclusion. Before long, the subject of slavery presented new challenges to Lowry's mission in Iowa. Lowry at first remained largely quiet on the matter while out west. "I had said nothing in public and scarcely anything in private on slavery," he later wrote. However, "it was known that I received the *Philanthropist* through the mail, and that was sufficient." He soon received a notice requesting him in Yellow Springs "and assist other ministers in the organization of a Presbytery for the Territory of Iowa." During the meeting, slavery became a major point of division among the ministers in attendance. "Desiring that the Presbytery should from its organization have a clear record against slavery, I presented a series of resolutions to that effect which were seconded by my uncle." A long debate ensued, as many members of the Presbytery were pro-slavery. Many Presbyterians at this time, including Rankin, were embroiled in a deep theological controversy that arose in the late 1830s. Those who adopted a strict Calvinistic view of pre-determination and rejected the spread of revivalism in American churches fell into what was considered the "Old School" of thought. Those who fell in the "New School" of thought adopted a more liberal view of salvation through Christ—that it is accessible to all those who repent, not just the godly select. Typically, though not always, the New School Presbyterians were more open to abolitionism and rejected biblical arguments in defense of slavery. "I was New School and an Abolitionist," Lowry wrote, revealing the source of his troubles in Iowa.

The next day, as the debate over Lowry's resolution over slavery concluded, one of the ministers provided final remarks in opposition to the resolution. He offered "a very long Bible argument in support of slavery. It was very bitter. The little church was packed." After Lowry offered a rebuttal, they finally voted. It was a tie. After hearing the results, the moderator, Reverend W. W. Woods, addressed the church. "I did entertain doubts respecting the introduction of the question of slavery at this time, but the attempt to prove that slavery is ordained of God is so abhorrent to every sense of justice that I am glad the subject has come before us for settlement. I therefore give the casting vote in the affirmative."

Lowry was pleased by his influence over the Presbytery in favor of abolition, and his wife was proud of him. Amanda had attended the meetings and watched her husband grow in confidence as he argued against slavery. They rode home triumphantly, but it would prove painfully short-lived. As they rounded a corner of a cornfield, a cow crashed through their path. Their horse was "young and spirited," and the cow "frightened him, causing him to break out of the road on a run across a small field toward a heavy rail fence." In the chaos, Amanda worried she might be trampled or crushed, and jumped from the wagon into the field. She cleared the wheels, but as Adam went to calm the horse, he noticed Amanda hadn't moved. He rushed to her side, but as he reached her, he discovered she was "unable to stand and suffering great pain in her back." Amanda injured her spine as she jumped out of the buggy, paralyzing her from the waist down. After facing harsh winters, disease, and the ever-present threat of political violence over his abolitionism, Adam had grown into a bold but tactful fighter on the Iowa frontier. But it was his wife's life-changing injury that forced him back to Ripley. Overcome with melancholy, he returned to his father and family in Ripley in the fall of 1843. Years later, a more jaded

Lowry cynically wrote that he "left Ripley for my work in Iowa with five cents and household goods and returned with no such goods and just ten cents in my pocket. Such was the ending of my ministry in Iowa." Despite his misfortune, he held on to his faith and remained confident that he had done the Lord's work in Iowa. "The experience had its lights and shadows, its great joys and its great sorrows. I have always been glad I have been privileged to add a little to the growth of that noble state."

* * * * *

Rankin tried to be a source of comfort for his grieving son and daughter-in-law. Under such circumstances, it would be easy for Adam and Amanda to be consumed with depression, lose faith, or give up fighting for such a demanding cause as abolitionism. They were not to be deterred. In the years to come, Lowry continued to work for the cause locally. The following fall, John B. Mahan became gravely sick. This, many in the Ripley and Sardinia communities knew, was nothing new for him. Illness had become a staple of his life, constantly lingering, particularly following his incarceration in Kentucky at the outset of the legal battle with William Greathouse. As he was imprisoned, he developed a severe cough and cold. He soon discovered this to be tuberculosis. The horrible conditions of the Kentucky jail cell eroded his immune system. Although he recovered after his release, he never regained full health. In the years following the trial, his tuberculosis would occasionally return, but Mahan would often recover. He continued in his work for the Ripley line of the Underground Railroad and contributed toward the Liberty Party's growth as the election of 1844 drew near. Then, on August 14, 1843, his firstborn daughter, Mary Jane Mahan, died in Manchester, Ohio after falling ill. Mary Jane's death shook Mahan to his core, and in his grief, Mahan completely retreated from his abolition work. The conductors in the area stopped sending fugitives to him, knowing he was no longer up to the task. While Mahan's poor health presented challenges in his abolition work, there was always a spark that motivated his will. Now, consumed by his daughter's death and his apparent retirement from abolitionism, his will had never been weaker. In the fall of 1844, his tuberculosis overcame him. On December 15, John Bennington Mahan passed away.[166]

Mahan's death sent shockwaves through the abolition movement. *The Liberator* soon re-published a notice of Mahan's death, alerting the anti-slavery community at large that a great titan of the cause was with them no more. "Many readers of the [Pennsylvania] *Freeman* will recollect the imprisonment and trial to which our friend Mahan was subjected in 1838," read the letter. "The memory of such a man will live after him, and impart new energy to the surviving co-laborers in the cause."[167] Mahan quickly became a symbol of martyrdom in the abolitionist community. Elijah Lovejoy was murdered by an anti-abolitionist mob in 1837. Mahan, in contrast, was driven to poverty and poor health not by impassioned zealots, but by the state itself. It was the governor of a free state that allowed him to be extradited from Ohio. Mahan's death put the dominance of the slaveocracy over the lives of freemen on full display. He was buried in the Sardinia cemetery. On his tombstone, it read "In Memory of John B. Mahan, died December 15, 1844, aged forty-three years eight months and nine days. A victim of the slave power." The community around Ripley agreed wholeheartedly with the sentiment.

* * * * *

As the abolition movement mourned the loss of Mahan, they also grappled with the 1844 election. The death of President Harrison and the subsequent ascension of John Tyler to the White House had vindicated Lowry and the other supporters of the Liberty Party. Embarrassed that they had inadvertently lent a hand to a supporter of slavery, thousands of abolitionists across the country were willing to give the Liberty Party a second chance. The abolitionists came to believe that working within the Whig party was futile. The 1844 election again saw James G. Birney leading the Liberty Party ticket. On the other hand,

President Tyler had managed to infuriate both Whig and Democrat leaders, leaving him without a party affiliation. Tyler had burned his bridge with the Whigs the moment he stepped into the executive office. Following the death of President Harrison, Tyler felt the presidency was his, and he had no obligation to fulfill campaign promises made by Harrison. This most infuriated Henry Clay, who despite being unable to secure the presidency for himself, had largely set the policy agenda of Harrison's administration. On the other side of the political aisle, the Democrats viewed Tyler as a turncoat for joining the Whigs during Andrew Jackson's administration. Tyler, politically homeless, attempted to form a third party to support his election bid, but it ultimately failed. The Whigs elevated Clay as their nominee. It was believed that the Democrats would nominate Martin Van Buren again. During the convention, Van Buren failed to gain the necessary two-thirds majority to secure the nomination. A political dark horse, James K. Polk, slowly became the convention favorite, and on the ninth ballot, he secured the nomination.[168]

More than any other issue, the annexation of Texas dominated the 1844 election cycle. Abolitionists and Whigs alike were vehemently opposed to the possibility of annexation. Since Texas declared its independence in 1836, it had been seeking annexation from the United States. Jacksonian Democrats, likewise, had supported annexation from the earliest days of the Texas Revolution. Acquiring Texas was the next natural step in America's manifest destiny to stretch across the continent, they believed. The less-spoken, though equally motivating reason that many supported annexation was the spread of slavery. Mexico had already abolished slavery in 1829, but it was reintroduced in Texas after independence was declared. Given the vast Texas territory, many feared it could be divided into several states, allowing Southerners to dominate Congress. The inclusion of Texas represented a great threat to abolitionism, and members of the American Anti-Slavery Society recognized this immediately. In 1837, the Ripley Anti-Slavery Society adopted resolutions in "an effort to prevent the annexation of Texas to this Union." They resolved to "take measures to circulate petitions for signatures and forward the same to Congress for the abolition of slavery in the District of Columbia, and against the annexation of Texas to the United States." Furthermore, they resolved that "the annexation of Texas to the United States (if it should take place)" would be equivalent to "virtually dissolving the Union."[169]

As much as the Whigs and abolitionists opposed annexation, the Democrats supported it even more passionately. Texas fever was sweeping the nation, especially in the West. Polk's eventual nomination was undoubtedly due to his early and vocal support for annexation. As the 1844 election approached, it became apparent to the Democrats that Polk was the man to continue the Jackson's legacy. It was a powerful and unifying sentiment. As Clay prepared to confront his political opponent from Tennessee, the abolitionists felt little comfort. Many still viewed Clay as a hypocrite, deferential to the slave powers. After the disaster that was Tyler's accidental ascension to the presidency, few abolitionists could stomach another Whig vote. As election day passed, the influence of the abolitionists was clear. In 1840, Birney secured approximately 7,400 votes. In 1844, that number exploded to more than 62,000 votes. This turnout especially stung for Clay, who lost the popular vote by about 38,000 ballots. In the electoral college, 170 votes went to Polk, and 107 to Clay. A clear depiction of Birney's influence over Clay's loss was illustrated by New York, where voters grew tired of Clay's flaky position on slavery and annexation. Disillusioned, thousands of voters who would have otherwise gone to Clay cast a ballot for Birney, ultimately allowing the state to tip toward Polk, handing him New York's thirty-six electoral votes.

As the Whigs licked their wounds following the results of 1844, President Tyler believed the election was a mandate for him to again push for Texas annexation. While he wasn't on the ballot, Tyler had advocated annexation for the majority of his term. The Senate had rejected his Texas annexation treaty in June of 1844, but in a lame-duck session of Congress, it was reintroduced as a joint resolution. This time, after much debate, it finally passed, and President Tyler signed the bill on March 1, 1845. Two days later, on his last full day in the White

House, he sent a courier to Texas with an annexation offer. Before the end of the year, Texas was admitted into the Union as a powerful new slave state.

* * * * *

Abolitionists in Ripley were anxious over the recent development in Texas, but Rankin's present stress stemmed from recent controversy in the Presbyterian Church. He was overwhelmed and conflicted regarding his role as both an anti-slavery activist and a minister of the gospel. For years, it made him uncomfortable that slaveowners were permitted to fellowship with non-slaveowners. "Let then all the various denominations of Christians exclude from church fellowship all who persevere in holding slaves, under any pretext whatsoever;" he proclaimed at the Granville convention a decade earlier. "And let all the gospel ministers lift up their voices against slavery...." Rankin's hope was that, at least within the Presbyterian church, he and the other abolitionist ministers might inspire an internal cleansing, washing the stain of slavery out of the congregation. What actually came of this campaign was a division within the church community. Many were beginning to suggest that the best path forward was not church unity, but church secession. This greatly disturbed Rankin. Both the church and the abolitionists needed strength if they were to succeed in their respective missions. Strength, Rankin believed, could only be obtained if they resisted further division. Factionalizing would only serve to hurt their cause. Rankin published a letter in the *Cincinnati Journal* stating that it brought him "painful emotions" to see his church community embrace the spirit of schism. He characterized church secession as sinful and in blatant rebellion of the example of Christ and doctrine taught. If that weren't enough, it was against the Constitution of the Presbyterian Church, he wrote. Furthermore, "nothing can be gained by secession as it respects the purity of the great body of the church. It will lessen rather than extend the influence of the seceders." Rankin believed that secession would not only bring ruin to the church but would expose the country to unparalleled levels of vice and immorality.[170]

Rankin made his pleas for unity in the fall of 1836, but despite these efforts, the church ultimately fell victim to a schism the following year. During the general assembly in Philadelphia in 1836, the "Old School" faction determined the 1801 Plan of Union to be unconstitutional. This plan joined the New England Congregationalist Churches with the Presbyterian Church to better spread the gospel to the frontier. Synods formed in the Western Reserve were part of this plan, thus a vote was taken to expel them. In 1837, the general assembly refused to acknowledge the Western Reserve synods and was denied recognition. This solidified it for the followers of the "New School" faction. They gathered in a nearby church and formed their own general assembly. Both called themselves the true Presbyterian Church, setting the stage for further conflict.[171]

The division in the Presbyterian Church caused Rankin's heart to ache. It was little coincidence that the rapid return of the slaveocracy in the early-to-mid-1840s coincided with a growing number of church factions. But that aside, even the way the two theological schools divided felt like wasted potential. Neither school separated over slavery. Rankin considered himself theologically in line with the Old School, but their refusal to rebuke slaveholders was intolerable. Far more abolitionists were gravitating to the New School. Despite certain theological differences, Rankin believed it would be the path of least resistance to lobby the New School to prohibit slaveholders from membership. This became a much greater challenge than he initially anticipated. In 1838, Rankin and other local Presbyterian ministers in the Ripley area, such as James Gilliland and Jesse Lockhart, formed the Presbytery of Ripley under the New School Synod of Cincinnati. This resulted in Rankin's election as a commissioner to the New School General Assembly in 1839. Here, he hoped he would finally be able to convince the church to take a firm stand against fellowship with slaveowners. Indeed, slavery was a major point of discussion during the assembly. However, the New School rejected formal opposition to slavery. The most that Rankin and his anti-slavery allies could manage was the approval of a resolution to yield to the deferment of "the lower judicatories the subject of slavery, leaving it to them to take such order thereon as in their judgment will be the most judicious and *adapted to remove the evil*" (emphasis theirs). This wasn't enough for Rankin. A growing number of those within the Synod of Cincinnati suspected that working within the New School was a waste of time. In subsequent meetings in 1840 and 1843, no progress would be made. The Presbytery of Ripley didn't even bother to send a commissioner in 1843.

As the Ripley Presbytery protested the New School over their refusal to condemn slavery, a minister by the name of William Graham made his own protest against the abolitionists. In the fall of 1843, Graham made a speech condemning abolitionism and defending slavery on biblical grounds. It didn't cause much of a stir until the following spring, when the speech was published as a pamphlet. Rankin was outraged. The Presbytery of Ripley immediately sought Graham's suspension from preaching. A trial was set, and in September of 1844, it was found "that the pamphlet of [William] Graham does contain sundry great and dangerous errors." The Graham case was elevated to the Cincinnati Synod, where Graham refused to recant his defense of slavery. With Graham unwilling to budge, they resolved that he "ought to be, and hereby is suspended from the exercise of the gospel ministry, until he retracts the errors contained in the specifications laid in the charges…and gives to his Presbytery satisfactory evidence of repentance." While six ministers protested the verdict by voting in the negative, they were in the minority. Rankin and twenty-seven others voted in the affirmative.[172]

There were some members of Rankin's congregation who harbored pro-slavery sentiments. They were none too pleased with his role in the suspension. "We have had great affliction in our church at this place," Rankin wrote to his brother, Alexander Taylor Rankin, on December 2, 1845. "The prime movers were Dr. Beasley and D. P. Evans. The one exerted his medical and the other his monied influence to drive me from the place."[173] Beasley and Evans sought to get Rankin removed as minister of their church. "The basest slander and intrigue were also employed. By fraud they gained a vote of one majority for my dismission." Much of his congregation rose to his defense, with 104 members signing a petition to keep Rankin as pastor and asking the Presbytery not to interfere. "The Presbytery wholly disregarded the prayer of the majority and dissolved the relation." The Presbytery then "organized us into a second Presbyterian church." The Second Presbyterian Church in Ripley found great support in the community, but it signified the deepening divisions in the church. "If the Presbytery had not organized the second church we should have done it ourselves and renounced our their jurisdiction." Rankin also noted that if the Synod hadn't suspended Graham after his trial, they would have left immediately. "This presbytery will finally leave its present connexion unless slaveholders shall be excluded from connexion of the constitutional body."

The last straw came in 1846 when Graham appealed his suspension to the general assembly. After examining the case, the Assembly for the New School ordered that the suspension be reversed and Graham be permitted to preach. On December 12, 1846, Rankin organized the abolitionist community in Ripley to officially call for "an evangelical anti-slavery convention" for the purpose of forming an anti-slavery church. The convention would take place in Cincinnati in May 1847. Four of Rankin's sons—Lowry, Calvin, David, and John Jr.—signed their father's petition. In addition, Isabella's husband, John Wilson, and her father-in-law, William Humphreys, attached their names. Some notable conductors did as well, such as Theodore and Thomas Collins. In January 1847, Rankin published the petition in the *Watchman of the Valley*, a Cincinnati newspaper, with a note to the editors. "I send you the following, in favor of a convention," he opened. Rankin emphasized that these signers belonged to many different churches and that their purpose was not to form a new denomination. Rather, they sought to "form an evangelical anti-slavery alliance, composed of different denominations." As he closed his short message, he offered his hope that "many others will send in their names in favor of our convention."[174]

In Cincinnati on May 27, 1847, Rankin chaired the convention that resulted in the formation of the Presbyterian Church of America. It would be often referred to as the Free Presbyterian Church. In an ironic twist, the same man who penned articles a decade earlier condemning church secession as unconstitutional and unbiblical was now leading the separation. Old Schoolers and New Schoolers alike would be permitted to partake in fellowship as Free Presbyterians, as long as they were committed to abolition. The New School Synod in Cincinnati attempted to discipline the members of the Ripley Presbytery, censuring them for leading the effort to secede. The Ripley Presbytery responded by asking them to remove their names from their rolls. In the formation of the Free Presbyterian Church, a Declaration of Human Rights was adopted, which definitively declared the church's anti-slavery principles. Notably, it prohibited slaveholders and pro-slavery advocates from fellowship in the church. Also, "no Church, Presbytery, or Synod, tolerating slaveholders or the advocates of slaveholding in its communion, can be a constituent part of this body."

Forming a new church at this scale was no small task, and it consumed much of Rankin's time and energy in the summer and fall of 1847. In November, much of that work began paying off. Three free presbyteries came together, forming the Free Synod of Cincinnati. Rankin continued to work on the development of the Free Presbyterian Church as the new year approached. On the heels of this, Rankin's world came to a crashing halt. Christmas day 1847 became one of the worst days of his life. His son David, whom Rankin had married to Mary Ann Wiley nearly seven years earlier, passed away after a long-fought battle against typhoid fever. While not unexpected, David's death consumed the Rankin family. Rankin and Jean were crippled in sorrow. They had never lost a child before, and at his death, David was a mere twenty-eight. David's passing left his wife, Mary Ann, widowed with three children. Their first, Mary Franklin, was almost six. Bella, their second, was three. Their third, John, was born a year and a half earlier. *The National Era* ran an obituary for David on February 3, 1848. "His death has been deeply felt by his aged parents," it read, "in whose affection he shared most deeply. This is the first, out of fourteen children, one of them adopted, that they have been called to follow to the grave. He left a wife and three helpless children, to deplore the loss of a loving husband and a tender father. He died in peace; and although in the prime of life, yet it is believed has attained the great end of existence—eternal life."[175]

Making matters especially painful, Rankin was still recovering from the loss of his mother, Jane Rankin, who had died almost two years earlier in January 1846. In an instance of cruel irony, Rankin's first child to pass bore the same name as his first sibling to pass in 1814. Rankin knew his son to be a special man, and anticipated great things from him. He accepted the finality of David's fate, believing that God's master plan was at work. Still, the mourning process was an agonizing one. Rankin had inquired David about his salvation as his health started to deteriorate. David assured him that it was long settled. In his autobiography years later, Rankin wrote simply that David, "when the father of three children, died in the hope of eternal life." It's a brief tribute, but Rankin could not imagine a better summary of his son's life and death. Still, even after so many years, it was painful to recount the loss of his son at such a young age. The death of David Wilmont Rankin left an unmistakable mark on the rest of his father's life.

* * * * *

1849 brought the arrival of a new resident to Ripley, ready to begin a new stage of life with his wife. With this resident's arrival, Rankin and the local conductors would find a powerful ally. As the newcomer stepped into town, he was acquainted with some of the townsfolks of Ripley. Back in 1845, one of the Collins brothers, Eli, had received a knock on his bedroom door in the middle of the night. Eli opened the door to a group of four: two girls, a guide helping them safely navigate the streets, and a young black man named John Parker. Rather than fleeing north himself, Parker was tasked with ensuring the girls found their way to the Ripley line. This was Parker's first-time helping fugitives escape, but what he found in Ripley was a pleasant surprise. Initially, he was very hesitant to help the girls, averse to the danger ahead and believing it foolish to participate. By the nature of his skin, the risks involved for Parker would far exceed the risk involved for others, such as Rankin or the Collins brothers. John Parker's neighbor in Cincinnati, also a free black man, came to him soliciting help with a fugitive rescue. Parker flat-out refused. Despite being turned away, his neighbor proceeded to plan the rescue. A few evenings later, Parker's neighbor informed him that word had gotten to the girls that he was on his way, and he wanted Parker to join his mission. Again, Parker refused, but his neighbor persisted. Perhaps he felt sympathy for the girls now that they knew plans were set. Perhaps he knew his neighbor would not quit asking until he agreed. Whatever his reason, Parker finally relented—despite believing it to be "quite a foolish thing for me to even try to do." After delivering them to the house, Parker watched as Eli took them down a darkened alleyway, as had been done so many times before on missions such as these. Parker never saw the girls again, but Collins later assured him that he got them safely to Gilliland's safe house. Parker was so impressed by the efficiency of the Ripley conductors that he moved to Ripley a few years later.

By the time he had been introduced to Ripley, Parker was a free man. However, his freedom did not come easily. For much of his childhood, he experienced a life all too familiar to slaves in the south. He was born in 1827 on a plantation in Norfolk, Virginia. His father was "one of the aristocrats of Virginia." In 1835, when Parker was eight, he was sold further south to Alabama. He was ripped away from his mother, never to be seen again. From an early age, Parker had a defiant streak in him, more than most other slaves he encountered. The cruelty he experienced from masters and overseers fueled his indignation rather than breaking his spirit. "How I hated slavery as it fettered me, and beat me, and baffled my desires," he wrote years later. "But in the end that unknown ancestor of mine gave me the will and courage to conquer or die." He was too young to work the cotton fields when he arrived in Alabama, so he was purchased by a doctor in Mobile to help around the house and office. The doctor, Parker noted, was "a gentleman of the Old South, kindhearted and very thoughtful of me." He treated Parker well, and he "responded to it and gave him no trouble." His rebellion against slavery in Alabama was more subtle than it was in Virginia. Parker became good friends with the doctor's two sons, who, in turn, taught him how to read in secret. This was the most significant development in Parker's pursuit of freedom. Despite it being highly illegal to teach slaves to read and write, Parker always had "several books in hand" from that moment on.

In 1843, Parker was sixteen when he finally found the opportunity to escape from bondage. His first attempt failed, but he maintained his determination. For two years, he would repeatedly attempt to escape, be caught, and go on the run. Finally, in 1845, he purchased his freedom for $1,800. Parker left the Deep South for Jeffersonville, Indiana, where he worked as an iron molder for some time, then moved to Cincinnati. As he settled in Ohio, the region's booming iron industry allowed him to find gainful employment. As he became associated with the free black community in Cincinnati, hints of Underground Railroad activity became frequent. After his reluctant introduction to the broader network of conductors in Ripley, Parker returned to Cincinnati incapable of leaving the Underground Railroad out of his mind. He thought often of the girls he helped escape to freedom. It was likely he had flashbacks to his own childhood as he returned. How sweet it would have been had a man like Parker rescued him from the hardships of his life on the Virginia plantation when he was a boy. In the years after his introduction to Ripley, the adventures of the Underground Railroad gravitated toward Parker. In 1847, Levi Coffin had made Cincinnati his new home. The man that John B. Mahan had sent so many fugitives to in Indiana was now ready to continue his work on the front lines of the Ohio River. Parker became acquainted with Coffin in Cincinnati and harbored an immense respect for "how resourceful" the Quaker abolitionist was as he helped fugitives escape. Still, the more connected to the Cincinnati community he became, the more he felt pulled to return to Ripley. Except for Coffin, the Ripley network of conductors were widely more efficient and united than what he experienced in Cincinnati. Ripley also had an iron foundry, which Parker determined he could work at if he lived there. After his marriage to Miranda Boulden in 1848, they made plans to relocate to Ripley.

Parker seamlessly integrated into the network of Ripley conductors. It wasn't long before he found himself leading extremely dangerous missions rescuing fugitives. What made Parker especially valuable was his willingness to often cross the river into the heart of slavery to conduct his rescues. Rankin quickly took notice of Parker, and the two of them developed a deep mutual respect. "The real fortress and home to the fugitives was the house of Rev. John Rankin," Parker wrote years later, "perched on a high hill behind the town. A single-story brick house, it sheltered Rev. John Rankin, a man of deeds as well as words." Rankin, Parker noted, was the "undoubted leader" of the Ripley abolitionists. Scarcely a night went by when Parker wasn't helping fugitives escape. Many he sent up the hill to Rankin's hilltop fortress. So routine had Parker's activities become that when one of Rankin's sons came urgently knocking on Parker's door near daybreak one Sunday, he could instantly tell that something was wrong.

"I had been told to bring all my firearms," Parker recalled, "which I did, including an old musket. I knew something was seriously up, because this was the first time I had ever been called on to come armed with anything but small arms." As the Rankin boy proceeded to explain, a group of five fugitives "either miscalculated the time or wandered from their route." No matter the reason, they arrived on the banks of the river "too late to be ferried across" and sat helplessly on the shore for all to see. Rankin caught wind of their predicament. Walking out of his home that morning, Rankin prepared to head for the home of Thomas Collins to work on a rescue plan. As the sun rose across along the Ohio River, he stopped in his tracks. There on the riverbank, cowering, praying for someone to rescue them from the punishment that surely awaited them once they were caught, Rankin spotted them. As he stood along the hillside, staring at their helpless state, something stirred inside him. He had been active as a conductor for over twenty-five years in Ripley, but as many people as he had helped, he had always done so from his side of the river. How many poor souls made it all the way to the Kentucky banks of the Ohio River, just to be captured before crossing? Was there more that could have been done? Perhaps there was, or perhaps not. What he could have done differently in the past ultimately didn't matter. As he gazed across the river that morning, Rankin had resolved to ensure that those five fugitives wouldn't be taken back into bondage, no matter the cost.

As Parker walked through the door of the Collins home, he could sense an uneasiness in the air. Sitting in the front room, there was Dr. Alexander Campbell, along with Eli, the wealthy businessman Tom McCague, and Dr. Alfred Beasley. Rankin was in the center of "the council of war," as Parker called it. "They were gravely discussing the situation when I entered." Rankin, Parker recalled, looked as if he had seen a ghost. "I can still see the pale face of Rev. Rankin" as he laid out his rescue plan. To everyone's surprise, Rankin's plan was to cross the river "heavily armed in broad daylight," secure the fugitives, and fight back against any who would try to stop them. He volunteered himself, six of his sons, and, to his surprise, Parker. Anyone else willing could join them in their rescue mission, Rankin told them.

Rev. John Rankin, circa 1840. Throughout the 1840's, John Rankin had his convictions tested like never before. He started to consider the possibility that slavery can only end through a violent conflict.

Rankin's proposal was utterly reckless, and several in the meeting knew this. "The question was," Parker wrote, "how would the citizens of the town take this invasion of an armed force into the friendly State of Kentucky?" Even if this extraction could be pulled off without incident, there would be bounty hunters on the Ohio side keeping an eye out for runaways. The hunters could easily watch Rankin and his sons march through the streets of Ripley with these fugitives as they headed toward Rankin's home. It would expose the Ripley line and open the community to a new wave of violence. Rankin may have been prepared for a gunfight, but the damage to their Underground Railroad efforts would be insurmountable. All these hypotheticals kindly assumed that an all-out war wouldn't break over the extraction between Kentucky and Ohio. With a bounty still on Rankin's head, the slaveholders across the river would be looking for any justification to attack Ripley in such a manner.

Campbell and Beasley made these points and more to Rankin. Ultimately, reason prevailed. The "council of war" determined that any action taken in broad daylight would be too risky, and could damage the entire operation of the Ripley line. If the runaways were still sitting on the Kentucky shore by nightfall, they would act then, but no earlier. Rankin knew this to be the right move, but he walked away discouraged. Parker, for his part, had been worked up by Rankin and was prepared to carry out his role in the extraction. "I am afraid I was disappointed, because I was sure the group would be captured before night." Rankin walked out of the Collins house and prepared for his Sunday sermon, sharing Parker's fear. As he preached, his thoughts dwelled on the fugitives across the river. His congregation could tell something was awry, and those who knew of the dilemma became worried that Rankin may accidentally reveal their dire situation. McCague crossed paths with Parker after the service. McCague shared that he became worried during Rankin's prayer that "the wrought-up preacher" would accidentally unveil "the presence of the slaves and their serious situation in his appeal to the Almighty for their protection during the day." Rankin, however, felt comforted after his prayer, sharing in discussion with Parker that he was confident "they would be watched over and protected."

Ironically, the others who attended the "war council" that morning felt anxious in anticipation. Their gaze frequently fell upon the spot the fugitives huddled that morning. "It was a long day for all of us," Parker noted. As nightfall finally came, Parker armed himself as he joined six others in crossing the river, hoping the five fugitives were still there. As they landed in Kentucky, Parker recalled how they "found them all right, scared and hungry." Quietly, they loaded them on one of the boats and rowed back to Ohio. Swiftly, they brought them through Ripley, where the council from that morning was staying, confirming the success of the mission. From there, they went to Rankin's house, where Jean ensured the five were properly fed. They were then taken to Gilliland's station at the Red Oak Church. As dawn broke on Monday morning, the "war council" could confidently say that their extraction brought no unwanted attention. The five moved up the line and disappeared, as so many had done before. If you asked Rankin how such a feat was accomplished, it's likely he would simply tell you they were "watched over and protected."[176]

THE DARK DECADE
1850–1861
IX.

S almon Portland Chase was in his first term as a United States senator from Ohio in 1850. The Ohio legislature selected Chase as one of Ohio's senators in Washington, not as a Democrat or a Whig, but as a Free Soil candidate. The Free Soil Party sprouted out of the Liberty Party and, unlike its predecessor, was doing surprisingly well electorally. Whereas the Liberty Party was extremely fixated on political abolitionism, the Free Soil Party represented more of a coalition, with slavery as the focus, but not the sole issue. With its slogan of "free soil, free speech, free labor, and free men," it attracted abolitionists, certainly. It also attracted small-town merchants, farmers, and laborers. Additionally, it spoke to the issue of civil liberties, which attracted many old-school Jeffersonians who had become dismayed by the Democrat's disregard for the principles of the freedom of speech and press during the Jacksonian era.

The Free Soil Party became particularly relevant in the wake of the war with Mexico. Following the admission of Texas into the Union, Mexico still considered the territory as its own. Tensions concentrated as a dispute over the true southern border of Texas arose. Texas, and by extension the United States, claimed it was at the Rio Grande. Mexico claimed the Nueces River further north as the border. After a failed diplomatic mission, President James K. Polk sent American forces led by General Zachary Taylor to the Rio Grande to defend land the United States declared was part of Texas. Seen as an invasion by Mexico, a skirmish broke out between American and Mexican forces. It was all President Polk needed to justify requesting a formal declaration of war, which Congress granted on May 13, 1846.

The war with Mexico realized all the worst abolitionist fears. Polk sought to conquer as much land as possible. This abundance of new territory would spark an unnerving domestic battle over the slave status of new states admitted. Months after the war was declared, Pennsylvania Democratic Congressman David Wilmot proposed an amendment to an appropriation bill that would permit the acquisition of territory in the wake of any peace negotiations with Mexico. Dubbed the Wilmot Proviso, the amendment would prohibit slavery from expanding into newly acquired territory following a peace agreement. As a "condition of the acquisition of any territory from the Republic of Mexico…neither slavery nor involuntary servitude shall ever exist in any part of said territory, except for crime, whereof the party shall first be duly convicted." The amendment borrowed heavily from the Northwest Ordinance of 1787. Although it passed in the House, it couldn't pass in the Senate. Notably, the vote in the House was divided by sectionalism rather than partisanship. Despite the failure of the Wilmot Proviso, Chase believed it would "exert a tremendous influence."[177]

Two years later, war with Mexico had concluded, and the land that made up California and New Mexico was to the United States. As Chase entered Congress in 1849, the country was again embroiled in a great debate over whether this vast new territory would support or prohibit slavery. Fuel was added to the fire when, to the outrage of the South, California applied for statehood in 1849 as a free state. Determined to maintain their political influence, Southerners refused to accept California's admittance without concessions. There were murmurings of secession, and unionists like Henry Clay began to panic. Dubbed

"The Great Compromiser," Clay began crafting a bill that he hoped would preserve the Union. In January 1850, he introduced an omnibus that combined eight individual measures. This included the admittance of California as a free state, a prohibition on the DC slave trade (though not a ban on slavery itself), and, most notably, a stricter fugitive slave law. The decades of work that John Rankin and others committed to the Underground Railroad infuriated southern slaveowners. Every slave that ran away cost them thousands of dollars. The Fugitive Slave Act of 1793 wasn't enough for them – they wanted northerners to be held liable for slaves who successfully escaped to Canada. California statehood would come at the expense of men like Rankin.

As the debate over Clay's resolutions was underway, Chase rose to speak "with unaffected diffidence" to "the important questions presented by the resolutions of the honorable Senator from Kentucky." Chase was quick to remind his Congressional colleagues how new he was to the legislative process. He had served on the Cincinnati City Council in 1840, but other than that, the Senate was his first elected position. "I speak from no eminence which will entitle me to command attention," he stated. "I claim for what I say that consideration only which is due to sincerity of belief…." He proceeded to make an argument for a belief he had long maintained by this point. While Congress had no authority to pass legislation that affected slavery within the states, it could, Chase argued, "prevent its extension, and to prohibit its existence within the sphere of the exclusive jurisdiction of the General Government."

His position was for the federal government to be totally divorced from the institution of slavery. Not only was this constitutional, Chase argued, but it was also what the founders had envisioned from the beginning. The American Revolution, he asserted, "was waged not to vindicate privileges, but rights; not the rights of any part or class of the people, but the rights of all men —'the rights of human nature.'" Chase invoked the legacies of notable founding fathers such as George Washington, James Madison, and Patrick Henry. The legacy of Thomas Jefferson, though, was one that Chase took a specific interest in.

Jefferson's role and influence in preventing slavery from expanding into the Northwest Territory "proved that the declaration of 1776 was not an empty profession, but a true faith." The Northwest Ordinance, he proceeded to argue, represented America's destiny to quarantine, and eventually vanquish slavery from the continent. He added,

> If a stranger from some foreign land should ask me for the monument of Jefferson, I would not take him to Virginia, and bid him look on a granite obelisk, however admirable in its proportions or its inscriptions. I would ask him to accompany me beyond the Alleghanies, into the midst of the broad Northwest, and would say to him: "*Si Monumentum Requiris, Circumspice.*"

> Behold, on every side, his monument. These thronged cities, these flourishing villages, these cultivated fields; these million happy homes of prosperous freemen; these churches, these schools, these asylums for the unfortunate and the helpless: these institutions of education, religion, and humanity; these great States, great in their present resources, but greater far in the mighty energies by which the resources of the future are to be developed; these, these are the monuments of Jefferson. His memorial is over all our western land.[178]

Clay's omnibus package was not long for this world. Despite his best efforts, the bill failed on July 31, 1850. Rather than appeal to all factions, it angered them. Northern anti-slavery men and Southern democrats alike were hostile to the bill. The seventy-three-year-old Clay, dealing with the tiring effects of tuberculosis, had little energy to start from scratch. Instead, an up-and-coming senator from Illinois by the name of Stephen Douglas continued to refine the compromise. Rather than a single omnibus package, Douglas introduced the major components of the compromise as five individual bills in September. The bills passed and were signed into law by President Millard Fillmore. Under normal circumstances, the admittance of California as a free state and the end of the DC slave trade would cause abolitionists to celebrate. The signing of the new Fugitive Slave Act into law on September 18 instead sparked outrage.[179]

The updated fugitive slave law sought to provide its 1793 predecessor with more teeth. Whereas the prior law offered legal protection for slaveowners to pursue runaways into northern states, it was difficult to enforce. The updated law denied the right to a trial by jury for any alleged runaway. It worsened the punishment for those who "knowingly and willingly obstruct" the capture of fugitives. Anyone caught attempting "to rescue…aid, abet, or assist" in the escape of a slave faced a fine of up to $1,000 or six months in jail. The penalty under the 1793 law, in contrast, would amount to a $500 fine. Perhaps most controversially, the new law commanded "all good citizens" to "aid and assist in the prompt and efficient execution of this law, whenever their services may be required."

Proponents of the Fugitive Slave Act believed that the risk of disunion had finally dissipated. The abolitionists—the individuals primarily responsible for driving the wedge, they argued—would finally be neutralized. But as word of the law spread, just the opposite happened. Not only were abolitionists across the country defiant, but even moderate anti-slavery proponents found themselves siding with the "radicals" in opposition of the law. On October 5, the Saturday before election day in Ohio, *The Ripley Bee* published the Fugitive Slave Act in full. Rankin and the Ripley conductors were indignant and refused to abide by the new law. *The National Era* reported on November 14 that "We observe in our exchanges reports of numerous meetings of the people in all the free States, called to denounce the Fugitive law."[180] These public meetings spread like wildfire in the north. Residents of Brown County held such a meeting a few days earlier on the tenth in Sardinia, Ohio. Coming out of the meeting, the attendees resolved that "the law, passed at the last session of Congress, relating to fugitives from labor, is at open war with justice, liberty, the Constitution of the United States, and the Word of God." Additionally, they declared that "all who voted in favor of that law are traitors to the Constitution and Christianity." Furthermore, "all who accept the detestable offices created by that law forfeit all claims to the regard and respect of their neighbors; and we hereby pledge ourselves that, knowingly, we will neither buy, sell, lend, nor borrow, with anyone, nor support for any office anyone, who may accept appointments under it."[181]

Fifteen years earlier, Rankin was giving lectures across the state and helping launch new anti-slavery societies. In the fall of 1850, he was again on the road, rallying communities against the Fugitive Slave Law. At the same time, Chase had returned to Ohio after months of debating the compromise in Congress. Opponents of the law were excited to hear from the senator who refused to compromise on the matter. In Greenfield, Ohio, Chase dropped in on a public meeting opposing the law where Rankin was speaking and Adam Lowry Rankin was appointed to a committee on resolutions. Rankin read the Fugitive Slave Law in its entirety to the crowd. The audience became animated and called upon Chase to speak. Chase, happy to oblige, approached the podium to address the meeting. He "spoke at some length" on the unconstitutionality of the law, further exciting the crowd. Some remarks followed Chase's address to the crowd, then the committee's report was "read, accepted, and unanimously adopted." They declared that "we hold it as a self-evident truth, that the authority of the most High God is paramount, and that his law is above all law." Therefore, the report concluded, disobedience to the enactment of the Fugitive Slave Law "is obedience to God." Chase would have certainly appreciated the Jeffersonian language used in the resolution. The meeting continued well into the night. As the sun set, they recessed briefly to light candles around the room. Rankin then approached the podium once more, speaking to the "unconstitutionality and wickedness" of the law.[182]

U.S. Senator Salmon P. Chase. After the Fugitive Slave Act passed Congress in 1850, Chase and John Rankin spoke together in opposition to the new law.

As Rankin and Lowry returned to Ripley, they continued to whip up local opposition. The Ripley Presbytery passed a series of resolutions, similar in language to those passed in public meetings across the north. On December 17, the Presbytery approved resolutions that declared the Fugitive Slave Law to be "practical atheism" because it "commands what God positively forbids" and is in "high-handed rebellion against his authority." Therefore, "it is the duty of all men to disobey it in defiance of all its penalties."[183] All resolutions that the Presbytery adopted were forwarded to *The Ripley Bee* for publication. At the Stone Church in Red Oak on Christmas Day, the "People of Brown County, Ohio, without distinction of party," pledged their support for the Constitution and "all laws made in conformity therewith." The Fugitive Slave Law was a "clear violation" of both "the letter and the spirit of the Constitution, and therefore cannot be binding upon us." They declared their "deliberate determination" to refuse any help that could be lent toward the enforcement of the law. It would be better, they asserted, for the government to "resort to its old practice of employing blood hounds to hunt down its human prey, than to command all good citizens to perform that service." Upon the arrival of the New Year in 1851, it was clear that the slave question was far from settled.[184]

* * * * *

September of 1850 brought heartache to Rankin for several reasons. The passage of the Fugitive Slave Law was troubling, but the death of his dear friend, Samuel Donnell, was heartbreaking. Rankin had been Donnell's friend since 1817, when Rankin had stopped in Carlisle, Kentucky and agreed to preach at the Concord Church. Donnell was an elder at the church and had established a longstanding reputation of opposing slavery by the time Rankin arrived. Inspired by the abolitionist minister David Rice's crusade against the institution during Kentucky's constitutional convention, Donnell "took an active part… in getting up associations through the county, and passing resolutions instructing our delegates to make provision in the constitution for the emancipation of the slaves." As Rankin and his family finished their journey to Ripley, Donnell moved with much of his church to Decatur County, Indiana. A new church was formed following their arrival, in which Donnell served as an elder for over the next twenty years, until his hearing loss forced him to step down. As the Presbyterian Church became consumed with schisms throughout the 1840s, Donnell was delighted to hear of Rankin's efforts to form the Free Presbyterian Church. Just before his death, he voted for his church to disassociate with the New School and join the Free Presbyterians in fellowship. The motion was carried unanimously.[185]

Rankin found himself reminiscing over his days with Donnell in Kentucky. "At this period, before the days of colonization, there were in the slave States many noble spirits," he wrote, "who stood up boldly for liberty." He fondly recalled how bold these Kentucky abolitionists were to openly advocate for "the doctrine of immediate abolition, which the enemies of liberty now call modern abolitionism, and pretend that it never existed until the days of Garrison." How distant those days of early abolitionism must have felt to Rankin as 1850 came to a close. This once robust and powerful movement was being torn apart by factions before his eyes. Rankin remained active with the American Anti-Slavery Society, but William Lloyd Garrison's growing radicalism pushed many supporters away. The abolitionists had been fracturing at a growing rate since at least the 1840 election. Disheartened by the splintering of the movement, Rankin sought to return to the fundamentals of what made the abolitionists such a powerful force in the first place.

Rankin had long been frustrated by the refusal of the American Tract Society to publish anti-slavery tracts. Founded in 1825, the society was formed to distribute Christian literature more widely to the public. At the time, the Bible was widely distributed, but few other options remained for those who wanted to dive deeper into theological literature. However, they "refused to publish tracts against slaveholding." Rankin concluded that another tract society should be formed with the explicit purpose of distributing Christian anti-slavery literature. The American Anti-Slavery Society had already demonstrated the proof of concept. Rankin's *Letters on Slavery* were among the first pieces of literature that they distributed. But they took a broad approach, not focusing on Christian abolitionism exclusively. Especially since the formation of the Free Presbyterian Church, Rankin's resolve to "cleanse" Christianity of the slavery influences had grown. At an anti-slavery convention in Chicago, he tried to gauge interest in the formation of a new tract society. There was significant interest after conversations with several attendees; however, no action was taken after the convention ended. Rankin finally took matters into his own hands. In the fall of 1851, he issued a call to officially organize a tract society that would be unafraid to publish literature opposing the "ruinous system of oppression" in America. On December 17, a meeting took place in the Vine Street Congregational Church in Cincinnati, Ohio to form the American Reform Tract and Book Society. Fittingly, Rankin was selected as the first president of the new organization. Immediately, raising funds for the creation and distribution of literature became an issue. For most individuals involved in the new society, churches refused to open their doors to allow them to speak. Schism still plagued the Presbyterian church, and several other denominations were undergoing a similar internal struggle over slavery. In the early days of the society's existence, it was up to Rankin to raise most of the funds needed. In this, he found more success than any other member.[186]

As it happened, Rankin wasn't the only Ohio abolitionist in 1851 interested in the disbursement of anti-slavery literature. On June 5, the first entry of a fictional story written by Harriet Beecher Stowe appeared in *The National Era*. On the front page, readers saw in bold letters: "**UNCLE TOM'S CABIN**: OR, LIFE AMONG THE LOWLY."[187]

For forty weeks, Stowe sent segments of this story, detailing the cruelty of slavery as well as its effect on Ohio communities across the river. Although a fictional drama, Stowe pulled from real-life examples that she had experienced or heard of through her close connection to the Cincinnati and Ripley conductors. There was one character in Stowe's chronicles that Rankin would have recognized quickly. In Stowe's story, the readers follow the journey of a slave woman named Eliza as she flees her master and escapes to the North through the Underground Railroad. As more of the story was released each week, Eliza soon found herself on the banks of Kentucky with her young son, prepared to cross the icy river in hopes of reaching "a large white house which stood by itself, off the main street of the village." She was told that "kind folks" lived there and that she would find no danger "but they'll help you— they'r up to all that sort o' thing." Stowe detailed the harrowing trek that Eliza made across the river on this cold, wintery night to the "large white house" on the hill behind the village. To the Rankin family, there was little doubt about where Stowe found her inspiration. While many details were changed for safety (Rankin's house was small and brick, for instance, not large and white), Eliza's journey was clearly modeled after the slave woman the Rankins found huddled around their fireplace in February 1838.

Harriet Beecher Stowe had known John Rankin for decades by the time *Uncle Tom's Cabin* was published. The character "Eliza" was inspired by John Rankin's account of the slave woman who crossed the Ohio River with her child in her arms.

As *The National Era* continued to publish segments of *Uncle Tom's Cabin* each week, Stowe was contacted by Boston publisher John P. Jewett. He was captivated by the story and convinced that if it were to be turned into a book, it would become a runaway bestseller.[188] His intuition proved accurate. On March 20, 1852, *Uncle Tom's Cabin* sold 3,000 copies in a single day. By the end of the year, over 300,000 copies were sold in the United States alone. In the United Kingdom, over 1.5 million copies were sold. Harriet Beecher Stowe became known the world over, and the debate over slavery grew with a fiery intensity. Immediately, supporters of slavery downplayed Stowe's depictions of slavery in the novel. Attempting to discredit her, critics claimed she overly dramatized the situations in the book to make slavery appear crueler than it was. Rankin and his family knew better, but there was little they could say in her defense without exposing much of their own involvement in the Underground Railroad. The following year, Stowe felt compelled to release *A Key to Uncle Tom's Cabin*.[189] She offered several "facts and documents" which she pulled from as she crafted the story of *Uncle Tom's Cabin*. "This work," Stowe asserted, "more, perhaps, than any other work of fiction that ever was written, has been a collection and arrangement of real incidents,—of actions really performed, of words and expressions really uttered,—grouped together with reference to a general result, in the same manner that the mosaic artist groups his fragments of various stones into one general picture." Stowe proceeded to offer citations for each of the major players and incidents detailed in the novel, including the character of Eliza, specifically her crossing of the icy Ohio River. Stowe recalled an incident the prior spring, as the backlash against her story was beginning to escalate. She was in New York when she had an interaction with a Presbyterian minister from Ohio. "I understand they dispute that fact about the woman's crossing the river," he said to her. "Now, I know all about that, for I got the story from the very man that helped her up the bank. I know it is true, for she is now living in Canada." Naming Rankin outright as the source of the story would have put him at serious risk of legal trouble or physical harm. For the time being, his official role would remain anonymous.

* * * * *

William Lloyd Garrison had long held an admiration for Rankin similar to that of Stowe's. Since Rankin's *Letters* had reached Garrison's hands, Garrison considered himself a disciple of the Ripley conductor. He wouldn't hesitate to point to Rankin as the reason for his coming to abolitionism. But after nearly two decades of anti-slavery advocacy, Rankin and Garrison were on notably separate paths. Throughout the 1830s, they diverged on a handful of issues, but the mission of building out the network of anti-slavery societies always seemed to make those differences secondary. Their differences became more publicly notable around the election of 1840. Rankin, who believed the political process should be used to advance the cause of abolition, rejected Garrison's political abstinence. Throughout the 1840s and early 1850s, Garrison only became more radicalized against political abolitionism. During the tenth anniversary of the American Anti-Slavery Society, Garrisonians convinced the society to adopt a policy of national dissolution. The executive committee, with Garrison sitting as president, issued an address which, among other things, suggested that the motto of "the banner of Freedom should be, NO UNION WITH SLAVEHOLDERS" (emphasis his). Rankin had worried that slavery may drive the nation to disunion, but for the American Anti-Slavery Society to openly call for the secession of the North was not something he could stand behind.[190]

Even Garrison's pupil, Frederick Douglass, found himself at odds with his mentor and friend over political and constitutional abolitionism. Following Douglass's escape from slavery in Maryland, he traveled to Nantucket, Massachusetts in 1841 to hear the famed Garrison speak at a meeting of the Massachusetts Anti-Slavery Society. After a series of speakers, Douglass was urged to address the crowd and tell the story of his experiences under slavery. In what was perhaps one of the most important decisions of his life, he agreed to do so. Most of those in attendance had never heard a first-hand account of slavery. "Flinty hearts were pierced," it was reported in *The National Anti-Slavery Standard*, "and cold ones melted by his eloquence. Our best pleaders for the slave held their breath for fear of interrupting him." Garrison was taken aback by the story of Douglass, but he was also inspired. In Douglass, he believed, the Anti-Slavery Society would have their secret weapon to destroy the system of slavery once and for all.[191]

As their friendship grew, Douglass bought into the Garrisonian view of abolitionism completely. To Douglass, slavery was a moral evil, not something to be reasoned or negotiated with. Garrison was one of the first people who fully understood this. Douglass was also encouraged by the network of abolitionists that the American Anti-Slavery

Society had successfully managed to spread across the country. He became one of the society's most effective speakers. As the decade went on and the debate between the Garrisonians and the political abolitionists concentrated, Douglass's viewpoint began to shift. The refusal of the Garrisonians to adopt a practical solution paired with their insistence on moral purity among their ranks seemed counterintuitive to the cause of abolition. If they were to demand a perfect solution without engaging in the political process, slavery may never be defeated. Additionally, Douglass's boundless intellectual curiosity led him to a different perspective on the Constitution than what Garrison held. Garrison asserted that the Constitution was a pro-slavery document. As Douglass continued to study the text and the positions that the framers held on slavery, concluded that his abolitionist mentor may be wrong. In 1847, Douglass made his first split with Garrison as he launched *The North Star* newspaper in Rochester, New York. Douglass insisted the reason was that it was beneficial to the cause for a black-operated abolitionist newspaper to exist. There was truth to this, but as he set out on his own, Douglass was free to adopt positions he never could under Garrison. During the 1851 annual meeting of the American Anti-Slavery Society in Syracuse, New York, Douglass made a public breaking from Garrison. He opposed a proposal which would have prevented any publication from being supported by the American Anti-Slavery Society unless it supported the view that the Constitution was a pro-slavery document. Douglass's "mind had undergone a radical change in reference to some points," reported *The National Anti-Slavery Standard* in their coverage of the convention. "He never thought that the fundamental principle of the American Anti-Slavery Society was the dissolution of the Union."[192] As to the nature of the Constitution, Douglass had "patiently investigated both sides of the matter," and determined it best to "apply to it those well known principles the legal interpretation of which would make it consistent with its preamble and object." In other words, Douglass rejected the Garrisonian view of a pro-slavery Constitution. Garrison was agitated by his former pupil's apparent betrayal. "There is roguery somewhere," he exclaimed.[193]

Although Rankin and Garrison had frequently fallen on opposite sides of issues over the years, their differences seemingly never affected their cordiality toward each other. However, Garrison was already on edge following the Fugitive Slave Law of 1850. His falling out with Douglass only furthered his frustration. So, in April 1853, when Garrison arrived in Cincinnati at the same anti-slavery convention as Rankin, conflict may have been inevitable. Garrison's presence at the convention immediately raised controversy. The convention opened on Tuesday, April 19, featuring both Garrison and Rankin as lead speakers. The two men had "a warm discussion" both "for and against" a series of "peculiar" resolutions that Garrison presented independent of the Business Committee he sat on. Among them included a resolution that the government and constitution should be "excommunicated, at whatever hazard, cost, or opprobrium" by abolitionists. He also offered a resolution calling for the anti-slavery movement at large to adopt the motto of "No union with slaveholders, religiously or politically." It wasn't clear exactly which aspects of Garrison's resolutions Rankin supported and opposed. Given Rankin's leadership in the formation of the Free Presbyterian Church, it is very likely that he supported Garrison's call for disunion with slaveholders in the church. However, based on Rankin's prior positions concerning political abolitionism, he likely opposed Garrison's call for the dissolution of the American Union. Rankin wasn't alone in his opposition, and the convention voted down both resolutions.

Whichever specific aspects of these resolutions Rankin opposed, it was clear that Garrison was greatly irritated by Rankin's disapproval. Lowry recalled how Garrison had made use of "some language bordering on the personal" in his "warm discussion" with Rankin. The convention president, Samuel Lewis, interrupted Garrison, fearful that "the warmth of the debate would result in the alienation of principal speakers for and against the resolutions [which were] before the convention" and believed that it "would be a calamity for two such champions of the antislavery cause as Rev. John Rankin and William Lloyd

Garrison to have [a] bitterness of feeling toward each other as a result of this discussion."

Garrison could read the room. As he responded to Lewis, he assured the convention that it is "out of the range of my purpose to be personal in my remarks. I have too great a respect for Mr. Rankin to wound his feelings and I am confident he is too loyal a Christian to wound mine." Furthermore, the idea of insulting Rankin was unfathomable to Garrison, he asserted, because he was Garrison's "antislavery father." John's *Letters on American Slavery*, Garrison reminded the convention, "was the cause of my entering the antislavery conflict."

As the convention came to an end, Lewis remained frustrated by Garrison. Lewis offered clarification in his closing remarks. "Your humble servant has tried to do his best, and be impartial to all who desired to speak." Garrison's debate with Rankin had noticeably gotten under his skin. "Doubts were expressed whether I would be willing to attend this Convention, if [William] Lloyd Garrison were invited. Now, I want it understood, that my feelings were hurt by the hint." Lewis welcomed the free spirit of debate, but had little time for rhetoric intended to insult. He extended additional praise to Rankin as he explored the church's important role in the anti-slavery cause. "Shall I hesitate about the value of the church, imperfect as it is, when I look upon Father Rankin, born and reared under the influence of slavery, yet taught by that word the principles of liberty, and made a light, set as it were, on a hill? No."

Afterward, Garrison may have experienced some guilt over his interactions with Rankin throughout the week. Perhaps he felt especially indebted to his "antislavery father." Following his split with Douglass, Garrison probably wasn't eager to make another split with Rankin. Whatever the reason, he approached Rankin with a gift. Garrison gave Rankin a copy of a book containing his speeches and writings. Inside the book, he wrote a note on the fly-leaf page: "Presented to Rev. John Rankin with the profoundest regards and loving veneration of his *anti-slavery disciple* and humble co-worker in the cause of emancipation, William Lloyd Garrison, Cincinnati, O. April 20, 1853." It was almost as if he were offering Rankin reassurance that no matter how far they may deviate on certain issues, Garrison would always harbor respect and gratitude toward his "antislavery father."[194]

William Lloyd Garrison and John Rankin didn't always see eye to eye, but Garrison's adoration and respect for Rankin was never affected. He wrote this note to Rankin in Cincinnati following an ideological dispute in 1853.

* * * * *

Lowry remained as active as possible in the anti-slavery cause during the early 1850s. Following his return from Iowa, he found employment acting as an agent for different newspapers and societies, including the *True American*. Originally published in Lexington, Kentucky in 1845, the *True American* was forced to relocate to Cincinnati after a headline entitled "What is Become of the Slaves in the United States?" elicited the scorn of pro-slavery mobs. Cassius Marcellus Clay, a fierce abolitionist, former Kentucky state representative, and Henry Clay's cousin, ran the publication. Lowry also served as a supply pastor for remote churches in the countryside, helping to establish and grow many congregations in the area, just as his father had upon their arrival in Ripley.

Lowry aided his father in whatever Rankin needed to help fight against the new Fugitive Slave Law in 1850. Shortly after the American Reform Tract and Book Society was formed, he worked for it as a general agent. In December 1852, however, Lowry's wife's health deteriorated. Amanda had been crippled for nearly a decade, virtually incapacitated since their return from Iowa in the fall of 1843. As Lowry decided to resign from the new tract society to remain close to his disabled wife, he returned to preaching locally. Finally, on April 10, 1853, Amanda Rankin died in Ripley, Ohio.

In a span of seven years, Rankin lost both a son and a daughter-in-law. Following David's death, his children had to learn to navigate the increasingly hostile world they found themselves in without a father. In the time between Amanda's accident and her death, she and Lowry produced three children, two of whom survived past infancy. Now these two would have to do the same without their mother. Overcome by grief, Lowry sought to escape from his sorrows in Ripley, accepting a position as pastor of a church he had previously helped organize in Clifton, Ohio. He spent some time traveling around the other parts of the country following Amanda's death as well, notably in New England. During his travels, Lowry came to know and build a new affection for a young lady named Margaret Donnell of Kingston, Indiana. Margaret was the great-niece of Rankin's late friend, Samuel Donnell. Born in 1831, she was also nearly fifteen years younger than Lowry. Her youth, however, seemed to awaken a new life in him. Lowry had been a faithful husband, but the unfortunate circumstance of his first marriage was difficult for both him and Amanda. While he tried to keep busy, he was frequently in a state of depression. Lowry's mental state was further tested following Amanda's passing. Getting to know Margaret was a refreshing change of pace from the last decade of his life, and one he didn't intend to let pass him. On Thursday, July 27, 1854, he had taken Margaret's hand in marriage.[195]

* * * * *

Meanwhile, as Lowry was processing grief and rediscovering love, the Whig Party found itself embroiled in an identity crisis. Following the compromise of 1850, Senators Clay and Daniel Webster had little wind left in them. Clay and Webster were not only two of the most important Whigs in Congress, they also rank highly among the most prominent senators in American history. Along with South Carolina Democrat John C. Calhoun, they formed the so-called "Great Triumvirate." Calhoun, a staunch defender of both slavery and nullification, died in March 1850, months before the passage of the new Fugitive Slave Act. Two years later, the great compromiser himself, Clay, passed away in June 1852. By October of the same year, the final member of the triumvirate, Webster, followed his predecessors to the grave. Already spiraling toward ineptitude since the compromise of 1850, the deaths of Clay and Webster determined the fate of the Whigs. Most Americans still wouldn't identify as abolitionists by 1854, but concern over slavery continued to grow with the American public. It was clear that the Whigs weren't up to the challenge set before them. The country needed a bold, new party to address the impending crisis.[196]

The Liberty Party, though it picked up steam in the 1844 election, was too narrow to attract a greater coalition than political abolitionists. The Free Soil Party showed promise as it began to win elections in many state legislatures, but it struggled to grow much beyond that or tip the legislative scales in their favor.

A new generation of political leaders sought to fill the power vacuum left in the absence of Clay, Webster, and Calhoun's leadership. A bill introduced in January by Senator Stephen Douglas of Illinois brought added urgency to the formation of a new party. Douglas advanced the cause of slavery in the halls of Congress, as did Jefferson Davis of Mississippi, before he left the Senate to serve as secretary of war under President Franklin Pierce. On the other side of the aisle, Chase and his friend Charles Sumner of Massachusetts took up the anti-slavery cause. The bill Douglas advanced through the Committee on Territories would become as great a threat to the anti-slavery cause as the Fugitive Slave Law had less than four years prior. Entitled "An Act to Organize the Territories of Nebraska and Kansas,"[197] the bill ensured that new states coming out of the Kansas and Nebraska territories would "be received into the Union with or without slavery, as their Constitution may prescribe at the time of their admission." In other words, the Missouri Compromise of 1820 would be repealed, and slavery would be permitted in new states formed north of the 36°30′ parallel. Four years earlier, southerners were outraged that California would be admitted into the Union as a free state, pointing to violation of the Missouri Compromise. Now, slavery proponents in Congress, led by Douglas, openly advocated repeal of the very same compromise. It was clear to many Americans, abolitionist or not, that proponents of slavery were no longer trying to merely preserve slavery in their own states. Instead, proponents of slavery now sought to spread the institution across the Union, until free states were choked out. Following the introduction of the bill, Chase, Sumner, and Representatives Joshua Giddings, Edward Wade, Gerritt Smith, and Alexander De Witt released an address entitled an "Appeal of the Independent Democrats in Congress to the People of the United States." They declared it was their duty as "Senators and Representatives in the Congress of the United States" to warn their constituents "whenever imminent danger menaces the freedom of our institutions or the permanency of our Union." The proposed Nebraska bill, they "firmly believe[d]," presented such a danger. "We arraign this bill as a gross violation of a sacred pledge; as a criminal betrayal of precious rights; as part and parcel of an atrocious plot to exclude from a vast unoccupied region immigrants from the Old World and free laborers from our own States, and convert it into a dreary region of despotism, inhabited by masters and slaves."[198]

Northerners were both angry and fearful regarding the implications of this new bill. Soon, just as had happened following the passage of the Fugitive Slave Law in 1850, public meetings sprouted up in communities across the country. In many of these anti-Nebraska meetings, the formation of a new political party took priority. During such a meeting in Ripon, Wisconsin, attendees suggested the name for such a party be "Republican." Rooted deeply in American history, the name drew inspiration from the Jeffersonian Republicans that defined the turn of the century, fifty years earlier. It took off like wildfire, and local Republican Parties began populating northern states.

* * * * *

The Nebraska debate and subsequent rise of the Republican Party in early 1854 directly influenced the success of the next Anti-Slavery Convention in Cincinnati that April. Rankin arrived at Greenwood Hall on April 12, 1854, to participate in what was reported to be "one of be largest and most enthusiastic Anti-Slavery gatherings ever held in the West."[199] As the convention proceeded, hardly a seat could be found open. "At all the evening sessions," reported *The National Era*, "every seat and every aisle were densely packed, and from five hundred to one thousand were obliged to go away without getting into the hall." A few decades earlier, Rankin would have been the main attraction at such a convention. During this spring assembly, however, there was one speaker that audiences regarded above the rest. "One of the most able and impressive speakers at the Convention was Frederick Douglas[s]," *The National Era* report continued. "It is wonderful, when we remember that thirteen or fourteen years ago he was a slave, that he has attained such eminence and influence in the country." Such a draw was Douglass that even Kentucky slaveholders crossed the river to hear him speak. Among the Kentuckians was former governor and US senator Thomas Metcalfe, present to hear from the powerful orator who escaped slavery. It is unclear if Rankin and Douglass had a quiet moment to speak with one another during the convention, but they almost certainly would have been aware of the other's attendance.

As official business was underway, the convention proceeded to declare that they "stand on the platform of the Revolution, and hold these truths to be self-evident:—'that all men are created equal; that they are endowed by their Creator with certain inalienable rights; that among them are life, liberty, and the pursuit of happiness.'" The convention then continued to pass a series of resolutions that condemned slavery broadly and the Nebraska bill specifically. "Resolved, that in seeking to repudiate the rule of the Missouri Compromise…slaveholders are acting entirely consistent with the genius of their Institution: that injustice, fraud, and robbery, form the groundwork of the slave system." Furthermore, the "present attempt to introduce slavery into Nebraska is but one step in a series of aggressions upon the rights and liberties of America, and one more act of subserviency on the part of Northern politicians with Southern principles." Embracing the principles of constitutional abolitionism, the convention demanded that the federal government "establish justice and secure the blessings of liberty" by prohibiting slavery in US territories, abolishing it in Washington, DC, repealing the Fugitive Slave Act, and prohibiting "the use of the inter-State Slave Trade upon the ocean and on all the National highways."[200]

The demands of the convention would ultimately fall on deaf ears. Despite a wave of opposition to the Nebraska bill, it passed through Congress and was signed into law by President Pierce on May 30, 1854. After the House passed the bill, *The Liberator* reported the distressing news on May 26. "The deed is done—the Slave Power is again victorious."[201] After detailing the nature of the vote, it defiantly declared: "A thousand times accursed be the Union which has made this possible!" The passage of the Nebraska bill caused the indignation of the Garrisonians to reach new levels. Making matters worse, the claws of the Fugitive Slave Law had recently been enforced in a rather public manner. On the evening of May 24, 1854, federal marshals arrested a fugitive slave by the name of Anthony Burns in Boston. Already agitated by the Nebraska bill, the capture of Burns instigated the abolitionist community to take up arms and attempt to storm the courthouse where Burns was held. A small group of twenty-five men attacked by breaking down the doors of the courthouse. The guards fought back, and one guard, James Batchelder, was killed in the skirmish. Police soon arrived to break up the riot and arrest many of the participants. President Pierce dispatched US Marines to ensure Burns would be extracted from Boston back to his Virginia slave master without incident. *The Liberator* was outraged: "Slave hunting defended at the point of bayonet – civil liberty prostrate before military despotism – Massachusetts in chains, and her subjugation absolute – the days of 1776 returned."

As the anniversary of American independence approached, Garrison had become so soured by the recent events that he felt America had little to celebrate. Still, he organized an Anti-Slavery Independence Day gathering in Framingham, Massachusetts. It attracted "almost unprecedented numbers" with "great unanimity and enthusiasm." The crowd that gathered on July 4 must have energized Garrison. Perhaps the heat that penetrated the event, "which was extreme," played a role in working him up as well. Garrison addressed the crowd. "Today, we are called to celebrate the seventy-eighth anniversary of American Independence," he told his audience. "In what spirit? With what purpose? To what end?" He declared American independence to be the "greatest political event in the annals of time," but betrayed by slavery's presence. Garrison continued to feed off the crowd's energy, which became more animated by his lengthy speech. Their excitement grew until Garrison finally reached his grand conclusion. He picked up a copy of the Fugitive Slave Law and proceeded to light it on fire. The crowd erupted into applause and praise. Garrison looked at the crowd and "using an old and well-known phrase, he said, 'And let all the people say, *Amen.*'" to which the crowd joined in unison, "Amen.". Then he repeated his actions with a copy of the decision in the case of Burns. Finally, and most dramatically, he picked up a copy of the Constitution. The crowd was worked to a frenzy as Garrison held it up and declared it "the parent of all other atrocities—'a covenant with death, and an agreement with hell.'" Without giving it a second thought, he set the document ablaze. "So perish all compromises with tyranny!" Waves of cheering and shouts of "Amen!" were deafening.

* * * * *

The Northern territories were reopened to slavery, and the federal government aggressively enforced the Fugitive Slave Law. Many in the North feared it would only be a matter of time until slavery was reintroduced in the North. Senator Douglas and his allies had embraced the concept of popular sovereignty in defense of the Nebraska bill. This was the notion that the fate of slavery should be determined by the people who resided in the state, and not the federal government. Problematically, abolitionists and slaveholders alike were rushing to Kansas following the passage of the bill to determine the fate of the soon-to-be state. Nearby Missourians flooded across the border, bringing their weapons and slaves with them. Countless armed abolitionists, prepared for the inevitable conflict that awaited them in Kansas, also made the journey. Among these anti-slavery migrants included a man named John Brown.

The Ripley community eagerly anticipated the latest correspondence out of Kansas. News from the territory trickled in until it was a near-weekly segment in *The Ripley Bee* and other local papers. "We arrived here about a week ago, and contributing our mi[ght] to prevent slavery [from] cursing the fairest part of creation," read one letter to the *Bee*. "Let me therefore say to one and all who ever design to come here, to come at once; no time is to be lost; you will find every assistance to get good claims rendered to you that is possible."[202] *The Independent American*, a Georgetown paper, reprinted a report of violence in Kansas by the *Chicago Tribune*. Fighting broke out over a land claim "that resulted, it is feared, fatally to two citizens of that territory." This was just the beginning. Violence would define the Kansas territory for the remainder of the decade.

In July, a public meeting was held in Brown County, open to all citizens "without distinction of party," to finally address the new Nebraska law. The anti-Nebraska meeting was led by local abolitionists such as *The Ripley Bee* editor Charles F. Campbell, Thomas McCague, William S. Humphreys, and Dr. Isaac Beck. Notably, Rankin took a back seat.[203]

They regarded the repeal of the Missouri Compromise a "breach of public faith, a gross outrage on the rights of Freedom, one of a series of measures intended to secure political power to the South, and to make Slavery the controlling interest of our country." They opposed the extension of slavery in "any territory now free" and demanded the reinstatement of the Missouri Compromise as well as the repeal of the Fugitive Slave Act.

By the time the Nebraska bill was signed by President Pierce, Rankin was sixty-one. He had devoted his entire life to the cause of abolition. He remained as active as he could, but his age was beginning to slow him down. He began to prioritize his role as minister over his activism. This and the time it took to build his tract society consumed most of his energy. His sons remained active in the Ripley community, which allowed him to focus his energies on other things. Calvin, for instance, became the Marshal in Ripley and had the daunting responsibility of keeping the peace during a decade of intensifying violence. One day in January 1855, Calvin got into a street altercation with an intoxicated Chancey Shaw. It had been decades since the former slave hunter helped the woman later remembered as Eliza escape to freedom. Chancey was a ruffian back then, and not much had changed in 1855. He was behaving disorderly when Calvin approached him with a warning that he would be arrested should he not control himself. Shaw, not taking too kindly to the warning, lunged at Calvin with a pocket knife. To avoid the assault, Calvin stumbled back and drew his pistol. He fired at Shaw three times, hitting a finger on his right hand once. In his drunken state, Shaw continued to pursue Calvin until the latter knocked Shaw out with an axe handle. After being subdued, Shaw was put under house arrest so his hand could heal.[204]

* * * * *

The decade was long and tiresome for Rankin. With each passing day, the advances that the slave powers made contributed to the increase in violence experienced throughout the country. Abolitionists were gaining certain grounds, but was it too late? In the fall of 1855, Salmon P. Chase had been elected as governor of Ohio on the Republican ticket—an important victory for the new political party. Chase swept Ripley specifically, with 477 votes in his favor, compared to 169 toward his Democratic opponent.[205] During his inaugural address, Chase reasserted his anti-slavery principles, especially as they pertained to the recent violence in Kansas. "The sole, special effect of the Nebraska-Kansas act upon the territories organized under it is to open them to the introduction of slaves." This, Chase prophetically proclaimed has led "to invasion, usurpation, violence, bloodshed—almost to civil war."[206] Over the next two years in Ohio, due to Chase's victory and Republican advances in the state, the legislature passed a series of "personal liberty laws," effectively nullifying aspects of the Fugitive Slave Law of 1850. These advances were bright spots in an otherwise dark era, however. Republicans didn't fare as well throughout the rest of the country, and they lost the presidential election the following year to Democrat James Buchanan.

Violence in Kansas had spread to other corners of the country as well, including to the halls of Congress. In May 1856, Chase's friend Sumner made a historic speech on the Senate floor entitled "The Crime Against Kansas." Sumner unleashed a scathing critique against the slave forces. "What could not be accomplished peaceably, was to be accomplished forcibly," he declared. During his speech, his remarks turned personal against Senators Douglas (Illinois) and Andrew Butler (South Carolina). Douglas, Sumner declared, was "the squire of slavery." As for Butler, Sumner suggested that he had "chosen a mistress to whom he has made his vows, and who, though ugly to others, is always lovely to him; though polluted in the sight of the world, is chaste in his sight? I mean the harlot, Slavery."

Butler's cousin, Preston Brooks, was a representative from South Carolina in the House chamber. Once he heard of Sumner's insinuation, he was infuriated, insulted, and embarrassed. Determined to defend his family's honor, Brooks marched from the House to the Senate chambers three days after Sumner's address with a cane in hand. Brooks found Sumner sitting at his desk in the Senate chamber. "Mr. Sumner, I have read your speech twice over carefully," he told the senator from Massachusetts. "It is a libel on South Carolina, and Mr. Butler, who is a relative of mine." Before Sumner could fully stand, Brooks proceeded to take his cane and beat Sumner senselessly until he was bloodied and unconscious. Sumner would survive the attack but would be unable to return to the Senate for nearly four years while he recovered.[207]

The following March, the Dred Scott decision was released and made matters worse for the cause of abolition. Dred Scott was a slave who lived in Illinois and Wisconsin for years with his master, John Emerson, until returning to Missouri. Scott believed himself to be free after years of living on free soil. Emerson died in 1843, so after failing to purchase his freedom, Scott sued Emerson's widow in 1846. In a 7–2 ruling, the Supreme Court declared that neither Scott, nor any black person, free or slave, had a right to sue because they were not US citizens. Furthermore, it declared, the federal government had no right to interfere with slavery in US territories anywhere before they acquired statehood. Thus, overnight, slavery was deemed all but untouchable in the eyes of the federal government, barring a constitutional amendment.

Rankin's attitude toward political violence had remained consistent in all the years he advocated for immediate abolition. He was extremely skeptical that violence would advance the cause of liberty for the slave. Since the night of his attack in 1841, Rankin dreaded the day that violence may be the only course left. Lately, both abolitionists and slaveholders had demonstrated an eagerness to rush to violence and finally put an end to the slave question. Despite all the setbacks abolitionists had faced in the 1850s, John believed there remained an opportunity to resolve the matter peaceably.

In August 1857, Rankin traveled to Cleveland, Ohio to participate in a convention to organize a National Compensation Emancipation Society. Popular in certain circles, and equally controversial in others, was the idea that to peaceably achieve immediate emancipation, slaveholders could be compensated for the loss of their slaves. Many abolitionists, including Rankin, believed that most slaveholders weren't going to voluntarily sacrifice their profits in support of what might feel like an altruistic mission of abolition. Even those slaveholders who were opposed to slavery, in theory, could uproot their entire enterprise overnight. Whether due to greed or necessity, they believed, slaveholders would need some form of compensation if immediate abolition were to be accomplished. At three o'clock that afternoon of August 25, the first session of the convention was underway. The declared purpose of the society, as adopted in their constitution, was "the extinction of slavery by a system of compensation to the slaveholder." They called for the people of the North to cooperate in a "generous and brotherly spirit" with the South, "and share liberally with them in the expense" that would be required to end slavery in this manner. They suggested that Congress should pass a bill that provides "the payment of such a vast sum of money to the Southern States" that would be necessary to effectively lift the slaves from their bondage "at the earliest possible day" that can be achieved "by peaceable means."

Rankin spoke in support of this cause at the Cleveland convention, hoping it may shift the course of the country away from the impending crisis it faced. *The Ripley Bee* reported that the attendance of the convention was "numerous and the interest increasing."[208] The report from *The Liberator* was less charitable. Garrison was a chief opponent of the plan, believing that compensation gave the slaveholder undue credibility in his claim to the slave. Compensating "Southern man-stealers" was exceptionally ridiculous in his view. "For many grave considerations," Garrison wrote, "we protest against the compensation movement."[209]

The National Compensation Emancipation Society spent the rest of the convention debating specifics of how to accomplish such a scheme. The society's first annual meeting was set for New York on May 12, 1858. Despite these final attempts to avoid bloodshed over slavery, war was beginning to feel inevitable. Kansas was practically a war zone already, and getting worse by the day. Details of assaults, robberies, murders, lynchings, raids, and massacres penetrated the newspapers. In October 1859, over two years after the Compensation Emancipation

Convention, John Brown returned from Kansas to lead a raid against the federal arsenal at Harper's Ferry, Virginia. His plan was to incite a slave revolt and overthrow the institution of slavery by force. He even sought the aid of Frederick Douglass, who believed the mission was doomed to fail, and thus declined to participate. The plan ultimately did fail, and Brown was tried for treason and hanged in December. On the day of his execution, he slipped the jailer a note which read "I, John Brown, am now quite certain that the crimes of this guilty land will never be purged away but with blood. I had, as I now think, vainly flattered myself that without very much bloodshed it might be done."

* * * * *

If Rankin had the opportunity to read Abraham Lincoln's short 1860 campaign biography, he likely would have related to the former Illinois congressman in several ways.[210] Like Rankin, his father and grandfather were pioneers of the American frontier. As Rankin began his journey to Ohio from Tennessee in the fall of 1816, Lincoln's father, Thomas, left Kentucky "for what is now Spencer County, Indiana." Both Rankin and Thomas Lincoln moved north to escape slavery, but also "on account of the difficulty in land titles in Kentucky." With these early similarities also came some notable distinctions. Rankin's opposition to slavery drove most actions he took. Abraham Lincoln, on the other hand, while certainly opposed to slavery, hardly identified it as the most significant driving force in his life. In his campaign biography, Lincoln's attitudes toward slavery were recounted in a story from his time in the 1837 Illinois legislature. "March 3, 1837, by a protest entered upon the 'Illinois House Journal' of that date, at pages 817 and 818, Abraham, with Dan Stone, another representative of Sangamon, briefly defined his position on the slavery question..." In their protest, Lincoln affirmed his belief that "the institution of slavery is founded on both injustice and bad policy, but that the promulgation of Abolition doctrines tends rather to increase than abate its evils." He also believed that "the Congress of the United States has no power under the Constitution to interfere with the institution of slavery in the different states." However, it did have the authority to "abolish slavery in the District of Columbia, but that the power ought not to be exercised unless at the request of the people of the District." Lincoln's position on slavery, it was added, "was then the same that it is now."

Many abolitionists recognized that Lincoln was not exactly one of them. His political hero was Henry Clay, and he valued stability and union over radical change. However, Lincoln also recognized that they no longer lived in the world of Clay. The Nebraska bill had a significant impact on the way he approached the issues. "The repeal of the Missouri Compromise aroused him as he had never been before," read Lincoln's campaign biography. It was evident to Lincoln now that slavery was not only a moral evil, but it also threatened the stability of the Union itself. Rankin, the ever-practical radical that he was, would have understood the value in such a candidate. It would be a value his colleagues would learn to appreciate as well. On November 6, 1860, Lincoln became the first Republican in history elected to the presidency.

Leading up to the election, Southern democrats warned that a Lincoln victory would be the final straw. They were prepared to secede from the Union. South Carolina did just that on December 20, 1860. Alabama, Florida, Georgia, Louisiana, Mississippi, and Texas joined their southern neighbor not long afterward. Following their secession, the Southern states agreed to meet in Montgomery, Alabama on February 4, 1861, to form a confederation of states. On that very date, the original Fugitive Slave Act had passed the House of Representatives sixty-eight years earlier. It was also Rankin's sixty-eighth birthday.

A NATION OF RIGHTEOUSNESS
1861–1865
X.

"War has commenced," *The Ripley Bee* declared on April 18, 1861, "by the act of South Carolina rebels."[211] After South Carolina seceded from the Union in December, Governor Francis Pickens, a cousin of the late Senator John C. Calhoun, demanded the federal government surrender Fort Sumter near Charleston. Its proximity threatened the "dignity [and] safety of the State of South Carolina," he claimed. A standoff ensued as South Carolina demanded the fort be abandoned. Major Robert Anderson refused, but was quickly running out of food and supplies. President Abraham Lincoln, following his inauguration in March, moved to resupply Fort Sumter. South Carolina warned that any attempt to resupply would be considered an "act of aggression." At around four thirty in the morning on April 12, militia forces opened fire on Fort Sumter. The Civil War had begun.[212]

The outbreak of war brought severe anxiety to the townspeople of Ripley. Since the 1830s, Ripley had been on the brink of armed conflict with their neighbors in Kentucky over matters far less pressing than the current crisis. Several prominent citizens, including John Rankin, had been attacked, kidnapped, and wanted dead or alive due to work against slavery. How would Kentucky respond with southern states seceding and waging war against the north? An emergency meeting was held in the Methodist church on April 23 to discuss "the preservation of peace on the border" with Kentucky. Three days earlier, the Ripley town council passed resolutions that asserted their determination to defend their "lives, rights, and property against invasions, attacks, or unlawful interference..." But, they declared, they were determined to "contemplate no hostilities against our neighbors of Kentucky." They urged the governments of Maysville, Dover, and Augusta, as well as Mason and Bracken Counties at large, to "take measures to cooperate with" the people of Ripley in "preserving the peace along the border and protecting the citizens on both sides." The neighboring Kentucky communities responded in kind. They fully endorsed the "friendly and patriotic action of the town council of Ripley" for seeking to protect not only themselves but also their neighboring communities across the river. As the townspeople of Ripley were reassured of the intentions of their Kentucky neighbors, they agreed to form a committee that would unite "the people of the border in common defense of homes and property" against both "individual crimes" and public war.[213]

With the border towns near Ripley secured by a pact of common defense, Richard Calvin Rankin was eager to get into the fight. On the same day of the emergency meeting in Ripley, a grand ceremony was held for "the departure of Captain [Jacob] Ammen's Company of volunteers." Calvin, wasting no time to enlist once the war broke out, was a private in Ammen's volunteer regiment. For those in attendance, emotions were high. It was both "exciting and affecting" and "solemn and sad" for parents, family, and friends of the volunteers to watch. Nobody, at this point, fully understood how long and gruesome the war would become. Still, the townspeople of Ripley surely felt an ominous feeling in the air. The volunteers faced an "arduous" and possibly "dangerous expedition" in front of them, but hopes of crushing the "wicked rebellion," diluted their fears. Calvin, for one, was never afraid of a fight. For over thirty years, he had evaded and fought back against bounty hunters. He took up arms when they attacked his father's home. As a marshal in Ripley, he was expected to keep the peace when the slavocracy had never been stronger. For nearly all his life, he had been in a state of war against slavery—enlistment didn't take a second thought.[214]

His older brother, Adam Lowry Rankin, was not in Ripley when the volunteers marched off to war. Following his marriage to Margaret Donnell, he accepted a position as a general missionary for the Congregationalist Church in Illinois. During his time as a missionary, he lived in Chicago for some time then moved his family to Salem, Illinois temporarily to be closer to them. "I rented a house from the editor of the Democratic paper," Lowry later wrote, "the only paper of the town and the official paper for the county as Salem was the county seat." It wasn't long before his presence caused controversy among local slavery sympathizers. The editor he was renting from, none too pleased with his company in town, ran an editorial calling him a "black Republican" and urging the people to "arise in a mass and in their indignation drive the Chicago intruder out of the county." Lowry very quickly could have become outraged. In their political climate, he could have been seriously harmed by the editor's call for a mob. Instead, he extended his hand when he saw the editor on a Monday morning. Suspicious, the man hesitated to return the gesture, but eventually shook his hand. "I said I was on my way to his office to thank him," Lowry later wrote. As he stood surprised, Lowry explained how he has been "kind enough without any cost to me to inform the readers of your paper who I am, what my business is, and have even told them what are my political affinities. Don't you see you have relieved me of the necessity of doing that?" In this moment of levity, any tension between them had dissipated. Before Lowry left, he told the editor that he was "going up to Chicago tonight and if you have any business there that I can attend to for you I shall be only too glad to do it. Good morning, sir."

Arthur Tappan Rankin, Lowry's younger brother, joined him in Salem to pastor at a church he helped organize. This "made it desirable that I should remain there." As 1861 rolled around, Lowry had been a missionary in Illinois for years. When he first learned of the attack on

Fort Sumter, he took a train to the city of Cairo—the southernmost tip of the state. "At the outbreak of the Rebellion two-thirds of southern Illinois was in sympathy with the South," Lowry later wrote. He would have to operate with caution. In many parts of the state, "it was dangerous to be openly a Union man." In the Salem paper, Southern Illinois was urged to secede and join the South. Many in authority started to worry that such sentiment of disloyalty to the Union would be widespread in the region. Following the attack on Fort Sumter, on April 15, President Lincoln called for 75,000 volunteers to enlist in defense of the Union. Rumors swirled around Springfield that conspirators in Cairo and Williamson County were planning to destroy a railroad bridge to disrupt troop movement from the north. Knowing of his missionary work, Illinois Governor Richard Yates relied on Lowry for a reconnaissance mission. Lowry was to go down to Cairo and determine if there was a legitimate threat to Union troop movements. "As you are in the habit of going over the road in your work, no one will suspect you," the governor wrote to him. As Lowry arrived in Cairo, he found Southern sympathies running rampant throughout the city. He conferred with the postmaster and a new school Presbyterian minister he had gotten to know since arriving in the state, both Union men. Between his conversations with them and his experiences in the town, Lowry believed the threat was serious. He telegraphed Springfield one word—*danger*. Not a moment was wasted. "The order was sent [by the Governor] to Chicago," dispatching "several regiments and a battery" to Cairo and the Big Muddy River, where the threatened bridge crossed. Both the town and the bridge were secured the night before the attack was believed to take place. While the citizens of Cairo "expressed great indignation" at the governor's distrust of their loyalties, Union troops were able to safely deploy from Illinois. These early days of the Civil War marked the beginning of "some of the most exciting" experiences in the life of Adam Lowry Rankin.[215]

* * * * *

John Rankin's concern over the safety of his sons was held privately. He cared immensely for each of his children, and the thought of losing another family member was heart wrenching. Death had again revealed its face to the Rankin family at the onset of the war. Mary Ann Rankin, the widow of Rankin's son David, passed away in 1859. Now orphans, their three children were left in Rankin's care. As he witnessed Calvin marching off to war, many thoughts likely raced through his mind. Was Rankin looking at his son for the last time, as he did his own brother, David, during the War of 1812? Perhaps he wondered if he had done everything in his power to prevent violent conflict in his fight against slavery. Any doubts or fears Rankin had developed would have been offset by his faith. It had long been his belief that God is the overseer of all things, and that His plan was in constant motion. Whether Rankin's sons would or would not be harmed in this great conflict was ultimately out of his control, and thus it was pointless to stress over it constantly. The same faith led Rankin to believe in a righteous purpose to this war. As much as he tried to avoid a violent conflict, it had arrived, nonetheless. If bloodshed must occur, he thought, it should at last vanquish the stain of slavery from American soil, once and for all.

When the war began in April, many assumed it would resolve quickly. As summer dragged on, those illusions began to fade. In Manassas, Virginia on July 21, Union forces lost the first major battle of the war. Twenty-five miles from Washington, DC, the Armies of the Potomac and the Shenandoah finally came to blows at Bull Run Creek. Outnumbered and outmatched, Union forces suffered 2,896 casualties. Despite immerging from the battle victorious, confederate forces also lost 1,982 men. News of the battle was sobering for Northerns and Southerners alike. President Lincoln was under pressure to resolve the conflict within ninety days—the length of the enlistment of the initial 75,000 volunteers. The battle at Bull Run squashed any hope of a swift victory. The following day, President Lincoln issued a call for 500,000 troops to serve for three years, rather than three months. Rankin, hearing the news of this escalation, could only shake his head. None of this would make a difference if the administration didn't address the cause of the war—slavery itself.[216]

In late summer, Rankin stirred up quite a controversy among Republicans and Democrats alike. Through the American Reform Tract and Book Society, he wrote a catechism addressing the recent outbreak of the war. "Question 1—What has broken up the peace of our nation and trampled our glorious flag in the dust?" The answer, of course, was "the slaveholding power." Entitled *A Catechism for Free Workmen*, Rankin blamed the recent insurrection against the Union squarely on the feet of slavery. "Will not the continuance of the slaveholding power reduce the slaveholding States to utter barbarism?" It already has "extinguished the sources of light" and has "abolished the moral sense of the people." The takeaway of the tract was clear to anyone reading it. If the rebellion was to be defeated and harmony among the states restored, slavery would need to be destroyed.

Rankin's tract had been "extensively circulated over Brown County, and indeed with similar ones all over the North," reported *The Southern Ohio Argus* out of Georgetown.[217] Many Republicans, however, weren't thrilled with it. The position of the Lincoln administration in the early days of the war was the preservation of the Union, not the abolition of slavery. The president's opposition to slavery hadn't changed, but he worried if he took action against slavery too early, many border states, like Kentucky, would secede with the rest of the South. Border towns like Ripley were full of Unionists who opposed secession but wanted to leave slavery alone. Rankin knew his position would be unpopular around his community. He was also certain he was right, and the people needed to come to terms with it.

He wrote an article in *The Ripley Bee*, published on August 29, making it clear that he and he alone took responsibility for the tract. "I wrote it without consulting any human being in respect to it." He wanted there to be no confusion concerning his position on the war and the Republican administration. "The Government did not wage war upon Slavery," he wrote. It waged war "to save itself" from dissolution, and to "secure the territory it justly owns." It has shown "no disposition to liberate the slaves" and has "exhibited no love for the colored race." There has been no evidence of repentance "on [the] part of the nation" for its role in the continuation of slavery, "even now when it lies under the most terrible judgment of God." Most Republicans, Rankin claimed, possessed "no more love for the negroes than have the Democrats." While this was Rankin's position, he was also quick to point out that the tract in question said "nothing in favor of the negroes," simply that it advocated for "the abolition of the cause of the war." As he defended his recent tract, he also felt compelled to make a note of his political loyalties. "I am a Democrat and the son of a Democrat, but I have never allowed myself to be owned by any party, so as to vote for everything that it might nominate," Rankin declared. "I have voted for Whigs, for Freesoilers, for Liberty men, and for Democrats." In other words, Rankin maintained an independent-mind, and would vote for anyone he believed would do the right thing, especially as it concerned slavery.

He closed with a message to those who wished him harm. "I say to those who threatened my life, they can not rob me of many days," he taunted his enemies. "I do not fear 'them that kill the body,'" he said. "They cannot kill the soul."[218]

Ironically, as Rankin scolded the Republican administration for not waging the war against slavery, Democrats complained that Lincoln had given in to the abolitionists. On August 6, the president signed the Confiscation Act of 1861 into law. Under this new law, courts were empowered to confiscate any and all Confederate property that could be used in support of the rebellion. Of course, this was only as enforceable as Union forces made advances in the war, but slaves were considered "property" under this law. In signing this bill, Lincoln risked conceding to Southerners that slaves are, in fact, property. He had hoped, however, to use their arguments as a tool for emancipation. "The result of Confiscation," wrote *the Southern Ohio Argus*, "since the Government does not propose to embark on the slave trade, *will be emancipation* (emphasis theirs). Who will say after this, that [US Representative from Kentucky] Crittenden was wrong in pronouncing the bill an abolition scheme?" By signing the bill into law, *The Argus* wrote, President Lincoln "at once" identified both "himself and his administration with abolitionism."[219]

* * * * *

In the same edition of *The Ripley Bee* as Rankin's recent article, a letter was published from Calvin. He wanted to provide the *Bee*'s "numerous readers" an opportunity to "hear how the Brown County Cavalry [is] getting along" and to offer "a slight history of our trip thus far." Throughout the war, Calvin provided frequent updates in letters written to *The Ripley Bee*. These war stories became very popular in and around Ripley. Indeed, he had demonstrated himself to be a very capable soldier. Before the end of summer, Calvin had quickly earned a promotion to sergeant. As the war trudged on, the War Department tasked Ohio Governor David Tod with raising a Cavalry Regiment for "Border Services" along the Ohio River and surrounding area. Brown County, along with most other border counties along the river, was responsible for raising one company in support of this order. By September 1862, the Seventh Ohio Volunteer Cavalry had all necessary companies filled. It was formally organized under the command of Colonel Israel Garrard. Richard Calvin Rankin became the Captain of E Company, quartered in Ripley.

Richard Calvin Rankin, Captain in the Seventh Ohio Volunteer Cavalry. Photo taken after the war. Throughout the Civil War, R.C. Rankin engaged in several battles in support of the Union.

As the Seventh OVC was being organized, Captain R. C. Rankin led E Company in defense of the region against Confederate forces. Captain Rankin's company "rendered valuable service to the city of Maysville, Ky, in defending her against John Morgan's command," Calvin later wrote. On September 20, they crossed the Ohio River "and marched to Brook[s]ville, Ky, a distance twenty-five miles, and participated in the attack and driving from the place, the rebels under [Second Lieutenant] Basil Duke…" The defense of Brooksville was a small but important skirmish to ensure Duke's forces didn't cross the river into Ohio, potentially threatening Cincinnati. If Duke had succeeded, Ripley certainly would have been in danger of attack. He had already "captured and burned" nearby Augusta, Kentucky. As Captain Rankin led his troops in a charge against Duke and his men, they captured a rebel soldier. Unfortunately, one of Calvin's men was also killed in the skirmish. "This may be recorded as the first blood the Seventh saw in battle," he later wrote. It wouldn't be the last time Captain Rankin and the Seventh engaged with Duke and his men. On this day, Duke retreated.[220]

Meanwhile, Lowry was about to join the fight in a different way than his younger brother. On October 11, 1862, Lowry was in Chicago when he received news that he was appointed as a chaplain for the Union Army and "was mustered in at once." After his regiment received their orders, Lowry said goodbye to his family. "The regiment left for Cairo, Illinois, by train from whence we went by steamer to Memphis, Tennessee." Once he arrived in Memphis, he and his regiment sang "Battle Cry of Freedom" as they marched in the streets. Once they arrived at their camp, Lowry's regiment received their assignment. "We were assigned to the First Brigade of the Second Division of the 15th Army Corps." The First Brigade was under the command of Brigadier General Morgan L. Smith. The commander of the Second Division was Major General William Tecumseh Sherman, while the 15th Army Corps was led by Rankin's former student, Major General Ulysses S. Grant.

During Lowry's time in the 15th Army Corps, he didn't lead men into battle as his brother did. However, he provided soldiers with much-needed spiritual support as they went into and returned from battle. He was also selected as postmaster for his regiment. "Congress authorized an officer in each regiment to endorse 'soldier's letter' and his official position on each letter, and the postage was collected when the letter was delivered," Lowry later wrote of his service in the war. "I was given the appointment both because I would have more time for the work and because it would enable me to become acquainted with every member of the regiment."[221]

Adam Lowry Rankin (front row, far left) with the 113th Illinois infantry during the Civil War. He served as a Chaplin for Union troops. (Ohio History Connection)

* * * * *

By July 1862, the issue of slavery weighed heavily on the mind of President Lincoln. The war, up to this point, had not gone well for the Union. Major General George McClellan, the general-in-chief of the Union Army for almost a year, had proven to be a disappointment to the administration. Lincoln and his cabinet could not comprehend why McClellan refused to destroy the Confederate Army despite encountering several opportunities to. Salmon P. Chase, now treasury secretary in the Lincoln administration, accused McClellan of being "the cruelest imposition ever forced upon a nation." McClellan "will never be ready to take Richmond," Chase complained.[222] Without a decisive victory in battle, Lincoln was hesitant to make any bold decisions concerning slavery. It could be seen as an act of desperation, and alienate the border states who maintained slavery but remained in the Union. Additionally, he still hoped Congress would act on the matter.

The Confiscation Act of 1861 set very few slaves free in practice. Some generals simply didn't have the supplies to care for captured slaves, and would send them back to their masters. Lincoln supported and advocated for Congress to pass a compensation emancipation bill in the spring of 1862, much like the plan Rankin had supported. Lincoln's plan had some notable differences. Lincoln wanted the States to carry some of the financial burdens of any compensation scheme. Lincoln still valued some elements of colonization at this point, and wanted to couple it with compensated emancipation. This bill failed to gain momentum, but a similar bill eliminating slavery in Washington, DC, did pass in Congress on April 16. "An Act For the Release of Certain Persons Held to Service or Labor in the District of Columbia," otherwise known as the District of Columbia Emancipation Act, abolished slavery within the district immediately.[223] Former slaveowners loyal to the Union were compensated $300 per slave. It also set funds aside for former slaves to be colonized to Haiti or Liberia if they so chose. In June, Lincoln signed a bill prohibiting slavery in all federal territories, North and South alike. A week after Independence Day, a second Confiscation Act was passed by Congress on July 12. Under this bill, all refugee slaves behind Union lines "shall be deemed captives of war, and shall be forever free of their servitude, and not again held as slaves." The president signed the bill on July 17.

Just a little over a year after the start of the war, President Lincoln signed policies into law that Rankin and his fellow abolitionists had spent decades trying to gain traction on. Many of Rankin's colleagues were pleasantly surprised at the conviction of the president to follow through on these issues. However, there was one glaring matter that had yet to be addressed—general emancipation. On August 19, 1862, *New York Tribune* editor Horace Greeley wrote a public letter to Lincoln on the subject. Entitled "The Prayer of Twenty Millions," Greeley expressed a concern that would have been shared by abolitionists across the country. "That the Rebellion, if crushed tomorrow, would be renewed within a year if slavery were left in full vigor," he warned the president. Greeley echoed what Rankin had written in *The Ripley Bee* the year prior. Slavery is the cause of the rebellion, and without defeating it, victory will be futile. Why then, wondered countless abolitionists, has Lincoln delayed issuing a proclamation of emancipation?[224]

Lincoln was an avid reader of newspapers, and he held reverence for Greeley. He knew Greeley's concerns were echoed by men like Rankin across the country. In Greeley's letter, he saw an opportunity to address the nation at large on the subject of emancipation. Less than a week after Greeley published his letter, Lincoln responded with his own in *The National Intelligencer*. On August 22, Lincoln wrote that he had "just read yours of the 19th... If there be any statements, or assumptions of fact, which I may know to be erroneous, I do not now and here, controvert them. If there be in it any interferences which I may believe to be falsely drawn, I do not now and here, argue against them. If there be perceptible in it an impatient and dictatorial tone, I waive it in deference to an old friend, whose heart I have always supposed to be right." Following this point of clarity, and a clear sign of respect for Greeley himself, Lincoln continued—"I would save the Union. I would save it in the shortest way under the Constitution. The sooner the national authority can be restored, the nearer the Union will be 'the Union as it was'... My paramount object in this struggle is to save the Union, and it is not to save or destroy slavery. If I could save the Union without freeing any slave I would do it, and if I could save it by freeing all the slaves I would do it; and if I could do it by freeing some and leaving others alone I would also do that. What I do about slavery, and about the colored race, I do because it helps save the Union; and what I forbear, I forbear because I do not believe it would help save the Union."

In modern times and in his day alike, Lincoln's letter has been mischaracterized as representing a disinterest in the outcome of slavery. His final section, often omitted from his response, provides insight into his true purpose. "I have here stated my purpose *according to my view of official duty*, and I intend no modification of my oft-expressed personal wish that all men everywhere could be free" (emphasis added). Lincoln, like all his predecessors, was limited in his power as president in what he could do against slavery. The war provided a unique opportunity to act in areas previously untouchable, but even this came with certain limitations. He could not, for instance, abolish slavery in the border states who weren't in rebellion against the Union. Only a Constitutional amendment could accomplish that. Despite his personal wish to see "all men everywhere" free, Lincoln reminded Greeley and like-minded abolitionists that his first duty as president was to preserve the Union and the Constitution. What Lincoln had neglected to mention was that he needed no further convincing that slavery was a threat to the Union. He had already made a decision on the matter. As he wrote his reply, his preliminary Emancipation Proclamation sat in the pocket of his coat.[225]

That July, the president informed Secretary of State William Seward and Secretary of the Navy Gideon Welles that he had been considering emancipation. Secretary of War Edwin Stanton's infant son had recently died, and Lincoln invited the two cabinet members to ride with him on the way to the funeral on July 13. There, Lincoln shared that he was putting emancipation under significant consideration. Welles wrote that Lincoln had come to believe that "we must free the slaves or be ourselves subdued." The next week, Chase wrote that the president was perplexed "almost as much as ever" by the slavery question, but believed he would soon "emerge from the obscurities where he has been grouping into somewhat clearer light." He was much closer to the "clearer light" than Chase anticipated. The next day, Lincoln informed his cabinet that he determined he would be taking "definitive steps in respect to military action and slavery." Over the next several weeks, he mulled over the details of his proclamation with his cabinet, waiting patiently for the right opportunity to announce it.[226]

* * * * *

"The most terrible judgment of God." That was the way Rankin described the war by the end of the summer of 1861. How accurate this was, the nation was only beginning to find out. On September 17, 1862, the most violent and bloody day in American military history took place at Antietam Creek in Maryland, about fifty miles from

Washington, DC. A combined total of 22,727 Union and Confederate soldiers were killed, wounded, or missing by the end of the battle. For comparison, American casualties following D-Day reached 6,603. More Americans died in battle on this one day than they had in every other war of the nineteenth century combined. To this day, September 17, 1862 remains one of the darkest days in American history. But through the darkness, a silver lining began to shine. The battle, as gruesome as it was, resulted in Union victory—the one Lincoln had been waiting for. "I think the time has come now," the president told his cabinet on September 22 after presenting them with a preliminary emancipation proclamation. "I wish that we were in a better condition. The action of the army against the rebels has not been quite what I should have best liked." Lincoln explained that he had made a promise to himself and his Maker that should the Confederate army be driven out of Maryland, he would issue the proclamation. "The rebel army is now driven out, and I am going to fulfill that promise." Before the end of the day, President Lincoln announced to the public that on January 1, 1863, all slaves in states engaged in active rebellion would be then freed. Over the next one hundred days, the Confederacy continued in their rebellion, with no signs of stopping. On January 1, President Lincoln kept his promise. "I do order and declare that all persons held as slaves" within States participating in an active rebellion against the Union "are, and henceforward shall be free."[227]

The next week, a catechism by Rankin was published in *The Ripley Bee*. In the wake of the proclamation, he discussed the merits of gradual vs. immediate emancipation. "It is evident by the President's late message that he, like every other honest and sensible man, knows that slavery is the cause of the enormous rebellion that has risen up against our Government," Rankin wrote, in a notably positive tone. The president, Rankin wrote in approval, now understood that "the abolition of [slavery] is indispensable to suppressing the rebellion and securing the Union." With this being the case, Rankin believed that "the time has come for the discussion of the question: 'Which is the better plan of emancipation—gradual or immediate?'"[228]

The question was especially relevant for Rankin. Lincoln's New Year proclamation was cause for great celebration among the abolitionists, and Rankin was happy to partake. However, it made little impact on his work on the Underground Railroad. The Emancipation Proclamation only affected states in active rebellion against the Union. Lincoln didn't have the authority to free any slave in states like Kentucky, which remained in good standing with the Union. Additionally, if Lincoln tried to free the slaves in border states without support from their state governments, they might secede as well.

As the war continued to rage in 1863, Rankin continued to help fugitives escape. Arnold Gragston escaped through Rankin's home not long after the Emancipation Proclamation was issued. Gragston lived in Dover, Kentucky on the plantation of Jack Tabb. For four years, Gragston had served as a conductor on the Kentucky side, choosing to live in slavery to help others gain freedom. "I figgered I wasn't gettin' along so bad so I would stay on Mr. Tabb's place and help the others get free." In the early months of 1863, after helping about twelve fugitives escape, Gragston's activities brought unwanted attention. "They set out after me as soon as I stepped out of the boat back on the Kentucky side; from that time on they were after me." After his operation was revealed, he couldn't return to his master in Dover. He and his wife decided to take their freedom for themselves, and they knew exactly where to go. Over the past four years, once on the Ohio shore, he sent fugitives to "a man named Mr. Rankins." Gragston knew that Rankin "had a regular 'station' for the slaves. He had a big lighthouse in his yard, about thirty feet high and he kept it burnin' all night. It always meant freedom for [a] slave if he could get to this light." He and his wife "quietly slipped across and headed for Mr. Rankin's" hilltop home. They continued north until they hit Detroit, where they chose to live.

Men like Gragston made Rankin anxious that in the wake of Lincoln's proclamation, the slaves in states like Kentucky would be forgotten. Gradual emancipation in the border states would have been "better than no plan," Rankin wrote. But he warned his readers that a gradual plan would "continue...that domineering spirit which has produced the present terrible war…" He maintained that the war was God's judgment for the sin of slavery. There was no better time to eliminate slavery than during the present crisis. "If the slaves have a right to freedom they have it now," he wrote, echoing arguments made from the earliest days of the abolition movement. "Hence to withhold it from them is injustice and oppression." Until every slave had won their freedom, Rankin knew there was still work to do.[229]

* * * * *

Joy and celebration erupted throughout abolitionist communities in 1863. The Emancipation Proclamation was the most widespread, unconditional anti-slavery policy ever enacted in the United States up until that point. Although there was still work to do, 1863 could be accurately considered a year of jubilee. As winter yielded to spring and spring yielded to summer, the Union Army also made a series of key military victories that only elevated attitudes in the North. Union forces under the command of Major General Grant defeated Confederate forces in Vicksburg, Mississippi, on July 4. Grant's victory in Vicksburg coincided with the defeat of Robert E. Lee's troops in Gettysburg, Pennsylvania, just one day earlier. After three days of brutal combat, Major General George Meade successfully repealed Lee's invasion of Pennsylvania in a crucial victory for the North. The one-two punch of Gettysburg and Vicksburg was a turning point in the war, and confidence in a Union victory soared.

Rankin also had personal cause for celebration. Calvin contributed to the defeat of Confederate General John Hunt Morgan and Colonel Basil Duke following the Battle of Buffington Island just two weeks following Union victories at Vicksburg and Gettysburg. Duke formally surrendered to the commander of the Seventh Ohio Volunteer Cavalry, Israel Garrard. Morgan, escaping from the battlefield, continued to move north, until he was finally captured following the Battle of Salineville on July 26. Captain R. C. Rankin was ordered to gather as many troops as he could muster, pursue, and capture many stragglers who escaped the battle. With "great credit" to "the colored people for the information they gave," Calvin managed to capture eighty-four of Morgan's troops, including two officers. [230]

On top of this, 1863 was the thirtieth anniversary of the American Anti-Slavery Society. A grand celebration was planned in Philadelphia for the anniversary in December. William Lloyd Garrison, Frederick Douglass, Susan B. Anthony, Henry Ward Beecher, and Levi Coffin were among some of the most notable participants of the convention. Of course, the society intended to invite as many of the foundational members as possible. Garrison personally invited Rankin to speak during the convention. It overwhelmed Rankin to think of all they had accomplished; he was about to turn seventy-one in February. He also had other responsibilities to attend to, as president of his Tract Society. Rankin elected to remain in Ripley, leaving the speech-making to a new generation of anti-slavery activists. However, understanding the significance of the occasion, he didn't leave Garrison empty-handed.

The convention opened on December 3, 1863, at Concert Hall in Philadelphia. The Philadelphia Female Anti-Slavery Society decorated the space in anticipation of the gathering. An American flag was fixated behind the center of the stage. Around the hall, large cards were placed with quotes from historic American figures like George Washington, Thomas Jefferson, Henry Clay, and James Madison, expressing their disdain for slavery. A large banner inscribed with the phrase "UNION AND LIBERTY" was hung over the convention—a notably different tone from Garrison's "No union with slaveholders!" motto. Lincoln's proclamation was the subject of many speeches and conversations. Garrison took the stage to read the letters sent by those who were unable to attend the celebration, with assistance from the society's secretaries. They opened with a letter from the American Anti-Slavery Society's first president, Arthur Tappan. Other letters by Theodore Weld and Ohio Congressman Joshua Giddings were read. One after another, they read the remarks of men and women who had become legendary in abolitionist circles. Finally, Garrison reached the letter he had received from Rankin. "The next letter," he told the crowd, "is from one who entered into the anti-slavery field at an earlier period than almost any of us. Long before my own mind was turned to this subject, he had fully comprehended it, and bravely and faithfully borne an uncompromising testimony for the abolition of slavery." Garrison looked up at the crowd, captured with a deep sense of appreciation for his "anti-slavery father," and remarked that "his name deserves to be held in lasting remembrance. I allude to Rev. John Rankin, of Ohio." Garrison then looked down at the letter in his hand. It was dated November 19, 1863, the very same day President Lincoln gave his Gettysburg address. Looking out over the crowd, Garrison continued to read Rankin's letter to the convention:

> Mr. Garrison—*Dear Sir*, Your invitation to attend the thirtieth Anniversary of the American Antislavery Society has been received. I regret that I am not in circumstances that will enable me to be present at your meeting. You and I have ever been united on the subject of immediate emancipation, while we have widely differed in other respects. I feel that my labors must soon close, I am now in the seventy first year of my age, and of course, must soon go the way of all past generations. From my boyhood to the present time I have opposed the abominable system of American slavery. For the liberation of the slaves I have labored long and suffered much reproach and persecution; but I regret none of the sacrifices I have made for the hapless millions that have been bought and sold as if beasts of the field, and deprived of all that makes existence desirable. Nearly forty years have passed away since I began to warn this nation of the ruin that would result from this horrible system of oppression; but now the day of blood has come. The son of God has come with his rod of iron and dashed those slaveholding Governments in pieces as a potter's

vessel is broken; and has made the general Government tremble on its foundation. "True and righteous are thy judgments O Lord."

I greatly rejoice in the President's Proclamation. No other man ever had the privilege of making a proclamation so magnificent. It is to lift more than those millions of people from the deepest degradation and misery to dignified life and station as rational beings. And although it is not broad enough to cover the whole field of oppression, yet it is the fiat that will end the system. He that is higher than the heavens has ordained it, and our brave soldiers in the field are the armies of the Living God to enforce it. Let us thank God and take courage; and not relax our efforts while there a slave in the land.

Receive My best respects.
John Rankin.[231]

The presidential election of 1864 vindicated Lincoln's execution of the war. For the first time since Andrew Jackson's victory in 1832, a sitting president won reelection. Lincoln defeated his former general-in-chief, George McClellan, who was selected as the Democratic nominee. To attract more border states, Andrew Johnson of Tennessee was attached to the ticket as the nominee for vice president. Johnson was a staunch Unionist, but he was a Democrat. Adam Lowry Rankin faced a dilemma very similar to the one he dealt with during the 1840 election. Lincoln's Emancipation Proclamation excited him, just as it had his father. He wanted to support Lincoln in his reelection bid, but Johnson was a bridge too far. "I did not want to aid in the election of Mr. Johnson," he later wrote. As the rest of his unit was given a thirty-day furlough to go home and vote, Lowry abstained from voting and watched over the camp. Johnson's inclusion to the ticket "was a mistake of grave character and one that the Republicans would regret," Lowry believed.[232]

Any concern about Johnson's influence over Lincoln's second term was quickly overshadowed by the news that Rankin and the abolitionists had been waiting their entire lives for. On January 31, 1865, Congress passed the thirteenth amendment to the Constitution. The war, everyone could clearly see, was coming to an end. The Emancipation Proclamation was a wartime measure. Once the war was over, there were certain to be many legal battles over the constitutional status of the president's proclamation. Additionally, slavery was never touched in the border states. The dangers of slavery from a national security standpoint were clear, but once peace was secured, the opportunity to eradicate the institution could be forever lost. President Lincoln, fresh off the heels of his landslide victory in the election of 1864, made the abolition of slavery via constitutional amendment his top priority. After weeks of political dealmaking, applause erupted in the house as the amendment passed 119–56.[233] Despite the content of the Thirteenth Amendment being notably brief, there was no mistaking the impact of the words:

> **Section 1.** *Neither slavery nor involuntary servitude, except as a punishment for crime whereof the party shall have been duly convicted, shall exist within the United States, or any place subject to their jurisdiction.*

> **Section 2.** Congress shall have power to enforce this article by appropriate legislation.

The Constitution's first mention of slavery brought about its abolition. The Constitution does not require the signature of the sitting president for an amendment to go into effect. However, the next day, Lincoln signed it in approval. "This amendment is a King's cure for all the evils," the president said. "It winds the whole thing up."[234]

The Liberator reported that a large celebration took take place in Boston on Saturday, February 4. "Grand Jubilee Meeting in the Music

Hall, to rejoice over the Amendment prohibiting Human Slavery in the United States forever," the headline read. For decades, Garrison had been an unapologetic advocate for disunion. During this celebration, he sang a new tune. "Freedom is triumphant!" he proclaimed to a cheering crowd. "THE PEOPLE have decreed the death of slavery! All the controlling elements of the country—national, state, religious, political, literary, social, economical, wealthy, industrial—are combined for its immediate extinction. There is no longer occasion, therefore, for the repetition of that persuasive song. As Jefferson said, in his inaugural message to Congress, 'We are all Federalists, we are all Republicans'— so, in view of the dominant Anti-slavery sentiment of the land, it may now be comprehensively declared, 'We are all abolitionists, we are all loyalists, to the back-bone.'" Much work still needed to be done, but the mood in early 1865 was triumphant.[235]

* * * * *

A public meeting was called in Ripley on April 17. Community members gathered at the Methodist Church that evening. Five years earlier, they anxiously met in the same spot to address the outbreak of the war. This was not a day of panic, however. The people of Ripley were in mourning. They gathered "for the purpose of giving expression of sorrow in consequence to the death of the Chief Magistrate of the nation."[236] Abraham Lincoln was dead. He was assassinated in Washington, DC on Friday by the stage actor, John Wilkes Booth. He was shot behind the head at Ford's Theater, passing away the next morning. It was a grim end to an otherwise joyful week. Six days earlier, Robert E. Lee surrendered the Army of Virginia to Ulysses S. Grant at Appomattox Court House in Virginia. The rebellion was all but officially over. In the wake of his assassination, abolitionists began to view Lincoln as the final victim of the slavocracy. "Slaveholders and their allies have done the deed," read *The Liberator*. "Slavery, that instigated the rebellion, that began and for four years carried on this civil war, has done it."[237]

At the public meeting in Ripley, "appropriate remarks were made by Rev. John Rankin and W. D. Young, Esq." Following this, a series of resolutions were drafted and approved. "Whereas, in the midst of our rejoicing for the glorious victories…the stunning intelligence of the murder of our good and great *President*…reached our ears." Therefore, "in the assassination of our beloved Chief Magistrate, '*a great and good man has fallen in Israel*,' and a whole people this day, in tears, attest their estimate of his worth and goodness, and the irreparable loss in his death." Lowry's camp in Memphis was even more distraught. "The terrible news of President Lincoln's assassination caused a deep sense of gloom," he later wrote. "The southern citizens of Memphis were greatly alarmed. The city was draped in mourning. Southern and northern citizens vied with each other in the extent of their draping. The northern soldiers were angry, sullen, and murmured vengeance, and the least indiscretion on the part of the southern people would have caused a deal of trouble, hence their activity in the display of mourning."[238]

Lincoln's assassination, the conclusion of the war, and the passage of the Thirteenth Amendment left Rankin conflicted. After decades of aiding fugitive slaves, he could finally rest knowing that no person would ever have to flee from undue bondage. Throughout his time in Ripley, it's estimated that over 2,000 fugitives came through Rankin's station on Liberty Hill in their northward journey. While we may never know the final number of those helped, these estimates place Rankin's hilltop home as one of the most active stations on the entire Underground Railroad. But now, abolition—the cause which he labored for his entire life—had finally been achieved. This victory came at a great cost. Hundreds of thousands of American souls, including, now, the president of the United States, had been forever lost. Hundreds of thousands of sons, brothers, and fathers, in the North and South alike, were prematurely forced to meet their maker. Or perhaps it wasn't premature. Perhaps their fate was destined to meet this ultimate end. These theological questions rattled in the minds of millions of Americans. There is no evidence that Rankin experienced spiritual doubt as the war concluded, but he did experience some remorse. A few years later, Rankin recorded his mixed feelings about the war in his autobiography. "I lived to see four million slaves liberated, but not in the way I had long labored to have it done. More than fifty years ago, when I was a citizen of Kentucky, I published an article in a religious paper issued at Chillicothe, Ohio, urging the setting of the slaves free by purchase. A thousand million dollars would purchase all the slaves in the union. Four thousand millions in property and money would have been saved, and what is vastly more important, a million lives would have been saved from a bloody death. The prime men of the nation were slaughtered and sorrow and weeping pervaded the entire country. Tens of thousands of families were clothed in mourning."[239]

Fortunately, Rankin's family was not among those clothed in mourning. Between 1861 and 1865, six of Rankin's sons and one of his grandsons fought for the Union in various capacities. "The Lord preserved them all; not one of them was visited with fatal disease, not one of them received a wound, and not one of them had his morals corrupted." Lowry remained in Memphis with his family throughout 1865, accepting an appointment as southern secretary for the American Tract Society. Calvin traveled to Georgia in July 1864 with the Seventh Ohio Volunteer Cavalry. They joined the Atlanta Campaign under Major General Sherman. He returned to Ohio the following July, after the capture of Jefferson Davis in Georgia. He would remain in Ripley after the war with his wife, America Whisner Rankin. John Thompson Rankin (or John Jr.) proved himself as heroic as Calvin. "He fought in some severe battles," his father later wrote. "He enlisted a colored regiment, and in various other ways did much service in subduing the rebels." Andrew Campbell Rankin was a surgeon in the Union Army "and performed much service for the sick and wounded soldiers." William Alexander Rankin and Arthur Tappan Rankin also served. Rankin and Jean took care of their grandson, John C. Rankin, once he became an orphan in 1859. After the war broke out, he enlisted as a private in the Union Army. He, like all his uncles, returned home safely.[240]

Rev. John Rankin with his children, 1872. (Front row, left to right: daughters Mary Eliza, Julia, Rev. John Rankin, his wife, Jean Rankin, and eldest daughter Isabella. Back row, left to right: sons Thomas Lovejoy, William Alexander, Andrew Campbell, John Thompson, Samuel Gardner Wilson, Richard Calvin, and Arthur Tappen Rankin. Adam Lowry Rankin was not present in the portrait. David Wilmont and Lucindia died before the portrait was taken, in 1847 and 1856, respectively.)

* * * * *

With emancipation settled, a new debate over suffrage and equal rights arose. Lifting the slave out of bondage was one thing, but could it really be expected that blacks receive the same rights as their white counterparts? To Rankin, the answer to this question must be an unequivocal "yes." The ratification of the Thirteenth Amendment was imminent, and millions of emancipated slaves would soon join civil society. Despite this, the spirit of slavery lingered. Rankin believed that equality before the law was the only way the United States could truly rise to its full potential. With the approach of autumn, abolitionist circles adopted the cause of universal suffrage.

On November 2, Rankin again traveled to Cincinnati for the thirteenth anniversary of the American Reform Tract and Book Society.

During the annual business meeting, the society officially changed its name to the Western Tract and Book Society. Rankin again presided as chair of the convention, as he had done so many years prior. Many subjects were discussed, including suffrage and the equality of emancipated blacks. Delivering remarks, Levi Coffin praised the society's indispensable work as the nation faced a great transitional period away from slavery. This society, he told them, was "intimately connected with the work of instruction of the freemen and ignorant poor of the South...." Rankin and the Western Tract and Book Society had hoped this year's convention would be especially notable with the attendance of Salmon P. Chase. Chase, however, was unable to attend. In 1864, Lincoln nominated Chase to fill a vacancy in the Supreme Court after Chief Justice Roger Brooke Taney died in October. The Senate confirmed his nomination the same day the president made it on December 6. After the war, Chase received more speaking invitations than he knew what to do with. His responsibilities as Chief Justice prevented him from accepting most of them. He didn't leave the Tract Society empty-handed, though. He wrote a letter expressing his gratitude for the invitation and apologizing for his inability to attend. He assured them that he takes "great interest" in the efforts of the Western Tract and Book Society to "diffuse light and knowledge among the people." This was especially necessary to the black population as they emerged from slavery. "Their future is identified, in God's providence, with the future of our nation."[241]

That concept—that is, that the emancipated slaves were forever tied to the fate of America—was a concept Rankin spent a lot of time thinking about in the coming weeks. A month later, on December 6, 1865, the Thirteenth Amendment was officially ratified by three-fourths of the states. As it passed this threshold, slavery was officially prohibited from all jurisdictions of the United States. Some still held on to the idea that liberated blacks could be colonized to Africa or the West Indies, but Rankin believed this was as foolish as ever. It simply wasn't practical to have millions of former slaves voluntarily emigrate to a foreign land they have no more of a connection to than white Americans had to the nations of Europe. "Their future," as Chase asserted, was tied to "the future of our nation."

As the New Year approached, Rankin picked up his pen, expressing his thoughts on this matter in an op-ed for *The Ripley Bee*. As a young man, Rankin offered his thoughts on any number of political, cultural, or social issues. Now, his public comments outside of the pulpit grew rare. "**READ AND CONSIDER**" opened the front page of *The Bee* on December 27. In an op-ed entitled "The Rights of the Negroes, The Question of the Day," Rankin filled more than two full columns on the front page with his defense of black equality. "Many objections are offered against permitting [black Americans] to exercise civil rights equally with the right race. Some of these will now be considered." Just as he had over forty years earlier in his *Letters on American Slavery*, Rankin proceeded to dismantle the popular arguments of the day in opposition to black civil rights. And just as he had in 1824, Rankin leaned on scripture for guidance. "This is the true rule of conduct toward our fellow man. 'Thou shall love thy neighbor as thyself,' is the law of him to whom vengeance belongs. No man can love his neighbor as himself, and yet hold him in a condition in which he himself would not be held. And as the nation is composed of individuals, the law that binds the individuals binds the nation." Because of slavery, "God has most terribly poured out his righteous judgment upon the nation, and if we persist in our oppressions he will visit us with greater vengeance. Righteousness exalteth a nation, but sin is the reproach of any people. *If we would be exalted as a nation, it must be by righteousness*" (emphasis added).

To Rankin, there was only one way America could finally become a nation of righteousness. "Let us have universal suffrage and let us evangelize and educate so fast as we can, and the nation will be safe under the protection of Him who is Lord of lords and King of kings."[242]

FREEDOM'S HEROES
1866–1892
EPILOGUE

"Having received an invitation to visit our children in Ohio, accompanied with the money for our expenses, my wife and I are now paying that visit at Ironton and vicinity," John Rankin wrote as he closed his autobiography in 1873. "Since I came to this place, I preached at Ironton in the forenoon, rode seven miles to Sheridan in the afternoon, preached at that place, and returned to Ironton and heard Mr. Calhoun in the evening. I went to bed and rested as comfortably as if I had performed no labor, and no blue Monday followed. Such is the strength the Lord has given me after being over eighty years of age."[243]

In 1866, Rankin decided it was time to move on from Ripley. Following the war, the subdivisions of the Presbyterian Church began to reunify. Much to his satisfaction, Rankin oversaw the reunification of the First and Second Presbyterian Church in Ripley. Without slavery, there was no longer any need for a Free Presbyterian Church. "Having served my church at Ripley forty-four years, I resigned my charge, not because my people desired me to do so, but because I did not wish to continue longer with them in old age. The church had given no indication of a desire that I should cease to be their pastor."[244] His departure was voluntary, but *The Ripley Bee* provided a little more context than what Rankin alluded to in his autobiography. On January 17, 1866, *The Bee* wrote that "It being deemed best by the Presbytery, that both the Presbyterian Churches in this place should unite, the two pastors, Rev. John Rankin and Rev. D Gould, were requested to resign, in order that no obstacle might be thrown in the way."[245] It seemed that both Rankin and the Presbytery understood that it was time to yield to a younger generation.

Shortly after his resignation, Rankin received a request to preach at the Presbyterian Church in New Richmond near Cincinnati in early 1866. Upon his arrival, he found the church on the verge of dissolution. "They had during the war employed a preacher who was disloyal, which caused divisions and weakened the church." Church membership, due to this, was on the decline. Rankin agreed to preach twice on the Sabbath, once in the morning and once in the evening. They then asked him to preach the next night, on Monday. Rankin's presence was a much-needed boost in morale in the church, and they asked him to lead a prayer meeting Tuesday morning and preach Tuesday evening. By the end of the week, Rankin had led an impromptu revival in the church, preaching every night that week. "The meetings were continued until a communion was held and thirty-two were added to the church, and some of them were very useful members." Seeing how much Rankin energized their church community, he was asked to become their pastor. He was initially hesitant, he told them. He had just stepped down from his position with the church in Ripley due to his age. He was getting too old to serve in any permanent position. On the other hand, he recognized how badly the church needed stable leadership. He told them he would accept their request, but only for a year, and only if they would have him live among them. They were more than happy to oblige. Before the summer, he moved to New Richmond, leading the Presbyterian church there to new heights. "I have never regretted having done so. I was happy in leaving the church in a better condition than when I began to preach for it."

After his services in New Richmond were complete, he traveled east to spend time with Jean, their son, Samuel, and his family in Glastonbury, Connecticut. In Connecticut, he enjoyed the ability to preach "as often as opportunity occurred." Samuel Rankin would remain in Connecticut with his family, following in his father's footsteps as a minister in Hartford. When he wasn't preaching, Rankin wrote tracts in support of the Republican Party. Before making it to Connecticut, however, he took a mid-Atlantic tour. He traveled to Pennsylvania in 1869, participating in the New School Presbyterian General Assembly. "The subject of uniting with the Old School body was largely discussed in the Assembly and excited great interest." In a near-unanimous vote, the assembly voted in favor of reuniting. The so-called "Thirty-Year War" within the Presbyterian Church had finally come to an end.

Nearby, the citizens of Gettysburg invited the Assembly to visit the battlefield. "The managers of the railroad generously furnished a train of cars and gave the Assembly a pleasant passage to the place," Rankin recalled. Merely six years earlier, this was the scene of carnage and bloodshed. Rankin already had mixed feelings about the war, but what he experienced at Gettysburg deeply affected him. "For the Union soldiers, a most beautiful cemetery was provided. The graves were in beautiful order and a marble slab was laid at the head of each grave of those whose names were known, but there was a considerable row of graves unmarked." He was overwhelmed with emotion as he considered how many young men were taken from this world in such a barbaric manner. "What silent, solemn sadness is there! What dear ones lie there! Husbands, sons and brothers far from home, silent in death. How many tender hearts have throbbed in anguish! A noble monument is there to hold in memory the deeds of that terrible day. Much is done to honor the brave men who died in their country's cause, but honor cannot reach the tomb nor cheer the bed of death."

After leaving Gettysburg, Rankin visited his niece in Baltimore, then made a short trip to Washington, DC. His former pupil, Ulysses S. Grant, had recently been inaugurated as president of the United States. Since the war, Grant had risen to a hero status few in the history of the country had ever achieved, then or now. Being in Washington at the same time his former pupil and hero of the Republic had assumed the highest office in the land was not an opportunity Rankin intended to pass up. Walking up to the White House and requesting to meet with the president is unthinkable for most Americans. In 1869, it was a much more common practice, and it was exactly what Rankin did. "I went to Washington and called on President Grant. I had no need of an introduction, for I knew him when he was a boy and he had often heard me preach." He also visited the recently completed Capitol Building while in DC. Rankin went to the House and the Senate and met with Schuyler Colfax, vice president of the United States and former Speaker of the House. While on Capitol Hill, Rankin made an amusing observation that he witnessed "no appearance of the intemperance about which so much has been said." Granted, how long he stuck around to draw this conclusion is unclear.

After his trip to Washington, Rankin finally arrived in Connecticut, where Jean, Samuel, and his family anticipated him. After spending a few months there, he and Jean went west to visit their other children. William Alexander lived in Lawrence, Kansas with his family. Rankin and Jean spent some time with them, as well as their daughter Mary Eliza, who lived in Prairie City, Kansas. They remained in Kansas throughout the winter of 1869, with Rankin preaching whenever he could find the opportunity. The arrival of spring in 1870 brought Rankin and Jean back to Ohio briefly, then on to Illinois. They met their youngest son, Thomas Lovejoy Rankin, in Peru, Illinois, and lived there for some time. Not long afterward, Thomas wanted to bring his own family to Kansas, but he insisted Rankin and Jean move with them. "He deemed us too old to be left to do for ourselves. I gave up my charge and we moved to Kansas." They moved in with their son Thomas near a village called Queeneme. Meanwhile, their daughter Isabella Jane Rankin had moved to Ironton, Ohio with her husband, John Wilson Humphreys. They invited Rankin and Jean to visit them for some time. Rankin was approaching eighty by the time he traveled to Ironton. It was time to finally tell his story. While back in Ohio in 1873, Rankin completed his autobiography.[246]

* * * * *

Ironton, Ohio, was a boomtown along the Ohio River that had recently exploded in population. Near the intersection of Ohio, Kentucky, and the new state of West Virginia, the city was outlined and established by the industrialist, John Campbell, in 1849. Chosen for the region's richness in iron ore, iron masters like Campbell would establish foundries throughout the area, bringing a wave of wealth and immigration. Ironton was also a pivotal stop on the Underground Railroad. Campbell and his wife, Elizabeth, were natives of Brown County. A Presbyterian, Campbell would hear Rankin preach in Ripley when he was a young man. Though he was not as vocal of an opponent to slavery as Rankin, his actions spoke more than enough for his anti-slavery sentiment. He became a very active conductor on the Underground Railroad. His cousin, Hiram Campbell, was another iron master who helped Campbell establish Ironton in the 1840s. He later recalled that "The [Underground Railroad] work was begun here before the town was laid out." Campbell and Hiram were "the moving spirits of [anti-slavery] activities of this region," especially following the passage of the Fugitive Slave Law of 1850.[247] Campbell would often use his vast wealth and resources as means to help fugitives escape through Ohio and into Canada. Many of the iron furnaces in the region would double as stations where slaves could lay low until the next leg of their escape. In nearby Galia County, Campbell would even use his proceeds from the iron industry to fund and support a refuge settlement for runaway slaves called poke patch. In this settlement, runaway slaves would find allies in the free black community that populated the area.[248]

Campbell would rely on key allies in the black community to help him successfully execute Underground Railroad operations. One man in particular, Gabe Johnson, was a black barber in Ironton. He used his barbershop as a stop where runaway slaves could find temporary refuge.

Johnson would often notify Campbell of the arrival of fugitive slaves as they arrived at his barber shop. At the appropriate time, Campbell and Johnson would often guide them through the woods at night to their next hideaway spot. At times, Johnson later recalled, he and Campbell would "[travel] those woods when the snow was a foot deep" aiding fugitives slaves.[249]

Ironton rivaled Ripley in Underground Railroad activity, and it quickly surpassed Ripley in industry. As the city grew, many of Ripley's younger families migrated to Ironton in pursuit of opportunity. Isabella and her family were part of this migration. The Humphreys had especially good reason to believe their move to Ironton would be a wise one. Isabella's father-in-law, William Humphreys, was Campbell's uncle. By the time Rankin and Jean arrived in Ironton to visit their daughter and family, their presence would have been celebrated by several prominent citizens.

Rankin had visited Ironton at least once before in 1869. On his way to Pennsylvania to attend the General Assembly of the Presbyterian Church, he stopped in Ironton and nearby Portsmouth, Ohio to raise funds for the Western Tract and Book Society. Ironton had a substantial churchgoing population, especially among the Presbyterians. As he visited his daughter, he got to know better the minister of the First Presbyterian Church in town, Reverend Henry Calhoun. During the days of the Underground Railroad, the Presbyterians were among the most active in Ironton's anti-slavery activities. The church's first minister, Reverend Joseph Chester, was the "most active [Underground Railroad] worker" in Ironton, according to Hiram.[250] Due to the church's unique history with anti-slavery activity, Rankin felt a certain kinship with the Ironton Presbyterians. He attended and preached at the First Presbyterian Church whenever the opportunity arose, becoming good friends with Calhoun. As much as Rankin enjoyed visiting with family and friends in Ironton, it soon came time for him and Jean to return to Kansas.

For the next five years, he and Jean lived a quiet life with their son Thomas and his family. Rankin mused a few years earlier that "I do as much preaching now as when I had a charge." When he had a charge in Ripley, he balanced his preaching with his anti-slavery activities. His preaching in the 1870s was both less stressful and less dangerous. In the fall, things took a turn for the worse. His beloved wife and confidant, Jean, had fallen ill. In her old age, recovery became difficult. Her condition worsened until finally, on December 28, 1878, Jean Rankin, passed away.

Christmas was already a difficult time of year for Rankin due to the death of his son on December 25, 1847. Now, thirty-one years later, almost to the day, he reexperienced the terrible grief of a loved one's passing. To escape the pain brought forth by the loss of his wife, Rankin's thoughts returned to Ironton. Before the summer of 1879, he had began his final journey back to Ohio, alone this time. Along the way, he would visit family and friends in Illinois, Indiana, and Kentucky. He would make a stop in Ripley to see Calvin, his wife America, and their children, before finally making it back to Ironton.[251]

Rev. John Rankin with his wife, Jean, in 1872. Other than his faith, nothing provided John with more support throughout his life than his wife Jean. "A more affectionate and industrious wife could not be found in any place," John wrote of Jean around the same time this photo was taken. She died four years later in 1878.

* * * * *

If you were to ask any abolitionist in 1835 who the father of abolition was, their most common response would be John Rankin. By 1880, as interest in the activities of the Underground Railroad had intensified, Rankin's legacy was slowly eroding. There was some effort, initially, to preserve it after the war. For instance, in 1868, one member of the Western Tract and Book Society, Reverend Andrew Ritchie, wrote a short biography, published through the society. The book, entitled *The Soldier, The Battle, The Victory*, provided a decent overview of Rankin's life. However, with such a title, the unsuspecting reader may assume it has more to do with the Civil War (or any war for that matter) than Rankin's involvement in the Underground Railroad. When Rankin published his own autobiography in 1873, his humility led him to downplay some notable episodes of his life. The attack on his home and family in 1841, for instance, amounted to a little more than a paragraph. Adam Lowry Rankin, who by this time had moved to California with his family, would write his own autobiography. In it, he would go much more in-depth on the instances which his father downplayed. However, he didn't write it for over a decade. Even when it was written, it would remain unpublished.

Additionally, due to the risks associated with living so close to slavery, the Ripley abolitionists had to take extra precautions. For years, Rankin lived under the threat of kidnapping and assassination due to the suspicion of his involvement in the Underground Railroad. As fugitives would escape through the Ripley line, he would often tell them "You cannot come back." Any trace of their activities would endanger not just Rankin's life, but the entire operation in Ripley. Rankin's ally, John Parker, kept "an accurate list of the names, dates, and original homes of the fugitives" who escaped through Ripley. After the 1850 Fugitive Slave Law, "agitation was at its highest, and active prosecutions began its enforcement." As a result, "everyone engaged in the work [of aiding fugitives] destroyed all existing evidence of his connection with it." Parker dropped his record book of the fugitives in the furnace of his iron foundry. "No one knew of its existence, especially its damaging contents."[252]

Compare this, in contrast, to William Still, the black conductor in Philadelphia who, along with Harriet Tubman, aided hundreds of fugitives in their escape. Despite the risk, Still maintained a robust record of those who came through his station, including names, letters, short biographies, and more. As the American centennial approached, interest exploded in the legendary network of slave escape routes. In 1872, Still released the stories and records he collected over the years in a book aptly titled *The Underground Railroad*.[253] This historic work ensured the legacy of the Underground Railroad would be preserved. Unfortunately, it also overshadowed Rankin and the conductors in the West. Due to the Fugitive Slave Act, the true history of the Underground Railroad is forever lost.

To complicate matters, some were actively trying to disparage Rankin's impact on the abolition movement. "It is a matter of well established history that Elizabeth Heyrick, a[n English] Quakeress, was the first to preach that doctrine (of immediate emancipation)," Illinois abolitionist A. J. Grover wrote on September 2, 1882. "And Mr. Garrison was the first man in this country to adopt Miss Heyrick's rallying cry." He continued to write that "if John Rankin or [Arthur Tappan] Rankin, D. D., have always been in full fellowship with the Presbyterian church, they were very inconsistent antislavery men, and their anti-slavery was a very harmless (to slavery) type…. I judge that A. T. Rankin, D. D., belongs to that inveterate (to the close of the war) pro-slavery denomination." Grover's criticisms, Arthur Tappan Rankin assumed, were meant to be read by his father. Rankin, however, "cannot now engage in controversy. His pen, once mighty in the cause of freedom, has lost its cunning. His tongue, once eloquent in defense of the oppressed, is enfeebled by age. The frame that stood erect before enraged mobs and endured pounding when he plead for the helpless is now bent by the hand of time. Far on in his ninetieth year, standing on the verge of the grave he waits his reward." Instead, Arthur wrote a lengthy rebuttal in a pamphlet entitled *Truth Vindicated and Slander Repelled*.[254]

Arthur refuted the assertions that Elizabeth Heyrick was the first to espouse immediate abolition, and that William Lloyd Garrison was the first to espouse it in the United States. "There is not a fact nor a scrap of history to prove" these claims. "Rev. John Rankin preached 'immediate unconditional emancipation' from the pulpit as early as 1817–18, taught it from the press in 1822, and never was a gradual abolitionist." Furthermore, Arthur pointed out, Garrison never tried to claim to be the first in America to espouse or even popularize immediate emancipation. "He only claimed to be a disciple; and co-worker in the cause." It was his father, Rankin, whom Garrison had always credited as the cause of his entry into immediate abolitionism. Rankin was far too old to care about such drama. As he approached ninety, he set his eyes on eternity.

* * * * *

"For thou art my rock and my fortress," King David writes in Psalm 31 (KJV), "therefore for thy name's sake lead me, and guide me.." Likewise, King Solomon writes "The name of the Lord *is* a strong tower: the righteous runneth into it, and is safe" in Proverbs 18:10 (KJV). It's hard to imagine that any other words in Scripture would have resonated with Rankin better than these. Few people had a more turbulent life than he. Financially, he never had much stability. His abolitionism put him under constant threat of mob violence, assassination, and kidnapping. His anti-slavery work frequently pulled him away from his home. Jean and their children went months without seeing their father. Not even engagement in his church would provide relief for Rankin—theological divisions over doctrine and slavery ensured that much. For most of his life, everything seemed to work against Rankin. Yet, there is no evidence that suggests he ever had a crisis of faith. Even as a boy, as he would experience great anxiety over spiritual matters, his doubts were more of himself than of the Almighty. Rankin's faith in God was his strong tower—a rock and a fortress. Understanding this faith is pivotal in understanding Rankin as a man. Because of it, Rankin turned his own home into a strong tower for "the righteous" as they escaped from slavery.

As he listened to Calhoun at the First Presbyterian Church in Ironton on Sunday, July 30, 1882, Rankin reflected much on his faith and life of trials. The church was packed with new faces and old members alike. The construction of a beautiful new sanctuary to accommodate more people had recently been completed. This was the day of dedication. "Everyone was delighted with the beauty and elegance of the house," reported *The Ironton Register*. Many prominent Irontonians were present for the dedication service, including Campbell, his wife Elizabeth, and his cousin Hiram. The husbands of two of Rankin's granddaughters were elders at the church. His granddaughter Mary Franklin Rankin, the orphan of David and Mary Ann Rankin, had married David Nixon. Rankin officiated their marriage on September 11, 1865. His other granddaughter, Eliza Humphreys, had married Civil War Colonel George N. Gray. Rankin would stay in their large Victorian home while in Ironton.

Following songs of worship, Calhoun approached the new black walnut pulpit, "rich in carving and exceedingly tasty in design." Rankin listened attentively as Calhoun read from Psalm 137:5–6 (KJV). "If I forget thee, O Jerusalem, let my right hand forget her cunning. If I do not remember thee, let my tongue cleave to the roof of my mouth; if I prefer not Jerusalem above my chief joy." Jerusalem, Calhoun told the crowded sanctuary, represented the church of God—the advancement of which was "far more important to mankind than all the triumphs, accomplishments, and enjoyments of hand or tongue." As he continued, Calhoun drew the attention of the audience to the beautiful craftsmanship of the new sanctuary, speaking "cheerfully of the noble work." But, he added, "This church was not built for me, nor for the generous-hearted men who so kindly gave their money, but for the children, and the rising generation, so largely represented here today, and whosoever may come here to worship." It was for those "who can give little or nothing as freely as those who can give much. There is no

distinction here – every seat is equally desirable and equally comfortable—and we invite all not connected with other churches to attend
here and partake in the blessings of the gospel." Equal treatment of
mankind, reflecting their equality before God. It was all Rankin ever
wanted to see in his life. Now, after almost nine decades, he sat in his
pew with immense satisfaction knowing that his divine purpose in this
world had been achieved.

A closing hymn was sung, then Rankin was called upon to give the
benediction. As he rose to the pulpit, reflecting on Calhoun's words, he
noticed the morning sun beaming through the stained-glass windows.
The colored sunlight embraced the congregation like a blanket, filling
the entire church with peace and tranquility. Bowing his head, Rankin
led the room in prayer.[255]

* * * * *

The boat's arrival in Ripley was delayed on March 20, 1886. It was
a Saturday night, and getting late, but six members of Ripley's black
community remained in the wharf. They were prepared to wait as long
as they needed to for the ship's arrival. Black crepe covered their arms in
mourning. As the boat finally arrived, not a moment was wasted. They
moved quickly to unload the coffin carrying the body of John Rankin.

For a little over six months, Rankin had been battling an aggressive
and painful cancer in his face that had grown to the point of complete blindness in one eye. Upon the arrival of his ninety-third birthday
in February, his cancer had begun eating away at his brain. He was
bedridden in Ironton at the home of George N. Gray and his granddaughter, Eliza. Finally, after months of agony, he drew his last breath
at around five in the afternoon on March 18, 1886. There was little
doubt where Rankin should be laid to rest. Arrangements were made to
return to Ripley.[256]

His family in Ironton returned with him. This included his daughter Isabella and her husband, John. Of course, Eliza joined them, as
did two of her own sons. Mary F. Nixon and her daughter did as well.

Calvin and his family still lived in Ripley. Arthur was already in town, having preached the Sunday prior. John, Jr. had traveled from Indiana for the funeral. Dr. Andrew Campbell Rankin traveled from near Chicago. Bella Cleveland, Mary Nixon's sister, crossed the river from Augusta with her daughter.

The funeral took place on Sunday, March 21, at the same Presbyterian Church Rankin spent decades helping grow. It was an emotional day for everyone in town. Hardly a soul in Ripley hadn't been affected by Rankin's influence. This was especially true for the black community. His four sons who were present, two of his sons-in-law, and the six black men who welcomed his boat at the wharf from the previous night served as pallbearers.

Reverend W. F. Gowdy gave the sermon during the funeral, which started at eleven o'clock that morning. The church was packed with black and white residents alike. Tears were shed by onlookers as his horse-drawn carriage passed through Second Street on their way to Maplewood Cemetery, where he would permanently remain. To those paying their respects, Rankin *was* Ripley. Before his arrival, Ripley was an old saloon town on the frontier. Rankin showed the people of Ripley their own humanity, and thus he led it to achieve its true potential. Rankin was a symbol of faith, courage, humanity, and freedom. Nearly everyone in town had their own reason to revere their finest citizen.

Later that week, *The Ripley Bee* reported on the death and funeral of Rankin. After detailing the funeral proceedings, they offered the following summary of his life: "In almost every town in the southern part of the state, the voice of Rev. John Rankin was heard in strong and fearless utterance against the curse of slavery, and for a quarter of a century he lived to see the slaves free men. He has at last passed to his rest above. His name will ever live in history and in the memory of those for whom he did so much."[257]

* * * * *

It was bright and sunny in Ripley on May 5, 1892, a perfect day for the occasion. Many members of the Rankin family, near and far alike, had traveled to Ripley for the unveiling of a magnificent bust and monument in honor of "the famous pioneer abolitionist," John Rankin. Richard Calvin Rankin was the marshal and master of ceremonies for the day, which started ten thirty that morning at the Presbyterian Church. The bust itself was sculpted by Dr. Andrew Campbell Rankin's daughter, and Rankin's granddaughter, Ellen Copp, who attended the Chicago Art School.[258] Unlike the melancholy that accompanied his funeral six years earlier, this was a day of celebration. The people of Ripley were jubilant. Festivities were opened with prayer and scripture reading. Hymns and other appropriate songs were sung throughout the day. Chambers Baird Jr. put together an appropriate sonnet, which was read during the ceremony:

> *Grand pioneer in Freedom's holy cause,*
>
> *The praise and honor thine, who battled long,*
>
> *And didst assail the citadel of wrong*
>
> *With dauntless faith, and courage without pause,*
>
> *Despite the throttling power of evil laws*
>
> *That made the bondsman's shackles doubly strong,*
>
> *And would make freemen slaves in common throng,*
>
> *Whilst cowards gave assent and meek applause.*
>
> *Dear Hero of our age, thy work is o'er,*
>
> *Thou canst and needst no more thy warfare wage,*
>
> *In peace and joy thou sawst thy latest sun;*

Thou hast the victor's crown for evermore,

And leav'st to us for blessed heritage

The faith well-kept, and good fight fought—and won.

The dedication ceremony for the monument to John and Jean Rankin, May 5, 1892. Richard Calvin Rankin served as Marshall and Master of Ceremonies that day. (Ohio History Connection)

Several speeches were given throughout the day. J. C. Leggett provided a thorough history of the Rankin family, stretching back to Alexander Rankin and the defense of Londonderry. "Where did [John Rankin] get that spirit of revolt against this evil [of slavery]?… It was the indomitable spirit of Alexander Rankin, of Londonderry, reasserting itself in a later generation through one of his descendants." Another speech was given by J. S. Atwood, who praise Rankin as the "grand and gallant hero of liberty." Arthur Tappan Rankin spoke at length not just on behalf of his father, but also his mother, who had been brought back to Ripley to lay alongside Rankin in their grave. Following an address by Reverend W. A. Jackson, the audience cheered as the monument was unveiled. Rankin's bust would now mark his grave for generations to come. Samuel Rankin, who had traveled all the way from Connecticut for the ceremony, then rose to speak. As he gazed upon the grand monument erected to his parents, his heart swelled with pride and emotion. "May this monument remain as a sacred shrine—the true Mecca to which our descendants unborn shall make their pilgrimages and gather new inspiration for life's noble work," he told his audience as he closed. He couldn't help but be captured by the beautiful simplicity of the monument's inscription.[259]

John Rankin
1793–1886
Jean Lowry, His Wife
1795–1878
Freedom's Heroes

"Freedom's Heroes," Samuel mused, "is all the epitaph they need."

The bust and monument of Rev. John Rankin, over his grave in Ripley, Ohio, sculpted by his granddaughter, Ellen Copp.

NOTES & SOURCES

While Reverend John Rankin was humble in nature, he was also a prolific writer on the issues he was passionate about. While writing this book, I encountered countless editorials, tracts, books, and some letters Rankin had penned. However, the most valuable record he left behind was his autobiography. *The Life of Rev. John Rankin: Written by Himself in His 80th Year* was one of three primary sources I pulled from throughout every chapter in this story. The other two are "The Autobiography of Adam Lowry Rankin" and *The Soldier, the Battle, and the Victory: Being a Brief Account of the Work of Rev. John Rankin in the Anti-Slavery Cause* by Reverend Andrew Ritchie. Unless otherwise cited, the quotes I pulled from John Rankin throughout the book are from his autobiography. The same can be said of Adam Lowry Rankin and his biography. Ritchie was heavily involved in the American Reform Tract and Book Society (later renamed the Western Tract and Book Society). He knew John Rankin well. Rankin had told Ritchie many of the stories he recorded in *The Soldier* directly.

There were two other sources that I relied on throughout the writing process. The first was the Union Township Public Library digital archives. They have digitized thousands of editions of local papers in Ripley and the surrounding region. A few dates as far back as 1816. Papers like *The Castigator* and *The Ripley Bee* were available to me from the convenience of my personal computer. This made the research process immensely smoother than it otherwise would have been. The second valuable source I relied on throughout the book was the Wilbur H. Siebert Underground Railroad Collection, held and maintained by the Ohio History Connection. Much like the Union Township Public Library, the Ohio History Connection has made this remarkable collection available online for public use. I managed to find countless interviews, articles, stories, and letters from original sources in this collection that made this book infinitely better than it otherwise would have been.

I do also want to note that while I have tried my best to include all relevant information that I could find on Reverend Rankin, this is far from a complete overview of his life. There are plenty of episodes throughout his life that I touch on in this book, but I simply didn't have the space or bandwidth to expand upon it as much as I would have liked to. There are plenty of letters and articles that I had to abbreviate to serve the story. There are likely other stories in his life that I simply didn't come across. I hope that this book will allow others to expand on those moments where I was not able to. That said, I'm immensely proud to be able to move John Rankin's story toward the recognition he deserves.

SELECTED BIBLIOGRAPHY

Books

Applegate, Debby. *The Most Famous Man in America: The Biography of Henry Ward Beecher*. New York: Three Leaves Press, 2006.

Bachman, J.W. *Rev. Samuel Doak*. Richmond: Presbyterian Committee of Publication, 1898.

Birney, William. *James G. Birney and His Times: The Genesis of the Republican Party, with Some Account of Abolition Movements in the South before 1828*. New York: D. Appleton & Co., 1890.

Blight, David W. *Frederick Douglass: Prophet of Freedom*. New York: Simon & Schuster, 2018.

Borneman, Walter R. *1812: The War That Forged a Nation*. New York: Harper Perennial, 2005.

Borneman, Walter R. *Polk: The Man Who Transformed the Presidency and America*. New York: Random House, 2009.

Brands, H. W. *Heirs of the Founders: The Epic Rivalry of Henry Clay, John Calhoun and Daniel Webster, the Second Generation of American Giants*. New York: Doubleday, 2018.

Clark, Thomas D. *Kentucky: Land of Contrast*. New York: Harper and Row, 1968.

Coffin, Levi. *Reminiscences of Levi Coffin*. Cincinnati: R. Clarke & Co., 1880.

Corum, G. L. *Ulysses Underground: The Unexplored Roots of U. S. Grant and the Underground Railroad*. West Union: Riveting History, 2015.

DeRose, Chris. *Congressman Lincoln: The Making of America's Greatest President*. New York, Threshold Editions, 2013.

Grant, Ulysses S. *Personal Memoirs of U. S. Grant*. New York: Charles L. Webster & Company, 1885.

Greenberg, Amy S. *A Wicked War: Polk, Clay, Lincoln, and the 1846 U.S. Invasion of Mexico*. New York: Vintage Books, 2013.

Hagedorn, Ann. *Beyond the River: The Untold Stories of the Heroes of the Underground Railroad*. New York: Simon & Schuster, 2002.

Heidler, David S. and Jeanne T. Heidler. *Henry Clay: The Essential American*. New York: Random House, 2010.

Hume, John F. *The Abolitionists: Together with Personal Memoirs of the Struggle for Human Rights, 1830–1864*. New York: Negro University Press, 1969.

Kaplan, Fred. *Lincoln and the Abolitionists: John Quincy Adams, Slavery, and the Civil War*. New York: Harper, 2017.

Mayer, Henry. *All on Fire: William Lloyd Garrison and the Abolition of Slavery*. New York: W.W. Norton & Company, 2008.

McCullough, David. *The Pioneers: The Heroic Story of the Settlers Who Brought the American Ideal West*. New York: Simon & Schuster, 2019.

Parker, John P. *His Promised Land: The Autobiography of John P. Parker, Former Slave and Conductor on the Underground Railroad*. Compiled and edited by Stuart Steely Sprague on behalf of the John P. Parker Historical Society. New York: Norton & Company, 1996.

Rankin, Adam Lowry. "The Autobiography of Adam Lowry Rankin." Handwritten but unpublished in the 1890s. Typewritten copy by Bella Rankin, granddaughter of Adam Lowry Rankin, made in 1931. Available from the Ohio History Connection.

Rankin, Arthur Tappan. *Truth Vindicated and Slander Repelled.* Ironton: The Register Office, 1883.

Rankin, John. *Letters on American Slavery: Addressed to Mr. Thomas Rankin, Merchant at Middlebrook, Augusta Co., VA.* Fifth Edition. Boston: Isaac Knapp, 1838.

Rankin, John. "The Life of Rev. John Rankin: Written by Himself in his 80th Year." 1872.

Rankin, Richard Calvin. *History of the Seventh Ohio Volunteer Cavalry (1881).* Ripley: J. C. Newcomb, 1881.

Ritchie, Rev. Andrew. *The Soldier, the Battle, and the Victory: Being a Brief Account of the Work of Rev. John Rankin in the Anti-Slavery Cause.* Cincinnati: Western Tract and Book Society, 1868.

Root, Damon. *A Glorious Liberty: Frederick Douglass and the Fight for an Antislavery Constitution.* Lincoln: Potomac Books, 2020.

Siebert, Wilbur H. *The Underground Railroad from Slavery to Freedom: A Comprehensive History.* New York: Macmillan, 1898.

Stahr, Walter. *Salmon P. Chase: Lincoln's Vital Rival.* New York: Simon & Schuster, 2021.

Still, William. *The Underground Railroad.* Philadelphia: Porter & Coates, Publishers, 1872.

Stowe, Harriet Beecher. *Uncle Tom's Cabin.* Boston: John P. Jewett & Co., 1852.

Stowe, Harriet Beecher. *A Key to Uncle Tom's Cabin.* Boston: John P. Jewett & Co., 1853.

The History of Brown County, Ohio. Chicago: W. H. Beers & Co., 1883.

Unger, Harlow Giles. *The Last Founding Father: James Monroe and a Nation's Call to Greatness.* Boston: De Capo Press, 2010.

Unger, Harlow Giles. *John Quincy Adams.* Boston: De Capo Press, 2012.

Unger, Harlow Giles. *Henry Clay: America's Greatest Statesman.* Boston: De Capo Press, 2015.

Wheelan, Joseph. *Mr. Adams's Last Crusade: John Quincy Adams's Extraordinary Post-Presidential Life in Congress.* Washington, DC: Public Affairs, 2009.

White, Jr., Ronald C. *A. Lincoln: A Biography*. New York: Random House, 2009.

White, Jr., Ronald C. *American Ulysses: A Life of Ulysses S. Grant*. New York: Random House, 2016.

Willey, Larry Gene. "The Reverend John Rankin, Early Ohio Anti-Slavery Leader." Ph.D. thesis, Department of History, Graduate College of University of Iowa, 1976.

Articles and Essays

Finkelman, Paul. "The Kidnapping of John Davis and the Adoption of the Fugitive Slave Law of 1793." *The Journal of Southern History* 56, no. 3 (1990): 397–422.

Grim, Paul R. "Rev. John Rankin: Early Abolitionist." Columbus: *Ohio Archaeological and Historical Quarterly, Ohio History Journal*, 1937.

Hale, Lance Justin. "Anti-Slavery and Church Schism among Protestants in Antebellum Central Kentucky." Online Theses and Dissertations. Eastern Kentucky University, 2012.

Martin, Asa Earl. "The Anti-Slavery Societies of Tennessee." *Tennessee Historical Magazine* 1, No. 4 (December 1, 1915). Published by the Tennessee Historical Society.

Price, Robert. "The Anti-Slavery Convention of 1836." Columbus: *Ohio Archaeological and Historical Quarterly, Ohio History Journal*.

Rankin, John. "A Review of the Statement of the Faculty of Lane Seminary: In Relation to the Recent Difficulties in That Institution." Ripley: Campbell & Palmer, Printers, 1835.

Willey, Larry Gene. "John Rankin, Antislavery Prophet, and the Free Presbyterian Church." *American Presbyterians* 72, no. 3 (1994). Published by the Presbyterian Historical Society.

Archives

Boston Public Library. Anti-Slavery Collection.
Boston Public Library: Boston, MA.

First Presbyterian Church: Ironton, Ohio.

Lawrence County Historical Society: Ironton, Ohio.

Library of Congress: Washington, DC.

Ohio History Connection: Columbus, Ohio.

Ohio History Connection. Wilbur H. Siebert Underground Railroad Collection.

The John Rankin House: Ripley, Ohio.

Union Township Public Library: Ripley, Ohio.

Union Township Public Library. Community History Archive.

ENDNOTES

1   "From George Washington to John Augustine Washington, 18 July 1755," *Founders Online*, National Archives, https://founders.archives. gov/documents/Washington/02-01-02-0169. [Original source: W. W. Abbot, ed., *The Papers of George Washington, Colonial Series, Vol. 1, 7 July 1748–14 August 1755* (Charlottesville: University Press of Virginia, 1983), 343.]

2   Like many in his day, Clay's views on slavery were both complex and apparently hypocritical. He consistently seemed to understand the immorality of the institution, however, even though he participated in it. There have been several excellent contributions recently which go much more in depth with Clay's struggle over slavery. As I crafted Clay's presence throughout this story, I largely pulled from three works: David S. Heidler and Jeanne T. Heidler, *Henry Clay: The Essential American* (New York: Random House, 2010); Harlow Giles Unger, *Henry Clay: America's Greatest Statesman* (Boston: De Capo Press, 2015); H.W. Brands, *Heirs of the Founders: The Epic Rivalry of Henry Clay, John Calhoun and Daniel Webster, the Second Generation of American Giants* (New York: Doubleday, 2018).

3   "Rather than relinquish our claim to the western territory...": David McCullough, *The Pioneers: The Heroic Story of the Settlers Who Brought the American Ideal West* (New York: Simon & Schuster, 2019), 7; Mary Cone, *Life of Rufus Putnam: With Extracts from His Journal, and an*

Account of the First Settlement in Ohio (Cleveland: W. W. Williams, 1886), 92.

4   The Treaty of Paris, September 3, 1783: National Archives. Specifically, Article II defined the borders of the vast Northwest Territory to prevent" all Disputes which might arise in future on the subject of the Boundaries of the said United States...."

5   "There shall be neither slavery...": "IV. Revised Report of the Committee, 22 March 1784," *Founders Online*, National Archives, https://founders. archives.gov/documents/Jefferson/01-06-02-0420-0005.   [Original source: Julian P. Boyd, ed., *The Papers of Thomas Jefferson, Vol. 6, 21 May 1781–1 March 1784* (Princeton: Princeton University Press, 1952), 607–613.]

6   "Jefferson's 'original Rough draught' of the Declaration of Independence." Julian P. Boyd, ed., *The Papers of Thomas Jefferson, Vol. 1, 1760–1776* (Princeton University Press, 1950), 423–28, https://jeffersonpapers. princeton.edu/selected-documents/jefferson%E2%80%99s-%E2%80%9Coriginal-rough-draught%E2%80%9D-declaration-independence#notes1a.

7   "Delighted with its high tone...": "From John Adams to Timothy Pickering, 6 August 1822," *Founders Online*, National Archives, https:// founders.archives.gov/documents/Adams/99-02-02-7674.

8   "The second was lost by an individual vote only...": "To James Madison from Thomas Jefferson, 25 April 1784," *Founders Online*, National   Archives,   https://founders.archives.gov/documents/ Madison/01-08-02-0009. [Original source: Robert A. Rutland, William M. E. Rachal, Barbara D. Ripel, and Fredrika J. Teute, eds., *The Papers of James Madison, Vol. 8, 10 March 1784–28 March 1786* (Chicago: The University of Chicago Press, 1973), 23–28.]

9   "We see the fate of millions unborn...": "IV. Jefferson's Observations on DéMeunier's Manuscript, 22 June 1786," *Founders Online*, National   Archives,   https://founders.archives.gov/documents/ Jefferson/01-10-02-0001-0005. [Original source: Julian P. Boyd, ed., *The Papers of Thomas Jefferson, Vol. 10, 22 June–31 December 1786* (Princeton: Princeton University Press, 1954), 30–61.]

10   *The Northwest Ordinance of 1787, July 13, 1787*, National Archives. The provision prohibiting slavery was included in Article VI: "There shall be neither slavery nor involuntary servitude in the said territory,

otherwise than in the punishment of crimes whereof the party shall have been duly convicted: Provided, always, That any person escaping into the same, from whom labor or service is lawfully claimed in any one of the original States, such fugitive may be lawfully reclaimed and conveyed to the person claiming his or her labor or service as aforesaid.

Be it ordained by the authority aforesaid, That the resolutions of the 23rd of April, 1784, relative to the subject of this ordinance, be, and the same are hereby repealed and declared null and void." https://www.archives.gov/milestone-documents/northwest-ordinance; McCullough, *The Pioneers*, 25–30.

11 "Sooner chop off his right hand…": James Madison, *Notes of Debates in the Federal Convention* (Philadelphia: [August 31] 1787).

12 *The History of Brown County, Ohio* (Chicago: W. H. Beers & Co., 1883), 54, 58; Ann Hagedorn, *Beyond the River: The Untold Stories of the Heroes of the Underground Railroad* (New York: Simon & Schuster, 2002), 8.

13 *A History of Adams County, Ohio* (West Union: E.B. Stivers, 1900), 612–613; *The History of Brown County*, 415–416; Hagedorn, *Beyond the River*, 9.

14 Following John Rankin's death, J.C. Leggett extensively researched Rankin's family lineage back to Alexander Rankin in anticipation of the unveiling of monument and ceremony in Rankin's honor. "Address of J. C. Leggett," *Rev. John Rankin: Dedication of a Bronze Bust and Granite Monument to His Memory* (June 1, 1897). Wilbur H. Siebert Underground Railroad Collection; John Rankin, *Abolitionist: The Life of Rev. John Rankin* (Lawrence County, OH: Task Force of the South Central Ohio Preservation Society, 1978), 3.

15 Rankin, *Abolitionist*, 3–5.

16 TO PASS S. 42, AN ACT RESPECTING FUGITIVES FROM JUSTICE AND PERSONS ESCAPING FROM THE SERVICE OF THEIR MASTERS. Second Congress, Section 2, Chapter 7, 1793 (Signed February 12, 1793); *The Constitution of the United States, with the acts of Congress, relating to slavery, embracing, the Constitution, the Fugitive Slave Act of 1793, the Missouri Compromise Act of 1820, the Fugitive Slave Law of 1850, and the Nebraska and Kansas Bill, carefully compiled* (Rochester: D. M. Dewey, 1854), 16–17.

17 Enacted into a Law at Philadelphia on Wednesday the first day of March, Anno Domini One thousand seven hundred Eighty Thomas

Paine, Clerk of the General Assembly, http://www.phmc.state.pa.us/portal/communities/documents/1776-1865/abolition-slavery.html.

[18] Paul Finkelman, "The Kidnapping of John Davis and the Adoption of the Fugitive Slave Law of 1793," *The Journal of Southern History* 56, no. 3 (1990): 397–422.

[19] Rankin, *Abolitionist*, 4.

[20] Several notable figures studied Dilworth's spelling book in their youth, including Noah Webster and Abraham Lincoln. Thomas Dilworth, *Dilworth's Spelling-Book, Improved: A New Guide to the English Tongue* (3rd edition) (Philadelphia: John M'Culloch, 1796).

[21] Rankin, *Abolitionist*, 4–7.

[22] Rankin, *Abolitionist*, 5.

[23] Mariam S. Houchens, "The Great Revival of 1800," *The Register of the Kentucky Historical Society* 69, no. 3 (1971): 216–234, http://www.jstor.org/stable/23377293; Rankin, *Abolitionist*, 8.

[24] Rankin, *Abolitionist*, 8–10.

[25] Douglas R. Egerton, *Gabriel's Rebellion: The Virginia Slave Conspiracies of 1800 and 1802* (Chapel Hill: University of North Carolina Press, 1993); "To Thomas Jefferson from James Monroe, 15 September 1800," *Founders Online*, National Archives, https://founders.archives.gov/documents/Jefferson/01-32-02-0094. [Original source: Barbara B. Oberg, ed., *The Papers of Thomas Jefferson, Vol. 32, 1 June 1800–16 February 1801* (Princeton: Princeton University Press, 2005), 144–145]; "From Thomas Jefferson to James Monroe, 20 September 1800," *Founders Online*, National Archives, https://founders.archives.gov/documents/Jefferson/01-32-02-0097. [Original source: Oberg, *The Papers of Thomas Jefferson*, 160–161].

[26] Hagedorn, *Beyond the River*, 23.

[27] J.W. Bachman, *Rev. Samuel Doak* (Richmond: Presbyterian Committee of Publication, 1898), 42–43. Tusculum (2013-10-24). "Samuel Doak: Tusculum University" (Office of the President); Rankin, *Abolitionist*, 11–12.

[28] Rankin, *Abolitionist*, 12.

[29] "Letter from General John Coffee to Major General Andrew Jackson, April 1, 1814, reporting on the Battle of Horseshoe Bend," John Coffee, 1772–1833, 1814 April 1, Andrew Jackson Collection, 1788-1942, VI-A-4-6, Box 3, Folder 1, 43023, Tennessee State Library and

Archives, Tennessee Virtual Archive, https://teva.contentdm.oclc.org/digital/collection/p15138coll33/id/83; Rankin, *Abolitionist*, 12–13.

30 "The militia of Kentucky...": *The Kentucky Gazette*, March 13, 1810; Ellery L. Hall, "Canadian Annexation Sentiment in Kentucky Prior to the War of 1812," *Register of Kentucky State Historical Society* 28, no. 85 (1930), 372–80, http://www.jstor.org/stable/23370018.

31 "We are, sir, from principle...": Brands, *Heirs of the Founders*, 41–42.

32 Walter R. Borneman, *1812: The War That Forged a Nation* (New York: Harper Perennial, 2005), 253–259; Theodore Dwight, *History of the Hartford Convention: With a Review of the Policy of the United States Government which Led to the War of 1812* (New York: N. & J. White, 1833), 377–378.

33 Rankin, *Abolitionist*, 13.

34 Rankin, *Abolitionist*, 13–15.

35 On Tennessee anti-slavery societies as well as John Rankin's involvement: Asa Earl Martin, "The Anti-Slavery Societies of Tennessee," *Tennessee Historical Magazine* 1, no. 4 (Dec 1, 1915), 262–265, published by the Tennessee Historical Society; Hagedorn, *Beyond the River*, 29.

36 Rankin, *Abolitionist*, 15–16.

37 Thomas D. Clark, *Kentucky: Land of Contrast* (New York: Harper and Row, 1968).

38 For more on Lewis Craig and the Baptist migration to Kentucky: Clark, *Kentucky*, 40–54; Robert B. Semple, *A History of the Rise and Progress of the Baptists in Virginia* (Richmond: Pitt and Dickinson, 1894), 40–41; Lewis Peyton Little, *Imprisoned Preachers and Religious Liberty in Virginia* (Lynchberg: J. P. Bell Co., 1938), 107–108; Dudley C. Haynes, *The Baptist Denomination* (New York: Sheldon, Blakeman & Co., 1856), 311–314.

39 *The Federal and State Constitutions, Vol. III Kentucky-Massachusetts* (Government Printing Office, 1909).

40 "Voting Rights in Kentucky, 1792–1799 - Free Negro, Mulatto, Indian Males," *Notable Kentucky African Americans Database* (University of Kentucky), https://nkaa.uky.edu/nkaa/items/show/2999.

41 *The Revised Statutes of Kentucky* (Frankfort: A.G. Hodges, 1852); Joan Wells Coward, *Kentucky in the New Republic: The Process of Constitution Making* (Lexington: University Press of Kentucky, 1979).

42 Rankin, *Abolitionist*, 16.

[43] Samuel Hopkins, *Works of Samuel Hopkins, D.D.*, Vol. 1 (Boston: Doctrinal Tract and Book Society, 1852); Rankin, *Abolitionist*, 17.

[44] Coward, *Kentucky in the New Republic*; KET Education, "Kentucky's Underground Railroad: Passage to Freedom," https://education.ket.org/resources/kentuckys-underground-railroad-passage-freedom/; Rankin, *Abolitionist*, 17–21. For the constitution of the Kentucky Abolition Society: *Abolition Intelligencer and Missionary Magazine*, Vol. 1. No. 6. October 1822.

[45] The story of the Rankin family being forced to leave Kentucky was compiled from two primary sources. I combined Rankin's account with the record of his son, Adam Lowry Rankin, in his unpublished autobiography, "The Autobiography of Adam Lowry Rankin," 21–22. Handwritten but unpublished in the 1890s. Typewritten copy by Bella Rankin, granddaughter of Adam Lowry Rankin, made in 1931. Available from the Ohio History Connection; Rankin, *Abolitionist*, 23–24; Paul R. Grim, "Rev. John Rankin: Early Abolitionist" Ohio History Journal (Columbus: Ohio Archaeological and Historical Quarterly, 1937); Hagedorn, *Beyond the River*, 33–34. For more detail on the panic of 1819: Harlow Giles Unger, *The Last Founding Father: James Monroe and a Nation's Call to Greatness* (Boston: De Capo Press, 2010), 296–297.

[46] "A motion for excluding slavery...": John Quincy Adams, *Memoirs of John Quincy Adams, Comprising Portions of His Diary from 1795 to 1848* (Philadelphia: J.B. Lippincott & Co., 1874–77), 502–503.

[47] "... fire that all the waters...": Daniel Walker Howe, "Compromise 2: Missouri, Slave or Free?" *American Heritage* 60, Issue 2 (Summer 2010); Henry M. Wriston, "Fire Bell in the Night," *Bulletin of the American Association of University Professors (1915–1955)* 35, no. 3 (1949), 434–449, https://doi.org/10.2307/40220364.

[48] The key section of the Missouri Compromise dealing with slavery appears in the final section: Sec. 8. "And be it further enacted. That in all that territory ceded by France to the United States, under the name of Louisiana, which lies north of thirty-six degrees and thirty minutes north latitude, not included within the limits of the state, contemplated by this act, slavery and involuntary servitude, otherwise than in the punishment of crimes, whereof the parties shall have been duly convicted, shall be, and is hereby, forever prohibited: Provided

always, That any person escaping into the same, from whom labour or service is lawfully claimed, in any state or territory of the United States, such fugitive may be lawfully reclaimed and conveyed to the person claiming his or her labour or service as aforesaid." *An Act to authorize the people of the Missouri territory to form a constitution and state government, and for the admission of such state into the Union on an equal footing with the original states, and to prohibit slavery in certain territories.* Approved March 6, 1820. National Archives.

49 "I have never known a question...": "James Monroe to Thomas Jefferson, 19 February 1820," *Founders Online*, National Archives, https://founders.archives.gov/documents/Jefferson/03-15-02-0378. [Original source: J. Jefferson Looney, ed., *The Papers of Thomas Jefferson, Retirement Series, Vol. 15, 1 September 1819 to 31 May 1820* (Princeton: Princeton University Press, 2018), 409.]

50 "...like a ball of fire...": "Thomas Jefferson to John Holmes, 22 April 1820," *Founders Online*, National Archives, https://founders.archives. gov/documents/Jefferson/03-15-02-0518. [Original source: Looney, *The Papers of Thomas Jefferson*, 550–551.]

51 Rev. Andrew Ritchie knew John Rankin personally and was deeply involved in the Western Tract and Book Society when he wrote the first biography of John Rankin. He wrote that "Mr. Rankin continued to labor in this field some four years, but toward its close the excitement on the slavery question became very warm in consequence of the admission of Missouri, into the Union, as a slave state." Rev. Andrew Ritchie, *The Soldier, the Battle, and the Victory: Being a Brief Account of the Work of Rev. John Rankin in the Anti-Slavery Cause* (Cincinnati: Western Tract and Book Society, 1868), 25; Rankin, *Abolitionist*, 24; Rankin, A.L., "The Autobiography," 22.

52 "Ripley was a very small village...": Rankin, *Abolitionist*, 24.

53 Cone, *Life of Rufus Putnam*, 65.

54 *The History of Brown County*, 354–355, 415–416.

55 *The History of Brown County*, 416.

56 *A History of Adams County*, 78–79; *The History of Brown County*, 285.

57 *The History of Brown County*, 415.

58 "...was spent in a free state...": Rankin, A.L., "The Autobiography," 22.

59 Stephen Middleton, *The Black Laws: Race and the Legal Process in Early Ohio* (Athens: Ohio University Press, 2005), 52–54; Walter Stahr,

Salmon P. Chase: Lincoln's Vital Rival (New York: Simon & Schuster, 2021), 53–54.

60 Rankin, *Abolitionist*, 40–41; Rankin, A.L., "The Autobiography," 25.

61 Rankin, *Abolitionist*, 25–32; Rankin, A.L., "The Autobiography," 23–24.

62 On Rankin and the Temperance movement: Rankin, A.L., "The Autobiography," 20; *The History of Brown County*, 420; Rankin, *Abolitionist*, 27–28.

63 "Dear Brother…": John Rankin, *The Castigator*, August 17, 1824.

64 John Rankin wrote twenty-one letters to his brother, but only thirteen appear in book form. The Union Township Library in Ripley, Ohio has digitized *The Castigator*, along with several other local papers used as reference in the research for this book. They are available for online viewing at https://ripleylibrary.com/. In this chapter, I wanted to offer the reader an opportunity to really peer into John Rankin's mind, both philosophically and theologically. The letters I included in this chapter were the letters that I believed achieved this most effectively. That said, all Rankin's letters to Thomas are worth reading. John Rankin, *Letters on American Slavery: Addressed to Mr. Thomas Rankin, Merchant at Middlebrook, Augusta Co., VA* (5th edition) (Boston: Isaac Knapp, 1838).

65 "This day's paper...": *The Castigator*, February 22, 1825.

66 "the Judas of the West...": Jackson Papers. Andrew Jackson to William Berkeley Lewis. February 14, 1825.

67 On the "corrupt bargain" of the 1824 election: Heidler and Heidler, *Henry Clay*, 178–185.

68 Rankin, *Abolitionist*, 41–42; Rankin, A.L., "The Autobiography," 25–26; Hagedorn, *Beyond the River*, 51–52.

69 "...murdered in Henry County, Kentucky...": *The Castigator*, August 8, 1826.

70 "...provide them with homes...": Rankin, A.L., "The Autobiography," 26.

71 Rankin, *Abolitionist*, 41.

72 Rankin, *Abolitionist*, 39, 41–42.

73 Rankin, A.L., "The Autobiography," 26.

74 Rankin's *Letters* apparently made its way to New England as early as 1825. Wilbur H. Siebert wrote in 1898 that "about the year 1825 they had fallen into the hands of the Rev. Samuel J. May, living at the time in Brooklyn, Connecticut, and he had read them with interest."

Additionally, while we don't know precisely when William Lloyd Garrison came across Rankin's *Letters*, Siebert wrote that he came to the doctrine of immediate abolition "during the summer of 1829, before his association with [Benjamin] Lundy at Baltimore...." This indicates that while there were not a lot of Rankin's *Letters* distributed before 1830, its influence was already widespread. Wilbur H. Siebert, *The Underground Railroad from Slavery to Freedom* (New York: Macmillan, 1898), 307–308; Rankin, A.L., "The Autobiography," 26; Rankin, *Abolitionist*, 43. Grim, "Rev. John Rankin," 225.

75 Early Lee Fox, *The American Colonization Society, 1817–1840* (Baltimore: Johns Hopkins Press, 1919).

76 "In Park-Street Church, of the Fourth of July, 1829...": *The Liberator*, January 1, 1831. Additional background on Garrison's conversion to immediate abolitionism: Henry Mayer, *All on Fire: William Lloyd Garrison and the Abolition of Slavery* (New York: W.W. Norton & Company, 2008), 60–70.

77 "We have met tonight...": John F. Hume, *The Abolitionists: Together with Personal Memoirs of the Struggle for Human Rights* (New York: Negro Universities Press, 1905).

78 Rankin's first letter reprinted: *The Liberator*, August 28, 1832.

79 In an article entitled "Insurrection in Virginia," Nat Turner's revolt was covered by Garrison in *The Liberator* in September 1831. In the same edition, Garrison published assassination threats he had received as result of his abolitionism. *The Liberator*, September 10, 1831; William Sidney Drewry, *Southampton Insurrection* (Washington: The Neale Co., 1900).

80 Grim, "Rev. John Rankin," 236; *The History of Brown County*, 449; Ritchie, *The Soldier*, 97–98.

81 Rankin, *Abolitionist*, 33–34; Rankin, A.L., "The Autobiography," 27–28; Grim, "Rev. John Rankin," 244; *The Castigator* ran several ads for Ripley College between 1830–1832. "This institution has now been in operation as a regular College, for two years, under the direction of a Professor of Languages and Mathematics," read *The Castigator* on October 16, 1832. The ad highlighted the board of trustees, which included Alexander Campbell, Archibald Liggett, and John Rankin.

82 Hagedorn, *Beyond the River*, 67.

[83] "The corner-stone upon which...": Anti-Slavery Convention. Declaration of the anti-slavery convention. Assembled in Philadelphia, December 4, 1833. Philadelphia Merrihew & Gunn, printers. No. 7 Carter's Alley. Philadelphia. Library of Congress.

[84] "The constitution of the American Anti-slavery Society: With the declaration of the National Anti-Slavery Convention at Philadelphia, December, 1833, and the address to the public" (New York: The American Anti-Slavery Society, 1838).

[85] "poor but earnest...": Robert Samuel Fletcher, *A History of Oberlin College from Its Foundation Through the Civil War* (Oberlin: Oberlin College, 1943), 43.

[86] Debby Applegate, *The Most Famous Man in America: The Biography of Henry Ward Beecher* (New York: Three Leaves Press, 2006), 94–95, 101–102, 107–108.

[87] William Lloyd Garrison wrote to Lyman Beecher in 1829, hoping to enlist the famed minister to the cause of abolition. Telling Garrison he had "too many irons in the fire already," Beecher gently but firmly turned him down. Applegate, *The Most Famous Man in America*, 105; Oliver Johnson, *W. L. Garrison and His Times* (Miami: Mnemosyne Pub Co, 1969), 44.

[88] "Ought the people...": Debate at the Lane Seminary, Cincinnati. Speech of James A. Thome, of Kentucky, delivered at the annual meeting of the American Anti-Slavery Society, May 6, 1834. Letter of the Rev. Dr. Samuel H. Cox, against the American Colonization Society, https://tile.loc.gov/storage-services/service/rbc/rbaapc/29400/29400.pdf.

[89] "why should not theological students...": Theodore Weld, *Cincinnati Journal*, May 30, 1834.

[90] "our Temple of God": *Cincinnati* Journal, July 11, 1834.

[91] "Inhibition of free discussion...": *The Liberator*, January 10, 1835; Stuart C. Henry, "The Lane Rebels: A Twentieth Century Look," *Journal of Presbyterian History* (1962–1985) 49, no. 1 (Spring 1971), 1–14.

[92] "a bad beginning...": John Rankin, *A Review of the Statement of the Faculty of Lane Seminary: In Relation to the Recent Difficulties in That Institution* (Ripley: Campbell & Palmer, 1835).

[93] Asa Mahan later reported in his autobiography that he and Theodore Weld tried to recruit Rankin to be the Professor of Theology at Oberlin College, but Rankin turned down their offer. Asa Mahan,

Autobiography: Intellectual, Moral and Spiritual (London: T. Woolmer, 1882), 192–193; Hagedorn, Beyond the River, 73–74.

94 Adam Lowry Rankin's first real experience with slavery is told in depth in his unpublished autobiography. Rankin, A.L., "The Autobiography," 28–31.

95 On the founding of Putnam, Ohio and the Muskingum County Emancipation Society, see: J.F. Everhart and Albert Allen Graham, *History of Muskingum County, Ohio, with Illustrations and Biographical Sketches of Prominent Men and Pioneers* (Columbus: J.F. Everhart & Co., 1882), 72, 146–147.

96 William Birney, *James G. Birney and His Times: The Genesis of the Republican Party with Some Account of Abolition Movements in the South before 1828* (New York: D. Appleton & Co., 1890), 163.

97 "Many western men...": Birney, James G. Birney, 168. Others have since compared Rankin to a "Martin Luther" type figure for abolition, including: Gilbert Hobbs Barnes, *The Antislavery Impulse, 1830–1844* (Gloucester: P. Smith, 1957), 213.

98 Proceedings of the Ohio Anti-Slavery Convention. Held at Putnam, on the twenty-second, twenty-third, and twenty-fourth of April, 1835. Beaumont and Wallace, Printers, 1835.

99 "There was an Englishman...": Rankin, *Abolitionist*, 51–52.

100 "I stayed over Sabbath...": Rankin, *Abolitionist*, 52. Additional resources pulled to craft the story of the Putnam convention include: Ritchie, *The Soldier*, 35–38; Grim, "Rev. John Rankin," 229–230.

101 Various papers across the country reported on the whipping of Amos Dresser, both in favor and outraged: *The Tennessean*, August 11, 1835; *The Cincinnati Daily Gazette*, August 25, 1835; *The Liberator*, September 26, 1835.

102 Bertram Wyatt-Brown, "The Abolitionists' Postal Campaign of 1835," *The Journal of Negro History* 50, no. 4 (1965): 227–238, https://doi. org/10.2307/2716246.

103 "I must...invite your attention...": Andrew Jackson, "Seventh Annual Message," December 8, 1835. The American Presidency Project, UC Santa Barbara, https://www.presidency.ucsb.edu/documents/ seventh-annual-message-2.

104 "Ripley Anti-Slavery Society Minutes Book." The transcript of the minutes from the Ripley Anti-Slavery Society has been scanned and

digitized by the Ohio History Connection, available for online reading. All references to the societal minutes or proceedings have come directly from this source.

105 "The duty of the church...": John Rankin, *An Address to the Churches, in Relation to Slavery: Delivered at the First Anniversary of the Ohio State Anti-slavery Society* (Granville: Ohio Anti-Slavery Society, 1836).

106 Accounts of the Granville Convention of 1836: Robert Price, "The Ohio Anti-Slavery Convention of 1836," *Ohio History Journal* (Columbus: Ohio Archaeological and Historical Quarterly); Report of the first anniversary of the Ohio Anti-Slavery Society: held near Granville, on the twenty-seventh and twenty-eighth of April, 1836. Cincinnati: Ohio Anti-Slavery Society, 1836.

107 Destruction of Birney's press and the bounty for his capture: Birney, *James G. Birney*, 240–255; Middleton, *The Black Laws*, 109.

108 Salmon P. Chase disperses the mob in Cincinnati: Stahr, *Salmon P. Chase*, 63.

109 "Disgust and horror": Paul Finkelman, *An Imperfect Union: Slavery, Federalism, and Comity* (Chapel Hill: The University of North Carolina Press: 1983), 160; Stahr, *Salmon P. Chase*, 64.

110 RASS Minutes Book, August 11, 1836.

111 "The Seventy": Barnes, *The Antislavery Impulse*, 104–108.

112 "A gentleman rose up": Rankin, *Abolitionist*, 56.

113 Templeton's enrollment into Lane Seminary: Rankin, A.L., "The Autobiography," 32–33.

114 Adam Lowry Rankin's Underground Railroad activities at Lane and throughout Cincinnati is recorded in his autobiography: Rankin, A.L., "The Autobiography," 33–35.

115 Adam Lowry Rankin's account of the pursuit of Eliza Jane Johnson: Rankin, A.L., "The Autobiography," 35–36.

116 "Can friendship between the States be maintained...": *Cincinnati Journal and Luminary*, September 30, 1837.

117 In addition to the *Cincinnati Journal and Luminary*, several local and abolitionist papers picked up the story of Eliza's kidnapping. It caused a sensation throughout Ohio and Kentucky as tensions escalated. Notably, her kidnapping was reported in: *The Maysville Eagle*, October 18, 1837; *The Philanthropist*, November 14, 1837; *The Liberator*, April 20, 1838.

118 "For the present...": *Maysville Eagle*, November 4, 1837.

[119] "It would by the nation whose sovereignty...": *The Philanthropist*, December 26, 1837.

[120] "Resolved, that His Excellency...": "The Western Reserve and the Fugitive Slave Law," *Collections of the Western Reserve Historical Society*, Publication no. 101 (Cleveland: Western Reserve Historical Society, 1920).

[121] "It is now considered...": *The Philanthropist*, March 6, 1838. Additional details covering the Johnson case were reported in the following issue of *The Philanthropist*, March 13, 1838.

[122] "we should have a higher sense...": John Rankin, *The Philanthropist*, March 20, 1838. Rankin wrote it on March 14, and it was published on the twentieth.

[123] A $2,500 reward: *The History of Brown County*, 313; Grim, "Rev. John Rankin," 237. In 2023 dollars, this translates to roughly $82,000.

[124] A couple of excellent accounts of the postal campaign in 1835 and the gag rule in Congress: Joseph Wheelan, *Mr. Adams's Last Crusade: John Quincy Adams's Extraordinary Post-Presidential Life in Congress* (Washington, DC: Public Affairs, 2009), 92–94; Damon Root, *A Glorious Liberty: Frederick Douglass and the Fight for an Antislavery Constitution* (Lincoln: Potomac Books, 2020), 5–11.

[125] On the murder of Elijah Lovejoy: Fred Kaplan, *Lincoln and the Abolitionists: John Quincy Adams, Slavery, and the Civil War* (New York: Harper, 2017), 41–45. Extensive coverage of the Lovejoy murder was in The Liberator on December 8, 1837.

[126] RASS Minutes Book, December 25, 1837.

[127] We may never know all the exact details of the night Eliza crossed the Ohio River and traveled up Liberty Hill. Naturally, given the secretive nature of the Underground Railroad in 1838, it would be easy for some of the specifics of the night to get mixed up or lost to history. In telling this story, I tried to find consistent themes throughout the various accounts that John Rankin and many of his sons provided in the aftermath of the Civil War, when it became safe to tell these stories more openly. Fortunately, Ann Hagedorn's retelling of the Eliza story in *Beyond the River* made the search for the truth of the night much easier. John Rankin provided an account in his autobiography. Much like many other dramatic episodes in his life, however, it is notably lacking in detail. His account amounts to little more than a

paragraph (Rankin, *Abolitionist*, 59). His sons would often go more in depth, as did Rev. Andrew Ritchie in *The Soldier, The Battle, the Victory*, who had direct access to Rankin to ensure the truthfulness of his biography (Ritchie, *The Soldier*, 99–100). Rankin's sons probably provided the most thorough account of Eliza's escape. Samuel W.G. Rankin told the story to a reporter at the *Hartford Daily Courant*, which was published on November 23, 1895, and republished in the *Boston Transcript* on November 30, 1895. In 1892, Wilbur Siebert interviewed Richard Calvin Rankin, where he provided an additional account of the Eliza story. John Thompson Rankin provided what is likely the most in-depth account of the Eliza story. He provided accounts of the story to Wilbur Siebert and Frank M. Gregg, which can be found at the Union Township Library in Ripley, Ohio. In Hagedorn's book, she wrote in her notes that "When I found inconsistencies in the accounts, the default account was John, Jr.'s, because his version as told to Gregg and to Siebert, is the most detailed and the details are the most logical and accurate." As I researched this book, I was inclined to agree with her assessment.

[128] "45 years ago, people walked across a frozen Ohio River," *The Cincinnati Enquirer*, January 18, 2022.

[129] Full report on the Ohio river freezing, from the late nineteenth to the mid twentieth century: *Ice in the Ohio River at Cincinnati 1874 Through 1964* (Cincinnati: U.S. Dept. of Commerce, Weather Bureau Office).

[130] We know Chancey Shaw was the man who helped Eliza on the shore from a few key sources. John Parker confirmed it was Shaw in his autobiography (John P. Parker, *His Promised Land: The Autobiography of John P. Parker, Former Slave and Conductor on the Underground Railroad* [New York: Norton & Company, 1996], 125, compiled and edited by Stuart Steely Sprague on behalf of the John P. Parker Historical Society). Parker was not in Ripley in 1838, but confirmed that he received the story "directly from Rev. John Rankin, to whom Eliza told her story within an hour after she had made the crossing, as she sat by his fireside in his hilltop home." Additionally, as Frank Gregg interviewed John, Jr. to get the truth of the Eliza story, John, Jr. confirmed Shaw's role. He told Gregg that "A rough hand suddenly came out of the black night like a hungry devil and seized her. There was no voice, no presence, just a giant hand laid its weight upon her and held her. It was so sudden and

unexpected. The fugitive sank helplessly to the ground with a groan." Then, according to John, Jr., Shaw told Eliza, "Woman, you have won your freedom." As for the exact wording of Shaw's quote, I opted to use the wording from Parker's autobiography in this book rather than John, Jr's. The essence is virtually the same, but I believed Parker's fit slightly better in the story I was crafting.

[131] Levi Coffin, *Reminiscences of Levi Coffin* (Cincinnati: R. Clarke & Co., 1880), 147.

[132] During Wilbur Siebert's interview of Richard Calvin Rankin on April 8, 1892, Calvin recalled how the Stowes were "friends and frequent visitors at my father's house" in Ripley. According to Calvin, the Stowes were in town because the Cincinnati Synod was meeting at Ripley. As Rankin and the Stowes were catching up, the former told them the story of Eliza.

[133] Adam Lowry Rankin's involvement in the slave escape: Richard Calvin Rankin interviewed by Wilbur Siebert, April 8, 1892.

[134] "did not conceal him...": Rankin, *Abolitionist*, 57; Grim, "The Rev. John Rankin," 237–238.

[135] "Send her to Mr. Johnson's...": *Trial of Rev. John B. Mahan, for Felony*. Mason County Circuit Court of Kentucky (Cincinnati: Samuel A. Alley, 1838).

[136] Various primary and secondary sources detail the extraction and trial of John B. Mahan, which were used for this book: *The History of Brown County*, 314–316; Letter from Dr. Isaac Beck to Wilbur Siebert, December 26, 1892; *Trial of Rev. John B. Mahan; The Philanthropist*, October 2 and October 9, 1838.

[137] "This is more alarming than even the case of Eliza Jane Johnson...": *The Philanthropist*, written on September 18, 1838, published on October 2, 1838.

[138] "even more alarming...": *The Liberator*, October 12, 1838.

[139] "MAHAN IN IRONS": *The Liberator*, November 2, 1838.

[140] Not Guilty: *Trial of Rev. John B. Mahan; The Liberator*, November 30, 1838.

[141] Dunlop posted Mahan's security: Birney, *James G. Birney*, 432. Announcing Mahan's release: *The Liberator*, December 28, 1838.

[142] Ohio Fugitive Slave Act: Emmett D. Preston, "The Fugitive Slave Acts in Ohio," *The Journal of Negro History* 28, no. 4 (1943): 422–477, https://doi.org/10.2307/2714948.

[143] Grant and Rankin: Ulysses S. Grant, *Personal Memoirs of U. S. Grant* (New York: Charles L. Webster & Company, 1885), 28. Grant didn't mention Rankin by name in his memoirs, but he did mention attending school in Ripley before heading to West Point. Ronald C. White, Jr, *American Ulysses: A Life of Ulysses S. Grant* (New York: Random House, 2016), 21–22. Both Rankin and Adam Lowry Rankin mentioned Grant's time in Ripley and their relation to him; Rankin, A.L., "The Autobiography," 25, 28; Rankin, *Abolitionist*, 64.

[144] The proceedings of the Sixth American Anti-Slavery Society convention in New York, including John Rankin's entire speech, can be found in the convention minutes: "Sixth Annual Report of the American Anti-Slavery Society: with the Speeches Delivered at the Anniversary Meeting, Held in the City of New-York, on the 7th May, 1839" and the minutes of the meetings of the society for business held on the evening and the three following days.

[145] "I am...no friend of slavery...": Speech of the Honorable Henry Clay, in the Senate of the United States about abolition petitions, February 7, 1839.

[146] "I have not owned...": Hagedorn, *Beyond the River*, 192–193.

[147] Standoff at Rankin's house: *The Philanthropist*, April 28, 1840. An article entitled "Violence of Slave-Hunters" from "A Citizen of Brown County" appeared in the Cincinnati paper, providing in-depth knowledge of the standoff. It's possible that one of the Rankin boys penned the article. Hagedorn, *Beyond the River*, 193–197.

[148] Birney, *James G. Birney*, 132–133, 150–152.

[149] "I had become personally acquainted...": Adam Lowry Rankin described the election of 1840 and the political friction with his father in his autobiography (Rankin, A.L., "The Autobiography," 39–41).

[150] Harrison rally in Ripley: *The History of Brown County*, 441.

[151] "One of these two...": *The Philanthropist*, September 8, 1840. Rankin wrote several letters that appeared in The Philanthropist in the summer and fall of 1840. Additionally, many of his critics appeared in the following issues. I largely pulled from letters and critics published on August 4th and September 8th and 15th.

[152] RASS Minutes Book, 1840.

[153] Birney in England: Birney, *James G. Birney*, 366–367.

[154] William Henry Harrison, "Inaugural Address," *The American Presidency Project* (UC Santa Barbara, March 4, 1841).

[155] Death of General Harrison: Report of Harrison's death and commentary of President Tyler: *The Philanthropist*, April 21, 1841.

[156] John Rankin, *A Present to Families: A Practical Work on the Covenant of Grace as Given to Abraham, Designed to Promote Family Religion* (Ripley: C. Edwards, 1840); John Rankin, *An Antidote for Unitarianism* (Cincinnati: Weed and Wilson, 1841); Rankin, Abolitionist, 43.

[157] "The Whole Case Detailed," *The Philanthropist*, June 30, 1841.

[158] "A reward of three thousand dollars were offered for father, dead or alive": Rankin, A.L., "The Autobiography," 37.

[159] Rankin, *Abolitionist*, 60.

[160] "Can't I come back from Canada...": Rankin, *Abolitionist*, 57.

[161] William Cheek and Aimee Lee, "John Mercer Langston and the Cincinnati Riot of 1841," in Henry Louis Taylor Jr., ed., *Race and the City: Work, Community, and Protest in Cincinnati*, 1820–1970 (Urbana: University of Illinois Press, 1993), 45–48.

[162] Rankin, A.L., "The Autobiography," 37.

[163] The details of the attack on Rankin's home were pulled predominantly from the accounts provided by Rankin (*Abolitionist*, 60) and Adam Lowry Rankin ("The Autobiography," 38–39) in their respective autobiographies. Lowry provided far more details of the specifics of the night. I found it interesting how Rankin seemed to undersell the importance of the attack in his autobiography. It is a remarkable contrast to the righteous indignation he was filled with in the days following the attack.

[164] "As false reports are in circulation...": John Rankin, *The Ripley Telegraph*, written September 13, 1841, published September 14, 1841. Republished in *The Philanthropist*, September 29, 1841.

[165] Adam Lowry and Amanda Rankin in Iowa: Rankin, A.L., "The Autobiography," 43–47.

[166] Death of John B. Mahan: *The History of Brown County*, 675.

[167] "Many readers of the *[Pennsylvania] Freeman*...": *The Liberator*, January 17, 1845.

168 The election of 1844: Walter R. Borneman, *Polk: The Man Who Transformed the Presidency and America* (New York: Random House, 2009), 102–110, 120–128; David Zarefsky, "Henry Clay and the Election of 1844: The Limits of a Rhetoric of Compromise," *Rhetoric and Public Affairs* 6, no. 1 (2003): 79–96, http://www.jstor.org/stable/41939810; Heidler and Heidler, Henry Clay, 388–393; Birney, *James G. Birney*, 352–356.

169 RASS Minutes Book, December 25, 1837.

170 John Rankin and the Free Presbyterian Church: Larry Gene Willey, "John Rankin, Antislavery Prophet, and the Free Presbyterian Church," *American Presbyterians* 72, no. 3 (Fall 1994). Published by the Presbyterian Historical Society.

171 New School/Old School divide in the Presbyterian Church: Albert Barnes, *The Church and Slavery* (Philadelphia: Parry & McMillan, 1857), 72.

172 Case of William Graham: *Watchman of the Valley*, October 30, 1845.

173 "We have had a great affliction...": Letter from John Rankin to Alexander Taylor Rankin, December 2, 1845, https://quod.lib.umich.edu/a/africanamer/africanamer.0003.48a/3?rgn=pages;view=image;q1=Rankin#?s=0&cv=2.

174 *Watchman of the Valley*, February 4, 1847.

175 Death of David Rankin: *The National Era*, February 3, 1848.

176 The majority of John P. Parker's story told in this book, including the ferry rescue incident, is drawn from his autobiography (Parker, *His Promised Land*), as told to Frank Gregg and edited years later by Stuart Seely Sprague. For narrative purposes, I've attached the account of the ferry rescue near his arrival to Ripley in 1849, but Parker doesn't provide an exact date, or even an exact year, when this happened. Parker does mention that it preceded John Brown's raid on Harper's Ferry "by several years." Given this and the place in Parker's autobiography in which he recounts this story, it is safe to say that this took place near the passage of the Fugitive Slave Act of 1850. We also know that it occurred in the summer. The Fugitive Slave Act was passed in September 1850. Rankin becomes increasingly involved in the Western Tract and Book Society and other similar societies in the 1850s, so the most likely summer that this rescue took place is either 1849 or 1850.

177 Full Wilmot Proviso: "Provided that, as an express and fundamental condition to the acquisition of any territory from the Republic of Mexico by the United States, by virtue of any treaty which may be negotiated between them, and to the use by the Executive of the moneys herein appropriated, neither slavery nor involuntary servitude shall ever exist in any part of said territory, except for crime, whereof the party shall first be duly convicted." National Archives.

178 Chase's objection to the 1850 Compromise: "Union and freedom, without compromise." Speech of S. P. Chase, of Ohio, in the Senate of the United States, March 26–27, 1850, on the compromise resolutions submitted by Mr. Clay on the 25th of January; Stahr, *Salmon P. Chase*, 156–167.

179 "Fugitive Slave Act of 1850." The Avalon Project: Documents in Law, History, and Diplomacy. Yale University, https://avalon.law.yale.edu/19th_century/fugitive.asp.

180 "We observe in our exchange...": *The National Era*, November 14, 1850.

181 "The law, passed at the last session...": *The National Era*, November 28, 1850.

182 Chase and Rankin in Greenfield, Ohio: *The National Era*, December 5, 1850.

183 "Practical atheism...": *The Ripley Bee*, December 21, 1850.

184 "The People of Brown County": *The Ripley Bee*, January 18, 1851.

185 John Rankin, *A Short Memoir of Samuel Donnell, Esq.* (Cincinnati: American Reform Tract and Book Society), c. 1854.

186 Ritchie, *The Soldier*, 75–77; The National Era, July 20, 1854.

187 *Uncle Tom's Cabin: The National Era*, June 5, 1851.

188 Harriet Beecher Stowe, *Uncle Tom's Cabin* (Boston: John P. Jewett & Co., 1852).

189 Harriet Beecher Stowe, *A Key to Uncle Tom's Cabin* (Boston: John P. Jewett & Co., 1853).

190 "No Union with Slaveholders": "Disunion: Address of the American Anti-Slavery Society," *The Anti-Slavery Examiner* (New York: American Anti-Slavery Society, 1845).

191 Douglass and Garrison's early alliance and friendship: David W. Blight, *Frederick Douglass: Prophet of Freedom* (New York: Simon & Schuster, 2018), 96–109; Root, *A Glorious Liberty*, 20–22, 25–26.

192 "...mind had undergone a radical change...": *The National Anti-Slavery Standard*, May 29, 1851.

193 The fallout between Garrison and Douglass is one of the most significant in American history. Many historians and authors have written about it. For this book, I pulled from several sources, but these were among the most informative: Tyrone Tillery, "The Inevitability of the Douglass-Garrison Conflict." *Phylon* (1960–) 37, no. 2 (1976): 137–149, https://doi.org/10.2307/274765; Blight, *Frederick Douglass*; Root, *A Glorious Liberty*.

194 The episode of Garrison and Rankin's dispute in Cincinnati was crafted through various primary and secondary sources. Adam Lowry Rankin detailed the incident in his autobiography (Rankin, A.L., "The Autobiography," 26). Several papers reported on it, including the *Daily Cincinnati Gazette*, April 20–24, 1853, and *The National Era*, May 12, 1853, which matched his account. As for the specifics of the argument they got into, I found some conflicting reports. It's likely that they butted heads more than once throughout the convention. What we do know with absolute certainty is the note Garrison left for Rankin on a fly-leaf page of a book of his speeches and writings. This is part of the Wilbur H. Siebert Underground Railroad Collection at the Ohio History Connection.

195 Rankin, A.L., "The Autobiography," 47–48.

196 The deaths of Calhoun, Clay, and Webster: Brands, *Heirs of the Founders*, 354, 364–370.

197 "An Act to Organize the Territories of Nebraska and Kansas": National Archives, May 30, 1854.

198 "Appeal of the Independent Democrats in Congress to the People of the United States": *Salmon P. Chase Papers: Speeches and Writings, 1849–1868* (January 19, 1854); Stahr, *Salmon P. Chase*, 191–193.

199 "one of the largest and most enthusiastic...": *The National Era*, April 27, 1854.

200 Additional report of the Anti-Slavery Convention in Cincinnati with Douglass and Rankin: *The Liberator*, April 28, 1854.

201 "The deed is done": *The Liberator*, May 26, 1854.

202 "We arrived here about a week ago...": *The Ripley Bee*, July 15, 1854.

203 People's Meeting: *The Ripley Bee*, July 15, 1854.

204 A Street Affray: *The Ripley Bee*, January 20, 1855.

[205] Ripley goes for Chase in 1855 election: *The History of Brown County*, 440.

[206] "The sole, special effect...": Salmon P. Chase, Inaugural Address of Salmon P. Chase, governor of the state of Ohio: Delivered before the Senate and House of Representatives (January 14, 1856).

[207] Both Sumner's "Crime Against Kansas" speech and report of his canning were reported in *The National Era* on May 29, 1856.

[208] "numerous and the interest increasing...": *The Ripley Bee*, August 29, 1857.

[209] "For many grave considerations...": *The Liberator*, September 4, 1857.

[210] Lincoln's campaign biography: Charles W. Moores, ed., *Lincoln: Addresses and Letters* (New York: American Book Co., 1914). "Autobiography written at the request of a friend as the basis of a campaign biography."

[211] "War Has Commenced": *The Ripley Bee*, April 18, 1861.

[212] Attack on Fort Sumter: Ronald C. White, Jr., *A. Lincoln: A Biography* (New York: Random House, 2009), 406–409.

[213] "...the preservation of peace on the border...": *The Ripley Bee*, April 23, 1861.

[214] Ammen's volunteer regiment: *The Ripley Bee*, April 25, 1861.

[215] Adam Lowry Rankin in Illinois during the outbreak of the war: Rankin, A.L., "The Autobiography," 49–51.

[216] White, *A. Lincoln*. 432–438.

[217] "extensively circulated over Brown County...": *The Southern Ohio Argus*, September 4, 1861.

[218] "I wrote it without consulting...": John Rankin, *The Ripley Bee*, August 29, 1861.

[219] "The result of Confiscation...": *The Southern Ohio Argus*, August 27, 1861.

[220] Richard Calvin Rankin, *History of the Seventh Ohio Volunteer Cavalry* (Ripley: J.C. Newcomb, 1881), 2.

[221] Rankin, A.L., "The Autobiography," 51.

[222] "the cruelest imposition...": Stahr, *Salmon P. Chase*, 397.

[223] "An Act for the Release of Certain Persons Held to Service or Labor in the District of Columbia": National Archives, April 16, 1862, https://catalog.archives.gov/id/299814.

[224] Horace Greeley, "The Prayer of Twenty Millions," *The New York Tribune*, August 20, 1862.

[225] There are plenty of accounts that detail the build-up to the release of the emancipation proclamation. However, in addition to the primary

sources, I found two accounts exceptionally helpful in crafting the version told in this book. White's *A. Lincoln* provides one of the best biographies of Lincoln in general. Specifically, his account of the Greeley/Lincoln editorial letters (White, *A. Lincoln*, 501–505) is a superb analysis of Lincoln's thinking about slavery as it relates to his duty as commander-in-chief. I also pulled inspiration from Stahr's *Salmon P. Chase* for much of the cabinet discussion in the weeks leading up to the announcement of the proclamation (Stahr, *Salmon P. Chase*, 400–412).

[226] "We must free the slaves...": Gideon Welles, *Diary of Gideon Welles, Secretary of the Navy under Lincoln and Johnson* (Boston; New York: Houghton Mifflin Company 1911), Vol. 1, 70; White, *A. Lincoln*, 493.

[227] "The Emancipation Proclamation," National Archives, January 1, 1863. The relevant section being: "And by virtue of the power, and for the purpose aforesaid, I do order and declare that all persons held as slaves within said designated States, and parts of States, are, and henceforward shall be free; and that the Executive government of the United States, including the military and naval authorities thereof, will recognize and maintain the freedom of said persons."

[228] "It is evident by the President's late message...": John Rankin, *The Ripley Bee*, January 8, 1863.

[229] "Narrative of Arnold Gragston: Underground Railroad 'Conductor' Enslaved in Kentucky, 1840–1865. Interview conducted ca. 1938 in Eatonville, Florida; Federal Writers' Project, WPA___Excerpts" in *The Making of African American Identity: Vol. I, 1500–1865*, http://www.nationalhumanitiescenter.org/pds/maai/community/text7/gragstonwpanarrative.pdf.

[230] Rankin, R.C., *History of the Seventh OVC,* 9.

[231] I pulled from two main sources in compiling the story of the thirtieth-anniversary celebration of the American Anti-Slavery Society. The Liberator reported the event on December 18, 1863. A detailed account of the speeches made during the convention can be found in *The National Anti-Slavery Standard* on December 19, 1863. The report of John Rankin's letter in *The Liberator* matches the original letter held in the Boston Public Library: Anti-Slavery Collection. Because of this, I primarily relied on this report.

[232] Rankin, A.L., "The Autobiography," 52.

[233] AMENDMENT XIII:

Section 1.

Neither slavery nor involuntary servitude, except as a punishment for crime whereof the party shall have been duly convicted, shall exist within the United States, or any place subject to their jurisdiction.

Section 2.

Congress shall have power to enforce this article by appropriate legislation.

Passed by Congress January 31, 1865. Ratified December 6, 1865. National Archives.

234 "This amendment is a King's cure...": Abraham Lincoln, "Response to a Serenade," February 1, 1865, https://quod.lib.umich.edu/l/lincoln/lincoln8/1:549?rgn=div1;view=fulltext.

235 "Freedom is Triumphant!": William Lloyd Garrison, *The Liberator*, February 4, 1865.

236 "for the purpose of giving expression of sorrow...": *The Ripley Bee*, April 19, 1865.

237 "Slaveholders and their allies have done the deed": Henry C. Wright, *The Liberator*, April 28, 1865.

238 Rankin, A.L., "The Autobiography," 52.

239 Rankin, *Abolitionist*, 61.

240 Rankin, *Abolitionist*, 60; Rankin, A.L., "The Autobiography," 52. Rankin, R.C., *History of the Seventh OVC*, 28–29).

241 "...diffuse light and knowledge among the people.": Salmon P. Chase, "Letter to the Western Tract and Book Society," *The Cincinnati Daily Commercial*, November 3, 1865.

242 "Read and Consider": John Rankin, *The Ripley Bee*, December 27, 1865.

243 Rankin, *Abolitionist*, 65.

244 "Having served my church...": Rankin, *Abolitionist*, 61.

245 "It being deemed best...": *The Ripley Bee*, January 17, 1866.

246 Rankin, *Abolitionist*, 62–65.

247 "The [Underground Railroad] work was begun here...": Hiram Campbell interviewed by Wilbur Siebert. Ironton, Ohio, September 30, 1894.

248 "Biographical Sketch of John Campbell," Ohio History Connection. Wilbur H. Siebert Underground Railroad Collection.

249 "[travel] those woods when snow was a foot deep...": Gabe Johnson interviewed by Wilbur Siebert. Ironton, Ohio, September 30, 1894.

250 "Most active [Underground Railroad] worker...": Hiram Campbell interviewed by Wilbur Siebert. Ironton, Ohio, September 30, 1894.

[251] John Rankin returns to Ironton: "John Rankin Day article, May 11, 1892." Wilbur H. Siebert Underground Railroad Collection.

[252] "...an accurate list of the names...": Parker, *His Promised Land*, 127.

[253] William Still, *The Underground Railroad* (Philadelphia: Porter & Coates, Publishers, 1872).

[254] Arthur Tappan Rankin, *Truth Vindicated and Slander Repelled* (Ironton: The Register Office, 1883).

[255] The entire account of the dedication was pulled from a transcript of the *Ironton Register* kept by the First Presbyterian Church in Ironton, Ohio: "A Day Long Looked For," *The Ironton Register*, August 3, 1883.

[256] John Rankin's cancer is reported in the diary of Mrs. Cora Young Wiles of Indianapolis, and later reported by *The Ripley Bee*, who was in Ripley the day of Rankin's funeral: "Noted Writer Recalls Rev. Rankin Funeral," *The Ripley Bee*, April 15, 1937.

[257] "In almost every town...": *The Ripley Bee*, March 24, 1886; An additional report of Rankin's death and funeral: *Brown County News*, March 24, 1886.

[258] "John Rankin Day article, May 11, 1892." Wilbur H. Siebert Underground Railroad Collection.

[259] "John Rankin's bust and monument dedication, June 1, 1897." Wilbur H. Siebert Underground Railroad Collection.

INDEX

Blythe, James, 46
Bonaparte, Napoleon, 29, 53
Boone, Daniel, 9
Boston, Massachusetts, 92, 101, 105, 150, 201, 212, 213, 241
Bradshaw, John, 11
Brockway, Nathan, 96, 109
Brooks, Preston, 216, 217
Brooksville, Kentucky, 229
Brown, Jacob, 63
Brown, John, 214, 219
Buchanan, James, 216
Buffington Island, battle of, 237
Burns, Anthony, 212
Bushnell, Horace, 112
Butler, Andrew, 216, 217
Butterworth, William, 129

Calhoun, Henry, 248, 253, 258, 259
Calhoun, John C., 153, 209, 221
California, 192, 193, 195, 210, 255
Calvinism, 21, 22, 47, 173
Campbell, Alexander, 61, 62, 66, 95, 96, 112, 115, 119, 120, 126, 134, 135, 144, 145, 147, 159, 188, 189
Campbell, Charles F., 214
Campbell, Hiram, 252, 253, 258
Campbell, John, 252, 253, 258
Cairo, Illinois, 224, 230

Canada, 31, 32, 95, 128, 139, 142, 144, 145, 146, 166, 193, 202, 252
Carlisle, Kentucky, 47, 58, 50, 51, 52, 198
Castigator, The, 67, 71, 72, 75, 82, 83, 84, 85, 86
Chase, Salmon Portland, 125, 156, 191, 192, 193, 196, 197, 209, 210, 216, 217, 231, 234, 246, 247
Chester, Joseph, 253
Chicago, Illinois, 199, 223, 224, 230, 260, 261
Chicago Tribune, The, 214
Chillicothe Presbytery, 96
Chillicothe, Ohio, 116, 244
Cincinnati, Ohio, 61, 100, 101, 102, 104, 112, 117, 118, 120, 129, 136, 182, 183, 185, 186, 187, 193, 199, 200, 205, 206, 207, 211, 229, 245, 249
   Mobs and riots, 123, 124, 125, 126, 127, 137, 156, 166, 167
Cincinnati Journal, 102, 103, 104, 179
Cincinnati Journal and Luminary, 133
Cincinnati Presbytery, 157
Cincinnati Synod, 181, 182, 183
Clay, Cassius Marcellus, 207

ACKNOWLEDGMENTS

I feel immensely honored to be able to push John Rankin's story forward to a more mainstream audience. He is, I believe, one of America's greatest heroes that has since been lost to history. It is my prayer that this book will help elevate him to his proper status. Fortunately, throughout the writing process, there were some terrific people who believed in this goal as much as I did. Their contributions, no matter how big or small, made this book possible.

As I embarked on writing this book, I was concerned about how much information I would be able to find to fill an entire biography. As I got started, however, those fears quickly evaporated. This is in no small part due to the help of my friend and research assistant, Charles Sanders. With a special talent for research, Charles was able to help me find the necessary primary sources in half the time it would otherwise have taken me. Charles was also one of the earliest believers in this project. As new discoveries were made, Charles was always especially eager to jump on the phone with me as we discussed the progression of the story. I'm especially grateful for his assistance and friendship.

From the outset, I knew I needed to connect with the John Rankin House and the people involved in preserving his legacy in Ripley. The days I spent in John Rankin's community were, without question, my favorite days throughout this process. The spirit of the Ripley conductors still persists in those tasked with preserving the community's rich heritage. As I reached out about this book, the people of Ripley were warm, supportive, and excited about the project. I'm grateful for the work they've done to preserve Rankin's legacy. Specifically, I'd like to thank Betty Campbell and Howard McClain at the John Rankin House and Alison Gibson at the Union Township Public Library in Ripley. Betty and Howard showed me through the Rankin House, providing key context that heavily influenced the setting of the book. Alison was a tremendous resource who helped me discover some of the activities of John Rankin during the Civil War in particular. So much of this story is indebted to them.

While I am on the subject of Ripley, I feel especially grateful to Ann Hagedorn. Ann's book, *Beyond the River*, was the last notable work which attempted fully to tell the story of John Rankin and the community of conductors in Ripley. She fell in love with the community of Ripley so much while writing her book that she decided to become part of it. Her book blazed the trail for this book to be possible. I reached out to Ann early in the writing process to discuss this project, hoping that she might be able to provide key insight that might help the book. Her response was immensely warm and encouraging. During one of my trips to Ripley, I had the opportunity to discuss the project in person with her. In these conversations, I explained to Ann how I wanted this book to provide a very personal look into John Rankin, as well as explore certain aspects of his story that have previously been untouched. While I knew there would be elements that overlapped with *Beyond the River*, I wanted this story to feel totally unique. Ideally, the two stories would complement each other. Ann was nothing but kind, supportive, and excited upon hearing this. Her encouragement gave me a certain confidence in this project that I didn't know I was missing. For that, I can't thank Ann enough.

Before writing the first word of this book, I knew I wanted to explore John Rankin's twilight years in Ironton, Ohio. Having grown up in Ironton, I was made aware of his death in my hometown, but not much else. His last twenty years or so, in fact, are largely underreported.

This made it so much more exciting to explore this subject in the epilogue. The first field visit I made, before even going to Ripley, was to the Lawrence County Ohio Museum and Historical Society. Formerly the home George N. Gray and his wife, Eliza, this was the same home where John Rankin took his last breath. I want to thank the Lawrence County Historical Society, and specifically Kay Rader, for showing me around the house and discussing the book with me. The First Presbyterian Church in Ironton provided perhaps the most valuable resource for this period of John Rankin's life. They provided a typed copy of the article on the dedication ceremony of the new sanctuary in the church, which I can confidently say is as beautiful as the story alludes. This story closed the book out better than I could have hoped. For this, I'm especially grateful.

Without Wilbur H. Siebert, much of the history of the Underground Railroad throughout Ohio would be forever lost. Siebert interviewed and recorded so many valuable details directly from the original source before their deaths. He died in 1961, well before I was born, but his contributions to American history will live on for generations to come.

I'd like to thank Alex Novak, acquisition editor at Post Hill Press, for believing in this project. Specifically, Alex recognized the potential in John Rankin's story and suggested I make this book a full-fledged biography. Both the book and my experience writing it were enriched by it. Thank you, Alex.

An additional thanks is owed to my managing editor, Caitlin Burdette. Caitlin and the wonderful editors at Post Hill Press worked diligently to help me present this story in the highest quality. I couldn't be more thankful for the work you've put into helping me bring John Rankin's story to life.

Beyond those above, there are many people and institutions who influenced the trajectory of this project. To Stephen Kent, Aaron Andrews, Aryssa Damron, Tom Spence, Chris Spangle, Chris DeRose, the Lexington Public Library, the Ohio History Connection, and so many others who helped me throughout this project in various ways, thank you.

I remember the exact moment I found the inspiration to write this book. I had just finished *The Pioneers* by David McCullough. David's book was filled with long-lost heroes in American history, as his stories usually are. Unlike most of his other books, however, *The Pioneers* took place practically in my backyard. I wondered to myself, "how many others in this region have been lost to history?" At that moment, I recalled the story of John Rankin. I didn't realize *how* impactful he was, but I knew his story was one that needed the same level of attention. As I prepared to write this book, I heard of the passing of David McCullough in August 2022. I never had the privilege to meet him, but I can't emphasize enough the impact he had on me or on this story. While giving a talk at the Library of Congress about his excellent biography on John Adams, McCullough told his audience that the better you know your subject, "the more you realize how extraordinary what they did was because they were so *human*." The emphasis on a character's humanity is something I thought about at every stage of writing this book. It made me feel more connected to John Rankin as a character, and I hope the reader will feel the same way. For his indispensable influence, I thank David McCullough.

I'd like to thank my father, Randy Franz, for whom this book is dedicated to. He first told me about John Rankin when I was barely a teenager. My father's enthusiasm for Rankin always stuck with me, and it made me realize how special of a figure he truly was. Throughout the writing process, he helped me find key stories and documents as they related to Rankin's time in Ironton. He occasionally has the privilege of preaching in the same church in Ironton that Rankin helped dedicate in 1882.

John Rankin wrote that "a more affectionate and industrious wife [than Jean] could not be found in any place." I believe that my wife, Danielle, could be described in much the same way. As I embarked on the time-consuming endeavor of researching and writing this book, she supported me from the beginning. From aiding me with editing, tagging along on my research trips, and supporting me on the long nights and weekends it often took to write this book, I couldn't have done it without her.

ABOUT THE AUTHOR

C aleb Franz has built a career as a writer, podcaster, and nonprofit professional. He often provides commentary on public affairs and writes on American history. His work has appeared in outlets such as *The Independent*, *Washington Examiner*, *RealClearHistory*, and more. He currently resides in Lexington, Kentucky, with his wife, Danielle.